The Unedited Diaries of Carolina Maria de Jesus

The
Unedited Diaries
of
Carolina Maria
de Jesus

Robert M. Levine
and
José Carlos Sebe Bom Meihy

Translated by Nancy P. S. Naro and Cristina Mehrtens

Rutgers University Press
New Brunswick, New Jersey, and London

Library of Congress Cataloging-in-Publication Data

Jesus, Carolina Maria de.
    The unedited diaries of Carolina Maria de Jesus / edited by Robert M.
Levine and José Carlos Sebe Bom Meihy ; translated by Nancy P. S.
Naro and Cristina Mehrtens.
      p.   cm.
    Contains selections from Meu estranho diário (Rio de Janeiro :
Editora Xamã, 1997) which contained selections from the 1958–1963
diaries, and are now published with new introductory material,
notes, and portions of the 1966 diary in addition.
    Includes bibliographical references and index.
    ISBN 0-8135-2569-1 (cloth : alk. paper). — ISBN 0-8135-2570-5
(pbk. : alk. paper)
    1. Jesus, Carolina Maria de—Diaries. 2. Blacks—Brazil—São
Paulo—Diaries. 3. Poor—Brazil—São Paulo—Diaries. 4. Blacks—
Brazil—São Paulo—Social conditions. 5. Poor—Brazil—São Paulo—
Social life and customs. 6. São Paulo (Brazil)—Social conditions.
7. São Paulo (Brazil)—Social life and customs. 8. City and town
life—Brazil—São Paulo. I. Levine, Robert M. II. Meihy, José
Carlos Sebe Bom, 1943–   . III. Naro, Nancy. IV. Mehrtens,
Cristina. V. Jesus, Carolina Maria de. Meu estranho diário.
VI. Title.
F2651.S253J474   1999
9812'.6100496'0092—dc21   98-4396
                                                    CIP

British Cataloging-in-Publication data for this book available from the British Library

The writings of Carolina Maria de Jesus have been translated and published by
permission of her daughter, Vera Eunice da Jesus Lima.
The 1958, 1961, 1962, and 1963 diaries, edited by Robert M. Levine and José
Carlos Sebe Bom Meihy, have been published in *Meu Estranho Diário* (Rio de
Janeiro: Editora Xamã, 1997).

Manufactured in the United States of America

To Craig and Carol Hendricks

Contents

Illustrations

Acknowledgments

My suggestion that we locate Carolina's children and find out what had happened to their mother in the last years of her life could not have succeeded without the indefatigable detective work of Juliano Andrade Spyer, a student in the University of São Paulo's oral history program directed by José Carlos Sebe Bom Meihy. Other students assisted as well, especially Andrea Paula dos Santos, Janes Jorge, Flávio Edson de Souza Brito, and José Carlos Sebe's able secretary, Maria Eta Vieira. Marisa Lajolo of UNICAMP (Campinas) has lent continual moral support and has joined the project as a collaborator in several ways. In Coral Gables, Florida, we would like to thank Quélia Quaresma, Elizabeth Allard, Sara Sánchez, and Elza Rezende for their help. A special acknowledgment goes to Cristina Mehrtens, who translated the sections covering 1964 and 1966 for this book. S. David Sperling of Hebrew Union College, New York, helped identify the Donatists. Although I wrote the introduction as well as the afterword to this book, they are based on José Carlos Sebe's analyses and are the result of lengthy discussions about the meaning of Carolina Maria de Jesus's writings. Nancy Naro contributed to this process as well. José Carlos Sebe painstakingly supervised the handling of the thirty seven unedited notebooks and shepherded the project to completion in Brazil, including published selections of Carolina's poems and plays.

Robert M. Levine

The Unedited Diaries of
Carolina Maria de Jesus

Introduction

Quarto de Despejo (The trash room), the diary of Carolina Maria de Jesus, a destitute black *favelada,* became a publishing sensation when it appeared in Brazil in 1960 and an international bestseller in more than forty countries.[1] The diary depicted the harsh life of the slums, but it also spoke of the author's pride in her blackness, her high moral standards, and her patriotism. Since the 1960s, more than a million copies of her diary are estimated to have been sold in bookstores around the world, although no accurate figures are available. Yet many Brazilians refused to believe that someone like Carolina could have written such a diary. She used complicated words (some, but not all of them, misused) and often lyrical phrasing, and she discussed the events of the world. Doubters preferred to believe that the book had either been written by Audálio Dantas, the enterprising newspaper reporter who had discovered her, or that he had rewritten it so substantially that her book was a fraud. With the cooperation of Carolina's daughter, Vera Eunice de Jesus Lima, however, recent research shows that, although

1. Carolina Maria de Jesus and Audálio Dantas during one of the journalist's visits to the favela. At this time her diary had been excerpted and printed in Dantas's newspaper, but her book had not yet appeared. *Photographer unknown.*

Dantas deleted considerable portions of her diary entries to produce the best-selling diary (as well as a second one, *Casa de Alvenaria,* a year later),[2] every single word that she wrote was hers.

In 1996 Vera turned over to us thirty-seven handwritten notebooks totaling more than forty-two hundred pages that her mother had written in her own hand during the late 1960s. Because the notebooks were falling apart and written on yellowing paper in fading ink, we decided to make photocopies of the notebooks to facilitate the microfilming. In April 1996, while photocopying the notebooks, José Carlos Sebe made a startling discovery: not only had Carolina made handwritten copies of her poems, fragments of plays, essays, short stories, and novels, but among the notebooks—sometimes appearing abruptly in the middle of something else—there were about 320 pages of her original diary entries. In the back of one of the notebooks, Carolina had written that she was copying her original diaries ten years after they had been published.

Although this opens up her redrafts to the possibility of having been rewritten by Carolina, a close comparison of the unedited diary entries shows that she had faithfully copied what she had written.

Because there are many gaps in the notebooks, we could not reconstitute in its entirety either of Carolina's published diaries. Some of the unedited entries cover the period from 1955 to 1960 dealt with in *Quarto de Despejo;* others cover the *Casa de Alvenaria* period from 1960 to 1961, and still others go beyond any of Carolina's published writing, through 1966. The final entries were written under the military dictatorship, to which Carolina seemed ambivalently favorable, although its repressive atmosphere smothered the reformist debate of the early 1960s that had contributed in part to the success of Carolina's original diary.

The Unedited Diaries of Carolina Maria de Jesus is a faithful translation of the diary entries found among the materials handed over to us by Vera Eunice de Jesus Lima. Because Dantas has kept inaccessible the original notebooks he found in Carolina's favela shack in 1958, up to now it has been impossible to verify the extent to which his editing altered her writing. *The Unedited Diaries,* then, provide the first opportunity to compare Carolina's entries with the published diaries. They reveal clearly that Dantas's extensive editing-by-deletion resulted in a one-dimensional picture of their author and her outlook on life. Readers of Carolina's diaries have long wondered why she seemed so docile and so forgiving. Others disparaged her for seeming to accept social injustice, seeing her as a selfish woman who cared only for herself and her three children.

We have selected typical diary entries from the hundreds of pages that Carolina copied over in her own hand and have reproduced each one in its entirety. Commentators often objected to the fact that she wrote awkwardly, with little consistency in punctuation or spelling, and that her writings, in the words of a prominent Brazilian literary critic, Marilene Felinto, were little more than "clichés born in the favela."[3] Carolina did, in fact, use words in unique ways. Like many intelligent but poorly educated persons, she loved fancy language, even though some of the big words she chose did not mean what she intended. Some of her phrases were archaic, others malapropisms. Her writings are filled with startling references to historical personages, the Bible, and mythology. Some Brazilians have pointed to her use of big words as evidence that her diaries were written for her, but there is no evidence whatsoever that anything was ever printed under her name that she did not write out by hand herself. The unedited diaries show this clearly. They do not read as easily as Carolina's published books because they have not been prettified, but as documents they are closer to Carolina's thoughts and as such hold much greater value for analysis.

Carolina typically refers to people without regard for Brazilian convention, writing out their full names and ascribing to them titles of address based upon her respect (or lack of respect) for them as people, and the spelling of names is frequently inconsistent. Sometimes she capitalizes words and names for emphasis, or she does not capitalize them for the same reason. She often repeats phrases; she starts off her diary entries in the same way (but so did Samuel Johnson); she dwells on how much things cost (after all, pennies made the difference for her family between eating or not eating each day), and she shows deep suspicion of people she does not know, because she fears that they will take advantage of her. She refers to Audálio Dantas, her discoverer (and in some ways her Svengali) by a variety of names depending on how she feels about him at a given time.

Our translation of Carolina Maria de Jesus's newly discovered diary pages deliberately preserves the author's distinctive writing style. Unlike David St. Clair, who produced the English-language version of *Quarto* and who called Carolina's language "direct, rough, and without artifice," we believe that her language is subtle and pointedly expressive, although stylistically varied at times to the point at times of contradiction.[4] St. Clair's *Child of the Dark*, which has been in print for more than thirty-five years and is known to a generation of university students in Latin American Studies, contains many errors, missed shadings of words, and missed emphases.[5] This book's translation attempts to come closer to the full meaning of her writing by closely following Carolina's style and grammar. Inconsistencies in capitalization and punctuation are preserved, as is the author's language. Carolina wrote as she talked: often in run-on sentences. In most cases, this format has been preserved in the translation. The use in the text of ellipsis points indicates where Carolina's text pauses or is interrupted. Our edits—which have been kept to a minimum—are enclosed in brackets. Entries are translated in their entirety, except for instances in which they were omitted for reasons of space. Names and Portuguese words not likely to be familiar to non-Brazilian readers are listed in the glossary.

The translations in this book represent about one-third of the written notebook material turned over to us by Carolina's daughter, Vera Eunice de Jesus Lima. They span the years from 1955 to 1966 and include large sections from *Quarto de Despejo* (*Child of the Dark*) and her second diary, *Casa de Alvenaria* (*I'm Going to Have a Little House*),[6] as well as for the period beyond 1961 when *Casa* ends. Among the thousands of handwritten entries in our possession (to be made available in Portuguese in the year 2000 on microfilm), we have selected segments from each of the three representative periods, rather than trying to translate and publish all of the diary entries.

The Story of Carolina Maria de Jesus

Carolina Maria de Jesus was born in 1915 in poverty to an unmarried mother in Sacramento in the rural hinterland of Minas Gerais. Although Sacramento was technically a city, it was more than anything else a tradition-bound, dusty small town locked into rigid class hierarchies, with blacks like Carolina at the very bottom. After her mother died, and after a childhood of constant travail, the young women, the great-grandchild of slaves, migrated to São Paulo in search of work and a better life. As a child she had become literate largely on her own, attending for a scant two years a private school paid for by a benefactress, the wife of a local landowner. She developed a passion for reading and shocked her mother by reading aloud words displayed in shop windows and the names of stores.[7] Later, her talent for reading (and the cruel rejection by her peers in Sacramento, who thought that a black girl enamored of reading must be a creature of the devil) fed her desire to write down her feelings and to tell her story. Beginning in 1955, she began to write a diary in notebooks fashioned from scraps of paper she found while foraging. Her diary entries, written with a powerfully personal narrative force, reflected a mixture of hope and ruefulness. She captured moments of poignancy in a touching manner: once, when they ran out of things to eat in their shanty, her daughter Vera asked Carolina to sell her to her godmother, Dona Julita, "because she has delicious food." Whether or not all diaries are subconsciously written for others, Carolina's handwritten diary fragments conveyed a richly felt sense of her personal life. She

was, as feminist scholars say, "constructing a self."[8]

Many of her diary entries reflect her bitterness at her miserable fate, although she fought against despair, often completing a description of a harrowing day by telling something that had made her happy, such as seeing the sunset or seeing the lights of the city at night. She wrote of death and of watching restaurant employees spill acid on garbage so that the poor could not take food. She wrote about excrement, drunkenness, sons who beat their parents, prostitution, undernourishment, and hopelessness. "Black is our life," she said; "everything is black around us."[9] She wrote about race: how she had always been discriminated against, about how she disliked idle people, about how she disliked most of her fellow blacks, whom she considered lazy. No revolutionary, she believed that if people worked hard within the system they could aspire to a better life.

During the 1950s Carolina tried frequently to find publishers for her writing. She sent a short poem to a newspaper, which was printed, but her other efforts to get her stories and plays and poems and novels published were rebuffed. Interviewed on Brazilian television after the success of her diary made her a celebrity, she said, on camera: "If I weren't so happy I would cry. When I first gave my manuscript to Brazilian editors they laughed at this poor Negro woman with calloused hands who wore rags and only had two years of schooling. They told me I should write on toilet paper."[10]

In April 1958 a São Paulo newspaper reporter, Audálio Dantas, discovered that she had written a diary about her hard life; he managed to edit it and publish some of the entries in his newspaper and, in August 1960, had it printed under the title *Quarto de Despejo.* It became the best-selling book in Brazilian history and brought its author worldwide fame. Her spirits soared. In a television interview she said: "Today I had lunch in a wonderful restaurant and a photographer took my picture. I told him: 'Write under the photo that Carolina who used to eat from trash cans now eats in restaurants. That she has come back into the human race and out of the Garbage Dump.'"[11]

Carolina's 182-page *Quarto de Despejo* describes in vivid detail the way its author survived by scavenging for trash. It refers not only to the trash found in slums but to the backroom in many Brazilian houses, an enclosed porch or a space under the back stoop, used for the storage of junk before its disposal. The title, then, refers to a nondescript place in the back where trash was allowed to accumulate, just as human castoffs and people considered rubbish were allowed to accumulate in the growing shantytowns of Brazil's cities. Even after Dantas's discovery of Carolina, she lived for nearly two more years in the favela, scavenging and raising pigs near her shack, with no royalty income.

Things changed considerably when the book appeared. *Quarto* sold nearly one hundred thousand copies within the first few months of its publication date, and sales might have been higher had not the metal plates warped from overuse. Within the next few years, the diary was translated into more than a dozen languages. Today, it is still in print in France, Britain, Japan, Germany, Cuba, and Russia. The

English version (*Child of the Dark*) sold well in hardcover and considerably better in paperback. It has been in print continuously since 1962 and has been on the assigned-reading list in Latin American studies courses and women's studies courses in the United States and Canada of a generation of college-level students, a fact that has not been lost on Brazilian critics who do not consider the book authentic ("Dantas or someone else must have written it") or significant ("After all, the book is out of date and exaggerates").[12]

Four months after Carolina's diary was published, she was honored by the *paulista* Academy of Letters and the University of São Paulo Law School. When she arrived early at the Academy building for the ceremony, she was turned away at the door by the black porter because he did not believe that a black woman had business there, even though she was dressed in fashionable clothing she had purchased on the elite Rua Augusta.

Only one group of contemporaries received her as a role model rather than an oddity. This was a small group of educated blacks in São Paulo, the Niger Circle, heirs of the Frente Negra (Black Front) of the 1930s. Circle members were black writers and intellectuals who published a small magazine, *Niger,* addressed, in their words, to the "Negro Collectivity." Invisible to the mainstream white cultural elite of the city, they humbly and graciously honored Carolina and placed her photograph on the cover of its September 1960 issue of the magazine.

In 1960 and 1961, Carolina received in royalties for her diary the equivalent of $7,338, an amount that would be worth five times that today and was enough for her to purchase a house. She continued writing diary entries, and in 1961 her publisher issued a second diary, *Casa de Alvenaria* (Cinder-block house), narrating her story from the point that her first diary was published to her life in the house of her dreams in the Santana neighborhood.

The sucess of *Quarto de Despejo* had made possible the purchase of her house, but her new neighbors rejected her, and she was continually hounded by curiosity seekers and people

2. Carolina in her shack in the Canindé favela. The boy on the right is probably her son João; the boy at the left near the shack is José Carlos. Vera is sitting on the ground, hidden by the boy running in front of the camera. *Photographer unknown.*

looking for handouts. Only a few years after her mercurial success she was forced back into poverty. During the early 1970s, she moved to Parelheiros, on the outskirts of the city, where she had constructed a house made of cement blocks on a plot of land on which she could grow vegetables and raise chickens. She and her family almost died of starvation until her children—João, José Carlos, and Vera Eunice—could bring in enough income to stabilize their fortunes, and she often traveled two hours by bus downtown where she scavenged for usable refuse, just as she had done in Canindé.

Carolina Maria de Jesus wrote four other books, which were published without success, and many poems, short stories, and memoir fragments. When she died in 1977, the obituaries in the Brazilian press scarcely hid their ambivalence about her. She had dropped from sight; even Audálio Dantas, her discoverer, had lost touch with her. Brazil had gone through a decade and a half of military dictatorship, and the social reformism that had been prominent in 1960 when her diary was published had evapo-rated, replaced by a polarization of attitudes marked at one end of the spectrum by the right-wing backers of the military, who favored economic development over social change, and at the other end by leftists, mostly driven underground, who ignored Carolina because she was not revolutionary enough for them. The obituary published in Rio de Janeiro's *Jornal do Brasil* illustrated this ambivalence:

> Carolina Maria de Jesus, the author of *Quarto de Despejo*, died yesterday . . . as poor as she had been when she began to write the diary that would turn into the major bestseller in Brazil of all time. . . . Her book royalties allowed Carolina in 1961 to purchase a brick house, a symbol—as she often pointed out—of her personal victory over hunger and misery. But her second book failed to attain the popularity of the first, and she began to quarrel with her friends and supporters, including the journalist Audálio Dantas, who had discovered her when she was scavenging for paper on which to write her diary and who had acted as her agent.
>
> Little by little, Carolina began to lose the resources that her book had brought her. She purchased everything in sight; she visited the famous, frequented the salons of the rich—but in time she began to irritate her hosts. . . . Her inability to adjust

to success cost her dearly. . . . Forced to sell her brick house for nonpayment of debts, she relocated her family to a rural shack along the Parelheiros road. There she raised chickens and pigs and lived in poverty, refusing, however, to become a burden on her now grown children. It was in this place that she was found yesterday, dead of an attack of acute asthma.

"When her body was discovered," the obituary concluded," the mayor of nearby Embú-Guaçú offered a valedictory. She was buried in the cemetery at Vila Cipó, a polluted industrial suburb near Parelheiros, the place to which she had escaped in search of fresh air and seclusion."

Carolina de Jesus was not the only nonelite writer to be overlooked by Brazilian critics and the reading public. In 1965, Maura Lopes Cançado published a diary, *Hospício é Deus*,[13] a narrative account of a troubled woman's experience in a mental hospital. Like Carolina, Maura had been born in the interior of the state of Minas Gerais, although Maura's father was a rich and influential landowner. Nonetheless, Maura's diary, which critic Reynaldo Jardim called a "cry for help," went largely unnoticed.[14] Brazilians did not care enough about her experience to buy her book, and her planned second diary never appeared. In 1983, Civilização Brasileira, one of the most important publishers in Rio de Janeiro, published *Ai de Vós!*, the diary of a domestic servant, Francisca Souza da Silva.[15] To prove that she actually wrote the book, the publisher reproduced a page of the diary manuscript written in the author's own hand. Francisca's diary was better written than Carolina's and not nearly as caustic, yet even the diary of a maid who played by the rules of elite society—she affected a self-effacing posture, accepting life's difficulties as a lesson teaching humility—her book was completely disregarded. Brazilians during the 1970s and 1980s showed little interest in women writing about their difficult lives.

In 1990 I recruited a team of volunteers in São Paulo to help find out what had happened to Carolina's family. Her book had been out of print since 1976, and most university students had never heard of her. The project succeeded finding and interviewing in depth not only Carolina's two surviving children, Vera Eunice and José Carlos, but talking with Audálio Dantas, her publisher, Paulo Dantas, the midwife who delivered her daughter, Vera, the child actor who had played José Carlos in a play about Carolina during the mid-1960s, and the social worker who knew Carolina and who had tried to help her. Several book projects about Carolina emerged from this effort; all royalties from them, including from this book, are being paid to Vera in trust for Carolina's grandchildren.

In addition, we attempted to find a home for Vera's deteriorating archive of her mother's papers, clippings, and photographs. Many of her papers and possessions have disappeared over the years, and those that remained were in precarious physical condition. In 1995 the United States Library of Congress agreed to microfilm the collection, using the facilities of the Brazilian National Library. Once Vera agreed to this plan, and once she became sufficiently trustful of José Carlos Sebe and me (in the past others, in her view, had taken advantage of her), she turned over the additional thirty-seven notebooks of unpublished writing by her mother.

Reception at Home and Abroad
Publicity aroused by our project led to a full-page story on Carolina's children in the weekly newsmagazine *Istoé* and led to the republication of her diary by Editora Ática in 1993. This edition was designed to appeal to a young persons' market. The cover—drawn by an artist in an idealized manner— depicted a handsome black woman and three children, draped like statues. Editora Ática also published a supplement for teachers that offered questions and answers about the book. This edition sold fairly well in Brazil and awakened a new awareness of Carolina Maria de Jesus.

Brazilian critics, however, continued to berate Carolina and to denigrate her significance. In October 1993, following the publication of the new Ática edition of her diary, the literary scholar Wilson Martins wrote a savage review *in the Jornal do Brasil* in which he dismissed *Quarto de Despejo* as a "literary mystification" and a fake.[16] Someone as ignorant as Carolina could never have written such a book, he argued. Martins attacked the book's "precious" language. He commented on Carolina's "casual lovers," disparaging her morals. Moreover, he insinuated that the real author of the book was Audálio Dantas. Dantas's outraged reply was published only six weeks later in the same newspaper.

"I kept the author's language and grammar without altering it in any way," he stated. "In the work of compilation there are long cuts, without significance. The essential, the important, remained. . . . What I did was something similar to editing a film." "The originals are preserved lest anyone challenges me," he concludes.[17] Given the evidence of the unpublished diaries, it is clear that Dantas's assertion is correct and Martins's allegations are wholly erroneous.

I wrote to Martins in Curitiba, politely telling him that there was documentary evidence to prove that Dantas had not put words in Carolina's mouth, and mailed him a draft copy of the manuscript of *The Life and Death of Carolina Maria de Jesus.*[18] Although Martins acknowledged receipt of the letter and manuscript, he did not change his mind: in a review in April 1995 of the Brazilian version of the study about Carolina, *Cinderela Negra,*[19] he repeated the charge that Carolina's diary was a "literary mystification" and chided foreign specialists who use it in their classes as naive and ingenuous.

The reaction to the campaign to revive interest in Carolina de Jesus in the form of the Brazilian publication of *Cinderela Negra* in the summer of 1994 and its English version, *The Life and Death of Carolina Maria de Jesus,* published in the United States early in 1995, differed enormously. Martins's angry attacks were answered only once, in a column in São Paulo's *Jornal da Tarde,* by the anthropologist Roberto Da Matta, who teaches at the University of Notre Dame.[20] Da Matta scolded Brazilian intellectuals for failing to acknowledge the symbolic importance of Carolina's cries from the depths of the lower class. His was the only defense of our books besides the favorable essay of the literary critic Marisa Lajolo in the preface of *Cinderela Negra*. All other Brazilian reviews of *Cinderela Negra* were perfunctory, never dealing with any of the important issues we raised.

In the United States, university faculty teaching courses in Latin American studies or women's studies embraced *The Life and Death of Carolina Maria de Jesus* as a useful classroom tool. The home page website established for Carolina on the University of Miami's Latin American studies home page drew more than one thousand visits in the first six months of its posting. Several teachers sent descriptions of how they used *Life and Death* together with Carolina's first diary, *Child of the Dark*.[21] One scholar at the April 1997 meeting of the Latin American Studies Association in Guadalajara asked for clarification about how each of the authors felt about Carolina de Jesus in the light of the different receptions the book received inside Brazil and outside. This was the response:

> The answer to the question asking for clarification about how José Carlos and I feel about Carolina Maria de Jesus's work now is that we agree without

qualification that her words embodied the voice of the Brazilian underclass. She was a special person, courageous for proving that she could live alone, protect and provide for her children, and maintain her independence. José Carlos underscores the symbolic value of her writing (she is the only poor Brazilian, for example, to have written plays). I place greater emphasis on her role as a spokesperson for the poor and for what the treatment she received teaches us about the dark side of Brazilian social structure. Here, probably, is where we still diverge. I feel that it is more urgent to deal with Carolina as a victim of social prejudices, whether or not her world—especially the world of the 1950s and 1960s—any longer exists. I emphasize the reasons that she was rejected—by persons on the right of the spectrum (probably because she was too feisty and did not play the passive role prescribed for women, especially those rising out of lower-class origins), and by intellectuals on the Left, who wanted her to be more politicized, an advocate of left-wing causes.[22]

The Real Carolina

In early 1996, Vera Eunice de Jesus Lima revealed to us that her mother had preserved forty-two hundred pages of writing—a mixture of copies of original diary entries, new diary entries (including some, as we have seen, as late as 1966, when Brazil was under military dictatorship), short stories, plays, and commentaries. Of all of these invaluable materials, the diary entries remain the most significant, for two reasons. First, it becomes clear that Dantas's deletions were so extensive that the Carolina Maria de Jesus who emerges from the pages of *Quarto de Despejo,* the international bestseller, was a different woman from the one that emerges from the pages of her unedited diaries. The former was docile, wistful, and seemingly reluctant to comment on the gritty realities of Brazilian politics. Dantas presented her through his editing as a woman who was aware of her miserable condition but who stood at a curious distance from the events she lived through; she comes across as a fatalist, a woman with a dream who stands isolated by her dreaming. The real Carolina, revealed in her unedited writings, was feisty, opinionated, and quick to blame politicians and officials for the wretched conditions in which the poor were forced to live.

Carolina embarrassed people who believed (or subscribed to) to the myth of Brazil's racial tolerance. Intellectuals displayed their own thinly veiled prejudices by pointing out that Carolina herself was intolerant. "I walked with her in the street a few times," her publisher, Paulo Dantas, said, "but I noted that she hated the common people." "Perhaps this hatred inside her existed," he concluded, "because it reminded her of things she wanted to forget." Although Carolina criticized lazy blacks—namely, the unemployed black migrants from the northeast who lived in Canindé— her writings are filled with expressions of pride in her blackness. She expressed sorrow for blacks who suffered hardship because of the discrimination against them. Few took her side when she pointed out in her writing that in Brazil blacks were still treated like slaves, but during the Centenary of Abolition public debates over slavery's legacy in 1988 many black militants and academics made the same rhetorical point, asserting that slavery had never really been abolished.

Few people understood the thickness of the protective shell

3. Carolina, surrounded by her children, signing autographs at a social function arranged by her publisher, 1960. *Photographer unknown.*

that Carolina had been forced to construct around herself in response to decades of fierce adversity. Audálio Dantas did not remain her patron for long. Carolina, he insisted, would not accept the relationship he needed to impose on her as her agent. She never asked to be defended or cared for—she was too independent for that. Dantas explained that he could not deal with what he considered Carolina's petulance and irascibility. His opinion is consistent with that of other journalists and intellectuals who gave up on her. Perhaps it is understandable that her diary continued to sell strongly outside of Brazil, where readers wanted to find in her words an expression of rage against poverty and suffering that Brazilians had grown tired of because they considered her attitudes simplistic and self-serving. She was a product of a society that tolerated the most glaring maldistribution of wealth in the world, yet she did not lend her voice to calls for massive social change. She simply wanted to escape from poverty with her children and to become a famous writer.

The unedited diary entries reproduced in this book depict the accurate Carolina. We have preserved her Joycean stream-of-consciousness language, her pithy characterizations, her allusions to antiquity. In her writing she was fearless. She is not too proud to admit that when she could not find enough scraps to sell, she went begging, because more than anything else she had to protect her children. She does not permit herself to be depressed, although she suffered from mood swings all her life. Even on days on which her family went hungry she tells her diary how much she loves her children, as if to fortify herself in her constant struggle to survive.

We intend not only to set the record straight by providing detailed translations of her unedited diaries but to explain why Brazilian elites were motivated to obscure Carolina's true personality and present her as something she was not. The book, then, is not only about Carolina Maria de Jesus but about Brazil as a whole as set down by her sarcastic pen.

Among the entries of Carolina's unedited notebooks dated 4 December 1958 is the following statement:

> This my Diary I wrote ten years Ago but I had no intention of popularizing myself i aimed to reveal my situation and the situation of my children that is the situation of the favelados.
> Carolina Maria de Jesus
> Carolina with an afflicted heart, due to the daily insipidity. Could it be that God will return to punish us and reprove us because of our errors, or will he forgive us with his go[od] . . .

These entries were written during the period
after Carolina's discovery by Dantas but before
her book *Quarto de Despejo* was published. She
had become well known in São Paulo (although
not outside of that city) after Dantas's
newspaper had printed several of her entries
edited by Dantas. Because she was not certain
that her book actually would appear in print,
this was a wait-and-see period for her. She was
still destitute, searching for paper, cardboard,
tin, even manure to sell to provide food for the
next day. Her daughter, Vera Eunice, was five
years old when these diary pages were penned,
her sons, João and José Carlos, a few years older.

1958

When they saw me many fled
supposing I took no note
Others asked to have a read
at the verses that I wrote

It was paper that I collected
to finance my living needs
In the garbage I resurrected
many books for me to read
So many things I wished to do
but prejudice checked my tracks
If I die I want to be born anew
in a country run by Blacks
Farewell, Goodbye! I am going to die!
And these verses I leave to my country
if I have the right to be once more alive
With happy Blacks I will find me

4. Carolina during one of her book signings, 1960. *Photographer unknown.*

30 October 1958 I got out of bed at 5 o'clock and went to haul water. What torture! There is a hole in my tin can and I don't know when I will be able to buy another. I lit the burner and put water on to heat for the children to wash their faces.

They detest cold water.

I went to buy bread and [get] water. Just in the mornings I am spending 30 [cruzeiros]. The children went to school and I went out with Vera since it is not raining. Vera went to the cold-storage plant to beg a sausage. I sensed that something was up since there are police in the streets.

I talked with a municipal worker. He complained that he paid 5 for the bus.

It can't go on like this. It was [Mayor] dr. Adhemar [de Barros] who upped the bus fares—not that he is against dr. Adhemar. All of them raise the fares but they are already badmouthing dr. Adhemar to keep him from Catete Palace [the presidency]. The people have to understand that the only decent politician in Brazil is dr. Adhemar.

The municipal worker took off his hat looked to heaven and said: God must help him get to Catete.

I went on. Looking at the *paulistas* [residents of the city of São Paulo] who amble about with sad faces.

I did not see a single smile.

Today can be called a sad day. I began to add up how much I will spend on the streetcar when I take the children to the city. 3 children and me, 24 return fare I thought of the rice at 30 a kilo, bread, and other expenses.

So I think: and if the majority go crazy thinking about life? A woman called me over to give me some paper. She told me that due to the fare increase the police were in the streets. She looked sad. I understood that the news of the fare increase made everybody sad. She told me:

They spend on the elections and afterwards they raise everything.

Auro lost the election, meat prices went up. Adhemar lost, fares went up.

A little each time, they put back what they spent.

The ones who pay for the elections are . . . the people! I went to Dona Julita. I saw her son Fausto for the first time. He is beautiful. She gave me coffee and food I heated it and ate it right there.

I think the worst thing in the world is to tolerate such a man. If the men knew how they burn women's patience, they would not be so pretentious.

She gave me a black sweater. There was a time when I got only red clothes. Now it's black. I got sick of red. I fished out lots of old scrap metal.

I left some in a depot and took some back.

When I passed the newsstand I read the students' slogan

—Juscelino [Kubitschek, the incumbent president] flays!!!

Janio [Quadros, the presidential candidate] kills!!!

—Adhemar steals!!!

—The city council upholds!!!

—And the people pay!!!

I thought over what dr. Adhemar said at a rally. Salaries go up a step at a time, but prices take the elevator. I took dr. Adhemar's sound words and made up this little rhyme:

Life is such a sacrifice!
for men who labor and thrift
A step at a time their salaries rise
while prices take the lift.

I think: could dr. Adhemar have forgotten his words! . . . Or is he fed up? thinking that he is great but that people don't give him any mind I arrived home at 11 o'clock heated up the food for the children Afterward I lay down to rest a little. Then I got up and went to ask Rosalina for the cart to go to Cruz Azul to sell some cans.

João and Vera went with me.

What torment! I can't manage a cart. The sacks fell out. On Pedro Vicente street a man who was throwing out his garbage gave me some cans. There is a school there I said to him: life goes on, right buddy? It was enough said for him to offer me the cans. The cart was already full and it was a sacrifice to take the cans. But I took them because when I decide to do something, I do it.

I am afraid of the *mineiros* [inhabitants of the state of Minas Gerais] because of their "leave it for tomorrow!" [attitude] I like to go to Cruz Azul. If I were to work there I would like it they are decent there. they asked for Rosalina when I left Cruz Azul I went to the paper depot to pick up a sack for my scrap metal. I put Vera and João into the cart.

I stopped along the railroad tracks to fetch the cans. because the guard let me leave them near the guardhouse. The guard asked me how much I would earn from the tin cans.

I answered 300. I am fed up with odd jobs.

He said that better this than nothing. I told him that the tins of cooking oil were 70, a good price. He said: instead of going up it comes down. Living is very expensive. Even women are expensive. When he wants a fuck the women want so much money that he passes it up. I pretended not to hear because I don't talk pornography.

I left without thanking him.

When I arrived at the shantytown it was 5 o'clock. I made coffee and went to buy sugar and a bit of wrapping paper for the notebooks that are going to New York.

I talked with senhor Eduardo I said I had sold the tin cans. I asked him which of his brothers had the most beautiful children.

—Mine!

I laughed and told him of the proverb about the owl. [He] smiled.

I wandered through the streets. I earned 40.

Vera found some bits of scrap metal.

I arrived at the shantytown at 11. I almost go crazy. I go indoors and there is nothing to eat. I don't approve of the increases because they wreak havoc on the life of the workers. In the past the politicians acted as agents for the people. Now they don't consult the people. When I came back to the shantytown I met Rosalina and she let me put the cans into her cart. Dona Armanda gave some vegetable fritters. I got home Tired and sad because the muse dislikes seeing her people oppressed. There was a time when limits were placed on workers' labor and the people lived happily. Today they work too much and are miserable As soon as I lay down I heard voices. I thought: a fight! Tomorrow I will find out.

31 October 1958 I got out of bed at 5 A.M. and went to fetch water. How nice! No line. Because it is raining. I noticed that the shanty-town women were upset and talking. I asked what happened They said that Orlando Lopes the current owner of the light network [electric power source in the favela] beat up Zefa And she reported him to the police and he was arrested.

I asked Geraldinho if it was true.

He said yes. If he [Lopes] beats up Pitita, he will see Pitita is the biggest whore in the shantytown.

That Orlando Lopes and Juaquim Paraiba were arrested. I heard the women say that people with children should behave themselves. At the door of Zefa's house there is a line of men. I made coffee and sent João to buy 10 worth of bread.

They went off to school, and I went out with Vera. The policemen are still on the streets. I met Nena and her mother Dona Dindita. Nena told me that Orlando really gave Zefa a beating. I went to fetch paper. Vera went to the cold-storage place to beg a sausage. I earned 106. Vera earned 6 cruzeiros because she entered the bar for a glass of water and they thought she was begging.

I paid the shoemaker for fixing Vera's shoes. Then I went shopping. I am shocked that rice is 30 a kilo. I bought rice, black beans and soap and the 100 cruzeiros disappeared I remembered the words of the black man who gave Vera 5 cruzeiros. That the paulistas are wrong, the strike should be a general one. fight the food prices that oppress us. That it is not only the CMTC [Municipal Transport Company] that exploits the people, exploitation is general.

At the bus stop I heard a man say he was a supporter of Adhemar. The others in the line reacted and an argument began First there were only 2. Then others. There is a rumor that Dr. Adhemar is in Rio de Janeiro. I think: when a politician's decisions displease the people he should not disappear He should stay around and explain why it was necessary to raise the fares He who does something and flees, is a rogue. The people are saying that Dr. Adhemar raised fares to get back at them for not voting for him. That he wants to chastise them. Politicians don't lose anything.

—When he loses at the polls he grabs the voters and tans their hides, and then, after using them in this way, forgets how they helped him get into office. . . .

When I got home the boys were already there. I heated the food. There was very little and they stayed hungry. I'm not irritable because I know that it doesn't solve anything. In all the streetcars they're put a policeman. And the busses too. The people don't know how to fight back. They should go to the Ibirapuera Palace [the mayor's office] and the state Assembly and give a kick to those shame faced political pygmies who don't know how to run the country.

I am unhappy because I didn't have anything to eat. I don't know what we are going to do [if] people work they are hungry [and] if they don't work they are hungry. Many people are saying that we must kill Dr. Adhemar That he is ruining the country. Whoever travels 4 times on the bus contributes 600 to the CMTC. Whoever takes the streetcar and the bus spends 1000 on transportation only. At this rate nobody can save for the future. In the morning when I was going out Orlando and Juaquim Paraiba were returning from jail.

1 November 1958 I got up at 5 and 44 [5:44 A.M.]. I went to fetch water. There was no line. I sent João to buy 10 worth of bread. I made coffee. João and José Carlos went with me. I went to the Incapre Cold Storage to get bones. Afterwards I went to the Pedacha [market] but got nothing since it had closed. After I went to the scrap metal deposit to sell some bits. I got 23. I went to the Guine bakery and Dona Madalena gave me bananas, sweet rolls 15 sweet rolls. Pieces of cheese, ham, and salami. I was pleased I found a sack of cornmeal in the garbage and brought it home for the pig. I am so used to garbage cans that I can't pass them by without fishing about inside. Today I didn't go after paper since I know I won't find any. An old man gets there before me. Yesterday I read the fable of the frog and the cow I have the impression that I am the frog That he wanted to grow to the size of the cow—I wanted many jobs.

They refused me due to my poetic talk, so for this reason I don't like to talk to anybody

Today I went begging

I got some *linguiça* [sausage] and other things I got home late and put the beans on to cook and began to clean the clay pots. João went to the market to pick up discarded greens I was making lunch when João arrived with vegetables and greens.

There are times when I really enjoy my children. And there are days when I would love to mince and remince them. Whoever has children. Rather whoever is poor needs to pluck up courage to survive. Work, beg what one cannot do is leave them starving. I soaped up the laundry and meant to wash it but I am cold and under the weather.

I sensed that the people still think we should revolt against food prices and not only loot the CTMC Whoever reads what Dr. Adhemar said in the newspapers that he lamented signing the increase says:

Adhemar is mistaken.

—He has no heart!

The hearts of politicians are like the tunnels of the Donatists.*

If the cost of living continues to rise until 1966 we will have:

—a revolution!

I try to keep João indoors to read so he won't go outdoors to play because he is very strong. When he pushes a kid they fall down and begin to cry. and they come to me to complain João wants to be a boxer. Healthy sport. I went to bed at 7:30 because I was exhausted.

If I had to be out at night I would never make it. I don't go to the movies since I have no money and don't feel like it. I was asleep when Lalau and her mother-in-law put on a show that woke me up. If the shantytown disappears Lalau and her family won't find anybody to rent to them because when they drink the foul jargon

---

* The Donatists were Christian heretics in 4th and 5th century Carthage who, presumably, burrowed out tunnels for hiding.

makes its entry you can tell that it's the grownups in the shanty-towns who distort childrens' morals. It's to be known! Poor favela children. Deolinda only stays at home if there is drink. If not, she will go out at any hour to buy it.

2 November 1958 I got up and went to the river where I washed clothes until 7:30. Darça went to wash clothes and we talked about the shameful goings-on in the favela. We talked to Zefa. She gets it from everybody. I spoke of the women who don't work but always have plenty of cash. We spoke of the romance between Lalau and Dona Maria. And Dona Maria says he's going with Nena. —That Nena is a fool.

I took the colored clothes and went to make coffee. I thought I had coffee. There was none—How horrible it is to be hungry and have nothing to eat.

We ate hominy grits. And José Carlos scraped some bones The bones they gave us at the Incapre cold-storage place.

I am horrified and agitated when I see my children hunting for something to eat. They look like dogs raiding the garbage bins A show that I watch with hate for the politicians who could fix prices for basic foodstuffs. João ate a sweet roll. I ate beans and manioc meal.

I made the beds. I dread going in my tiny bedroom because it is so cramped. I have to undo the bed in order to sweep.

I sweep the little room every two weeks. I put the beans to cook and went to finish the washing. Cirçe was at her window and asked me how I am doing. I told her that I'm fine And that the reporters of the tabloids are going to give me a furnished house. She told me that I won't get used to living in a decent House and to give it to her. I think: does Cirçe think me a fool? I finished washing the clothes at 11 o'clock. I hung the clothes on the rack. Then I felt sick. I could not sit down, I lay down. I was so tired and upset João went out. I didn't want to sweep the shack. I have no water to make lunch.

Ills multiply.

I decided to lie down a bit. I picked out a book to read. João and José Carlos appeared.

—Is lunch ready? Asked João. Looking at the stove.

I didn't make lunch because you both went off. Sundays they don't stay at home. I heated beans and manioc meal they ate.

I began to make lunch. I went to fetch a pail of water to make lunch.

I told João to peel garlic and clean the rice.

João disappeared. I sensed that he was off to the movies Lunch was ready, and my children didn't turn up. I ate little because I am tired.

I grabbed a book to read. Then I felt a chill. I went outside to sit in the sunshine It was too hot I sat in the shade. I washed a lot of laundry. I am tired.

After I wrote. Senhor Manoel turned up. He said to me: he didn't bring the 200 because he fell and hurt himself. I sensed he was lying. But I kept quiet. I wanted to be like the other Blacks who know how to be assertive. I don't. I told Senhor Manoel that I [would] cuss him out. He told me that on the 10th he will give me the cash. He went off about the favela I noticed that a lot of people have moved into the favela.

There is no more room.

i think if the favela sails away what will they do to house these shoeless ones. We of the favela are the shoeless feet. There are men here with 7 children and no work. And they eat of the good and the best. If the favela goes they can count on the politicians. They only need to say they are sick and that does it. I told a man that there is a rumor that the favela will go to make room for Avenida Marginal [a bypass]. He said: not yet. The town hall has no money. That Dr. Adhemar is a no-good politician. That another mayor will do something. That Dr. Adhemar does nothing. That he would make a good politician. But he is too greedy. That if he becomes President of the Republic Brazil will turn into a mixed salad That any sergeant will be in command. That he will mix with the no-goods. I told him that I would vote or am going to vote for Dr. Adhemar if I live until then.

João came back from the movies. I smacked him and he ran off. I have a headache. I spoke with Antonio the shoemaker about the suicide of Senhor Esmael. He said that those who drink . . .

3 November 1958 I got up at 5 o'clock. I turned on the burner and went out to buy bread and butter Senhor Eduardo was irritated because the milkman forgot to leave his milk. He asked me to ask dona Maria if she had milk for him.

I came back and told senhor Eduardo that she didn't He weighed my notebooks. They weighed 7 kilos, 700 [grams]. Tomorrow I will mail them to the United States. I bought 10 of coffee 8 of bread and 10 of Claybon [margarine]. I made coffee and changed the children's clothes they went to school and I went with Vera to fetch paper.

I went to Dona Julita. She was at mass. When she returned she gave me coffee, food, and newspapers.

Senhor João Pires was groaning. I got irritated since I can't stand his personality. And I, I can't banish him. I left Dona Julita's house at 9 o'clock. I will clean her house I asked senhor João if he wants me to fatten a pig for him. He can order it from Jaú. He said it was too much trouble. I told him it wasn't difficult. I got paper on the Rua Eduardo Chaves. In that house where they fix victrolas.

I asked the woman where her husband was. She answered:

—He is a good man. Some days ago he left without saying where he was going. I won't go after him. I don't miss him. If he doesn't come back he'll be doing me a favor.

I laughed thinking about the dilemma of wives.

she asked me if I am tired

—I am not tired. I don't envy married women

to get money to send the notebooks I got together 360 cans of oil and 60 of wax with lids.

—He* said: fantastic.

A man was drinking beer and I asked for a sip—He gave me

---

* Carolina wrote "he" in her diary but she probably meant to write "she."

some I got to the favela and heated up food for the children. Beforehand, I smelled and tasted it to see if it was bad. I reread some verses to put the accents. After that I packaged them up.

I and João, we started to sing. I sent José Carlos to buy a spool of thread to sew the notebooks because I filled one up. The spool cost 8 cruzeiros. I thought that one of these days it would go up to 10. I bathed the children. They went to bed. I washed the dishes and brushed my teeth and took a bath. Then I went to write—I felt tired and sleepy. I ate a piece of bread with butter and went to bed. I killed some fleas that were wandering about the bed and lay down. I didn't see another thing.

I slept for three hours straight. I woke to the voice of Juaquim [P]araiba, who was complaining about his girlfriend. But she doesn't like to make love in the dark. Only by day and at night near to some light.

I think: he is up to no good with that girlfriend.

How nice it would be if all the women decided to make love by daylight.

Today I am not agitated.

I ran into an acquaintance. A blond man who sold scrap iron in Salvador He said I was irritated

I told him that I am tired from working so hard. Day, and night.

4 November 1958 I got out of bed at 5 o'clock and went to fetch water. Adalberto was tipsy and talking to himself as he went by. i thought: he drinks so much that even sleep does not wear off the effect of the alcohol. After I bought bread made coffee and we went out hunting for paper.

The Newspaper says that there wouldn't be any school so I didn't send the children. i went by the Cruz Azul [market] to be paid. I got 325. I earned 65. I went to D. Julita She was in Santo Andre. Eduardo gave 5 to José Carlos. A woman who looks after the factory on the Avenida do Estado gave me paper. I bought a sandwich for the children. When I arrived home it was 11. I saw the bus that took the children to the Coca Cola factory. Mine were shoeless and not going.

I dashed home. I bought lettuce rice and cheese and got ready to mail the book—I went. I arrived at the post office and had to undo the wrapping since the post office doesn't handle wrapped-up bundles. The stamp salesclerk taught me how to make a package. The notebooks have to be visible. I went to a bookstore to undo the package. i bought 1 piece of lined paper to write the address i went to the post office there wasn't enough money to send the book. 100 short. I went to the court of justice to see if Vera's father had left child support money for me. He hadn't. I got irritated. When I was coming back I stopped at a newsstand. I saw a man calling the police idiots. May they prevail.

In the clichè,* a policeman beat up an old man. The newspaper said it was a policeman from the DOPS [security police]

I decided to take the streetcar home. i only paid the return fare, because when I went to the city a nice man paid my fare. In the bus was senhor Eduardo's mother-in-law. i thought I would sit near her because she is nice. Then I decided to sit near a man. We talked about dr. Adhemar. The only name that one hears due to the rise in bus fares. The man told me that our politicians are merrymakers.

I think that dr. Adhemar is fed up. And he decided to show his muscle to demonstrate the strength he has to punish us poor people. They don't bother with the upper Echelons. The king of politics was dr. Aleram Lurcasil Caucária a calm contestant who didn't get upset if he lost. If he won he didn't try to show off to avoid envy. I talked with the man who was going to write a letter to dr. Adhemar. May my letters calm his nerves.

I got home tired and aching. I met Vera on the street. My dear João, my model of a son, is no good. The shack was open, the shoes scattered over the floor. He didn't put the beans on to cook. I put on the fire and went to lie down. i put Vera to bed. She quieted

---

* Carolina wrote "clichê" but probably meant "guichê," a word borrowed from the French meaning, in working-class Portuguese, a doorway or closed space.

down after a beating. I slept from 4 to 6. José Carlos came home, I told him to heat up the beans, but because I called him low-down lazybones he didn't do it. I can't stand my children because they are lazy. It was 6:30 when João showed up. I told him to heat the beans. After I hit him with a chain and a pole. And I tore up the damned comic books. kind of reading that I loathe.

I made dinner and lay down. When I get angry they don't talk to me. I see that I only manage to be obeyed with force. José Carlos came in and asked me if he was going to get a beating.

Today no. Early tomorrow. Right now I'm too tired.

Today a rumor started that the Light [light company] is going to cut the power. and the water too to do away with the shantytown.

The women in the favela are a bunch of gossips.

5 November 1958 I got up at 5 o'clock and went for water. I made coffee and went to get bread. i put water on to heat to give the kids a bath. I don't know how they manage to get dirt into their hair. They went to school. And I went out alone. I didn't take Vera because she has a cold.

I walked quickly and went by the warehouse and said to Senhor Eduardo:

—Your mother-in-law told me that you are a saint. So bring on a miracle and come up with one hundred cruzeiros.

He told me to think only of him and it would work. I went through various streets. I went to Dona Julita to see if senhor João Pires was any better. I had coffee and Dona Julita told me that there was food i asked her to keep it, that I was on my way to the city to send the book to the United States and on the return, I would pick up the food.

I went to Satape. There was a lot of cardboard. I took it to the storehouse they weighed it and Julio paid me. He gave me the money and I counted 105. I was pleased and went home. I got there at 11. i made a salad from the tomato and watercress that senhor Luiz gave me. I heated up the food I was so hungry. but I didn't eat to save it for the kids. What torture. To be hungry have food and not be able to eat. —I cussed out the politicians. People are so hungry, and they still raise food prices. i changed clothes to go out. As I was leaving I thought I had better put on Vera's shoes or she would cut her foot. i thought: i am in a hurry and will be right back. Later I will put on her sandals. I grabbed the notebooks and a liter bottle, and went by the warehouse where I sold the liter bottle to senhor Eduardo for 3 cruzeiros to pay the bus.

When I got to the bus stop I met Dona Adelaide's Toninho. He works at the [S]araiva Bookstore. I said to Toninho: the publishers in Brazil don't publish what I write because I am poor and have nothing to pay them with so I am sending my book to the United States.

He gave me a number of addresses of publishers to look up.

—He paid my bus fare. I was pleased! I prayed that God would make Toninho happy.

I got to the Post Office they weighed the notebooks. 406. i thought: Not here, there is no table of rates. Yesterday it was 412. i thought about the Order and progress written on our flag but it doesn't prevail. I took the stamps. I glued them to the paper that the books were wrapped in There were so many stamps that the notebooks looked dressed up. I took it to the window. Registered airmail A. Gambini waited on me. Slip number 44,290 dispatching ticket number 837,936.

I thought about the coincidence of number 936 to my life. Why the register number is: 845,936. Senhor Gambini, told me to come by the post office. I told him: as soon as I received word from the United States telling me that the book arrived I would let him know. He told me to come by before that I was pleased: I told him that I was sending the originals to the United States, because the publishers in Brazil didn't help poor writers. An embryo that doesn't evolve. An atrophied embryo.

He smiled. I gave him Audálio's article to read.

I said goodbye, and left the post office so as not to pay bus fare, I walked thinking how nice it was of senhor Gambini to invite me Back!

A rare invitation since most men flee from me, or hide when

they see me! When a person flees from me, I begin to treat them coldly. I walked picking up bits of metal that I saw. I passed by Dona Julita's house and asked for food. She heated food for me and her daughter Dona Theresinha was there. She is very nice she told me she is sad over her father's illness It's just that her father is very good.

I told her that senhor João Pires came over to talk when he saw me looking for paper. And if he is driving, he stops the car to greet me. When I saw senhor João, I hid. After I saw that he didn't avoid me I looked out for him to greet him. Dona Julita gave me soup, coffee, and bread for the children. I ate there at D. Julita's.

It was three o'clock. I felt dizzy the furniture revolved around me It's just that my organism isn't used to good food When I was near the Incapre Cold Storage A lady called me over, and gave me some empty cement bags.

i went by the warehouse and bought 1 bread. When I got to the favela Vera had cut her foot. As soon as João saw me he told me I answered that I already knew. That I had been warned. She was sleeping. I looked at the cut. It was big. I decided to go to the pharmacy. The pharmacist didn't want to dress it. I took her, to the Central Hospital. They dressed it and gave her a shot against tetanus [misspelled *teto* 'roof']. I stayed at the Central an hour and a half. The nurse gives Vera 2 cruzeiros. At the Central there was a black man who began to complain of his wife. That due to incompatibility he was going to leave her. I asked him if they got along when they were engaged. He said yes. He complained that he can't live on what he earns. i thought: A worker, poorly paid doesn't find any pleasure in life. He gets neurotic and dissolves his household. The cost of living is a competitor at breaking up homes.

My home isn't broken up because there's no man there.

I asked Black if he had kids.

—No.

—Did he work?

—Yes.

i thought: they have no kids. And even so complain. He is lazy. And weak. He ruined his life from the beginning. God did the right thing, not to give children to lazy people.

The orderlies at the Central asked me if I still write. I answered yes. The male orderly said he knew me. And seeing that I am not lazy—I enjoyed the eulogy. i thought: I am out of fashion because the wagging tongues say, that poets are lazy. A haughty orderly asked me if I knew how to bless.

—I answered no. That Dona Alcelia blesses by name.

He wrote down his name for her to bless him: Adonis Assunção da Selva. When the doctor examined Vera's injection and told me that I could go home I was pleased. Vera said goodbye to the doctor and we went to the Largo São Bento to take the bus. It was 6 o'clock when I got to the favela.

I met José Carlos at the streetcar stop. I told him to go back home. He saw me in the bus and went running off. I got home and João came to tell me that senhor Manoel was waiting for me.

He began to question me. He wants to know if I sell the book if I will buy a house. because the reporters don't give houses—I can't stand the Portuguese because they are calculating. They are like the cats that love velvet pillows i asked João how much he got for the scrap metal bits that he went to sell 40. i took the money and went to buy macaroni for soup. Two weeks ago, I paid 20 for a kilo of macaroni. today, I paid 24 in a few days it will jump to 30. The prices are currently doing triple jumps. I bought 12 of minced meat, it didn't fill a cup. When I got home senhor Manoel had already gone.

He didn't leave me a cent so it's not worth waiting for the man. I can't stand a man who wants to wrap himself up in the shadow of a woman. i made the soup for my children. They slept before it was ready. When it was done I woke them up to eat. We ate and went to sleep. I dreamt of Dona Julita. That she had told me to go work for her and she paid me 4 thousand cruzeiros a month, for me to do the shopping[,] that senhor João Pires didn't want her to touch the money and wanted her to make his food. —I told him that I was going to put my children in an orphanage. And I only took Vera with me to work. —I woke up.

I couldn't get back to sleep. I began to feel hunger pangs. He who has pangs, doesn't sleep. When Jesus said to the women of Jerusalem: —Don't cry for me. Cry for yourselves. his words foresaw the government of senhor [President] Juscelino [Kubitschek]—a period of hardship for the Brazilian poor. Period when the poor had to eat garbage or sleep on an empty stomach. Jesus, prophetized that weak rachitic government. This light without oil that will extinguish itself.

—Have you ever seen a dog, when it chases its tail with its mouth and never catches it?

—It is just like Juscelino's government.

6 November 1958 I got up at 4 o'clock to write. When dawn appeared I went to fetch water. I made coffee and went out for bread. The warehouse was closed. Julio was there with a turkey and bread for senhor Eduardo.

As soon as he opened the door I walked in. I bought 12 of bread and came home to change the kids for school. I washed the pots swept the shack and went out with Vera. I went to work at Dona Julita's. I picked up cans and scrap metal bits that I found. i went by the chicken abattoir to order 2 kilos of feathers to make a fantastic costume [for carnival].

When I got to Dona Julita's it was 8:30. She gave me coffee. The rugs were already out in the sunshine. Vera went to talk to senhor João Pires. And I began to clean house. Vera started to say that she would like to live in a house just like Dona Julita's She made lunch. And I ate.

Vera said while she was eating: —What tasty food!

Dona Julita's food leaves me dizzy. I feel ill. She is pleasant. She was always pressing me to eat. She made manioc pap with milk, cornmeal and eggs for senhor João and gave me a little. When

I finished cleaning, she gave me food, soap, and other things cheese, fat and rice. That long-grained rice. The rice of rich people.

When I got home the kids weren't in. They hadn't eaten the food that I Left them. It was soup. I boiled the soup it hadn't gone sour i gave it to them.

José Carlos arrived. He gave me a letter from the director.

—These are the terms of the letter: "São Paulo, 6 November 1958.

Dona Carolina. I inform you that in spite of the warning that I gave you on 15 September, your son José Carlos has shown little improvement. He confronted a teacher in the classroom in a clear demonstration of undiscipline. For that he is suspended from classes on the 7th, 8th, and 9th of this month. Hoping that nothing out of ordinary ensues and conscious of your worthy guidance —I thank you. Sincerely, Arlindo Caetano Filho"

The teachers and the directors were receptive when I appeared at school. They didn't suspend students They disciplined students by consultation. José Carlos is sad when he misses class because he wants to learn. I give him some projects [to do]. He says he wants to graduate. He wants to know everything about culture.

7 November 1958 I couldn't sleep: Vera began to cough I got up and went to Dona Black Maria to ask for a Melhoral [a brand name for aspirin]. She gave me 1 Cibalena [another brand]. I was afraid to give it to Vera because [when] she had the injection at the Central Senhor João Pires told me that for 2 days she could not injure her-self because the injection could not be reapplied. I thought about the horrible life of Brazil's poor people. And I am also one of them.

I got up and went to fetch water at 5:30 A.M. I lit the stove and didn't go to buy bread since I had no money. I made a porridge of cornmeal and asked my children to do me the favor of eating it. They agreed to. Vera didn't want to. I went to ask Rosalina to lend me her cart to take scrap metal pieces to the depot. She said that she had lent the cart [to someone else]. That when the guy returned from the market I could use it. I got João ready for school and I went after the cart. I waited for the guy to empty it. I went to sell scrap metal bits. I took Vera and José Carlos.

As I approached the Guine bakery, there was a woman washing the pavement and cussing out dr. Adhemar —It is the mayor who ought to live on this dusty street. The only thing that he wants is our money. He ought to wet down the road. I am tired of cleaning the dust, and the house is always dusty—i thought of the Vicious Circle [because] if it rains, there is mud, the mayor is no good because he doesn't pave the streets. If it is sunny and there is dust, the mayor is no good because he doesn't wet down the streets. When will the people understand that when it rains it is muddy. And when it shines it is dusty. Political careers are thorny Senhor Manoel weighed the scrap metal pieces I earned 70. I bought bread, and a cup of coffee with milk for the kids. Two bars of soap 9 cruzeiros each. I was horrified! 1 bar of soap 9 cruzeiros—at this rate the poor is a candidate for dirtiness It only took Adhemar to back one price rise, everything went up. if dr. Adhemar wins over the people and the fare increase holds, things are going to get worse at this end.

Dr. Adhemar isn't affected because he doesn't use public transportation.

—He only uses it to inaugurate it. It is injustice to increase the only transportation of the poor.

The people ennobled dr. Adhemar's philanthropic qualities and said:

—Dr. Adhemar . . . he is a saint. Even my daughter Vera Eunice said: that he is a saint. I heard a lot of people say that body and soul dr. Adhemar was or is going to heaven. —Nowadays I hear people say he is going to hell. That he is the devil's assistant. —The people say: that dr. Adhemar is no good.

—That dona Leonor [the mayors's wife] is good.

So let's adopt the old proverb: for the saint they kiss stones.

I went after José Carlos who was taking his time. I told him to buy meat. When I passed the warehouse I saw the Municipal trucks moving people from the Municipal land. They are cussing dr.

Adhemar—but, they haven't paid rent for 4 years. They should have said: Thank you City Hall. But, more thankless are born than thankful

The weeds multiply easily. The owner of the dona Neusa candy factory watched the women fighting with the supervisor, and smiled

I said to him: now with Adhemar, force takes hold!

—Get off my place!

José Carlos was late because he went to school. He is so sad because the director suspended him for these 3 days: i could tell he loves school. Here is a verse for dr. Adhemar to beat on a drum:

—I was candidate for office:
And elect me they did not.
Now I am rebellious:
Claiming mine from what they've got.
All town lands are being cleared.
The favela poor are uneasy, I fear.

I went out to sell some cement bags. I took João along to learn the way to the depot i got 21. When I got home I sat down to rest The place is a mess Senhor Manoel arrived. I talked to him about the life of working as little as possible that I plan to have. I send João out to buy coffee and Claybon I swept the room and made the beds. I washed the dishes and went to fetch a can of water I talked with a northerner who is my neighbor who dr. Adhemar is ordering to clear the town lands. What I wonder is if he is going to clear the shantytown He told me that he heard we were going to Tremembé.

—I answered that the poor there don't want us—I think we can sing:

—The favela of Canindé
Is moving to Tremembé
But the poor from over there
Don't want us.

Today I won't go scavenging for paper I am very tired i spent the day here. Dona Francisca Kiss said: that I am gaining weight. I was appalled hearing this Eating so badly. How can I be putting on weight. Does air make you fat?

The way that prices are increasing, we have to get used to feeding ourselves with air A man who moved into the favela came to complain that José Carlos had thrown stones at his shack, and that his wife is dieting [pregnant?] and could collapse.

—I told him that birth is not a serious illness. That gypsies give birth and half an hour later go skiing.

—That's gypsies. He answered me

—No! It is not only gypsies who give birth and mount their horses . . .

i had Vera one day, and got up the next. because I need to work. The North American women work right after giving birth because the life there is really tough! But your wife is very lazy She has to begin to produce so you can rock the baby.

—He started laughing.

He's the one who hauls water. He lights the fire and makes coffee, and puts the beans on to cook. Now that his son is born he will have to wash the baby's clothes if he wants a clean baby if his wife only knew how terrible it is to keep repeating, I . . . I'm ill! if she is ill she should get treatment.

It is much better to see a healthy woman than to see one lethargic like a turtle. —I don't like lazy women.

8 November 1958 I got up at 4:30 and went to haul water because I need to leave much earlier to collect the papers at the houses. Yesterday I did not go out because I was tired. I made coffee and sent João to buy 3 of bread. He ate it all up. I did not wake up José Carlos. He was out until 10 o'clock. I was already sleeping when he began to drum on the shack.

I don't like anybody to wake me up. I sleep, if I wake up I begin to think up poems I got up and opened the door. He didn't want to come in saying that I was going to hit him and I never hit José Carlos. When I grab the chain he begins to cry. I remain motionless. yesterday I didn't take his tears into account and gave him 8 chain beatings. This was last night I know that mothers regret spanking a child. But . . . it's necessary. João went off to school and I went out with Vera. She went by the Incapre Cold-Storage place to beg a sausage. I collected paper. On the Avenida Cruzeiro do Sul I stopped to collect cardboard that was thrown nearby the railroad track. A guard from the town hall came up and we began to talk about dr. Adhemar He told me that dr. Adhemar is doing the right thing to drive people from the city's lands. The tenants have been there for ages, and pay very little and on top of that they sublet and that is against the rent laws. The income from the municipal properties doesn't benefit the town hall at all. He told me that he admires me! because I work. It's that on saturdays he sees the shantytown women lining up at the Cold Storage plant and never saw me there.

What kind of kids can they have, and what kind of time do they have to have kids: —But work . . . they can't. He thinks that the favelas should be eliminated. That the favela is the nest of the bandits. He told me that he has two sons and is content with his wife. I went to the depot I got 15. i went up the Avenida Tiradentes and found 100, i thought: instead of two [z]eros, there should be 3. But I was pleased. I went to Dona Julita to pick up paper. She was crocheting. i asked senhor João if he was feeling better.

—He said he was. And that he is sleeping. I told him that dr.

Adhemar is evicting people from the municipal land. That there are those who continue to sublet a portion. That there are people who live for 20 on public land, and haven't paid rent in 5 years. That those ingrates are cussing out dr.Adhemar. That they should thank the town hall and the mayor for living there without paying. But the world has more thankless than thankful:

—He agreed and said: that Christ wasn't even thanked.

I told Dona Julita that I had found 100, cruzeiros.

—She told me: You work for me. I'll give you 100, Give me this 100, and take 200.

—I didn't accept. I told her that today is the day that I earn more money, that the day that I need money I would ask her

She agreed. I won't take money from D. Julita because senhor João is ill. And they have helped me a lot. She gave me food, coffee and paper. i went past senhor Rodolfo's i told him that I had sent the book to the United States and that I was awaiting a reply. That he is getting fat. There was a lot of paper i carried it in 2 trips Afterward I went to the shoemaker i talked with senhor Sebastião about the price hikes and the cost of living He told me that he is sick With blood pressure [a high number] owing to too much work. That he thinks a lot and sleeps little.

hearing this I got frightened because I also think a lot and sleep little.

it's as if a wave of the little affects Brazil—eats little sleeps little—A team that carries us to the grave.

A lady who lives near senhor rodolfo's gave a wardrobe and some bottles and a fridge to me to sell at the junk dealer.

The wardrobe is to be moved today, and the refrigerator and the bottles tomorrow. After that I went to the Satope store. Vera began to cry. She said that she was tired. I told her to sit down at the door to the produce store and I gave her the slice of watermelon I had bought for her. She sat down and I went to the Japanese [-owned store] to shop. I bought 1 kilo and a half of beans, 2 of rice, $1\frac{1}{2}$ of sugar, 1 soap. I ask them to add up to 100, cruzeiros, sugar went up.

The fashionable word at the moment is "it went up!" It went up! This reminds me of the verse that Roque gave me: to include as my own in my repertoire of poetry.

Politician, when a candidate
swears he'll give a raise
And the poor see true to fate
"Increases" in their suffering!

I went to the depot to weigh the papers and got 40. i ended up with 100. I bought a sweet for Vera. It was one o'clock when I got home. i made food for the kids and went to Rosalina to borrow her cart to pick up the wardrobe. I am tired. But, I know that the poor cannot rest. I saw Policarpo's woman. The gossiper. Her tongue has grooves. She slammed the door in my face i began to cuss her out for her laziness. That she prefers to starve than work. It is terrible to argue with a lazy person. I took the cart. Cussing Policarpo's ugliness. Whoever says her children all have the same father—it's a lie! —Two years ago. When she moved into the favela she told me that only the little girl was Policarpo's. —She must have forgotten what she told me. Her first son, one can see is the son of a white person the daughter is ugly like policarpo who has a shovel nose of a Black. Nose of a nothing.

I took João, and José Carlos. Vera stayed behind because the sun is very hot. When I arrived to pick up the wardrobe a young fellow who lives there helped me take it down and gave me a mattress. And I said to him:

May God give you health and happiness, because you already are handsome.

—He smiled. i sensed that i that was a good thing for me to have said to him!

He couldn't fit the wardrobe in the cart. João was beginning to get irritated—He said: cursed be the hour that I came after this wardrobe! The owner of the shoe store helped me place the wardrobe in the cart. It fell because the cart slid. There were some workers from the Light company. one of them came over and gave me a rope. I began to secure. After I got some wire. But I couldn't do it. Paulistas stop and watch everything. People started to gather to see me. João got irritated with all the people. I looked at the workers of the Light company and thought: there are no men in Brasil! If there were, they would fix this for me. I should have been born in hell! I put the mattress inside the wardrobe. things got worse! The workers watched my struggle. And I thought: they are great for looking. i thought: I wasn't born to wait for help from

anybody. I have overcome so many things alone I'll overcome this
too! i have to handle this wardrobe. I wasn't thinking of the workers
of the Light company. —I was sweating and smelled the sweat I
jumped when I heard a man's voice in my ear

—Leave off! I'll fix it for you! I thought:

—Now . . . do it! I looked at the man and thought him handsome! He took the mattress out of the wardrobe and put it in the
cart After that he put the wardrobe on top and tied it with the rope
so it wouldn't slip. João was pleased and said: Thanks to this man!
Now the wardrobe goes! When he finished I thanked him and
pushed the cart. And in less than an hour I got to the favela.

I went shopping. I bought half a liter of oil, jerky, bread and
lard that came to: 100. i thought: today is the day of 100. I told senhor Eduardo that tuesday I would pay him 170 that I owe him. I got
home and made a meal for the kids. I bought 4 eggs. I fried 2. I
boiled one for José Carlos because he can't eat fried eggs.

I was cussing senhor Manoel when he arrived.

—He greeted me!

I told him: I was cussing you did you hear?

—No, I didn't.

I was telling my kids that I wished to be a Black.

—And aren't you a Black?

—I am!

But I wanted to be one of these scandalous Blacks to beat you
and tear your clothes. But, when I do something like that, my sound
judgment takes over. My judgment takes over because I don't drink.
because whoever drinks doesn't think clearly.

I told him what I did during the day. He doesn't talk. But he
values those who like to talk. When days pass and he doesn't
appear, I cuss him out. I explain when he shows up I want to beat
him and throw water on him. When he arrives I do nothing.

He said he wants to marry me. I look and think: this man is no
good for me. he is like an actor who comes on stage. I like men
who hammer nails fix things at home. But, when I am lying with
him, I think he is fine for me. He tells me that he will give me more

money! Who knows if I will be lucky with him. It could be that happiness makes peace with me.

I am tired. I bathed the kids. I made rice pudding, and heated water to take a bath. i thought of policarpo's woman's words that I smell of dried codfish when she passes me.

—I told her: that I work hard, that I had carried more than one hundred kilos of paper and it is very hot. And the human body is no good. Whoever works like me has to stink like skunk excrement and codfish because I sweat. If I spent the day standing in line I would not perspire She is white, and nobody wants her. I washed myself and lay down.

9 November 1958 I got out of bed at 4 o'clock and went to fetch water to wash the clothes. I did not buy bread. I made coffee. I soaped up the wash. The kids ate sweet rice pudding. I asked Rosalina for her cart and went to Avenida Tiradentes to fetch the fridge and the bottles that a lady from the North gave me. I took José Carlos and Vera. I didn't want to take Vera because she couldn't find her sandal and wanted to put on clogs and she doesn't know how to walk in clogs When I got to Rua Pedro Vicente I went to the greengrocer to buy lettuce. 2 tiny weights worth. 4 each one. I no longer am horrified by the calamity that has installed itself in Brazil.

I got to the house of the Northerner. That one who lives near senhor Rodolfo. I rang the bell twice. She appeared and told me to enter. I hastily climbed the stairs The kids came with me. She helped me carry the fridge. She told me that she could not exert herself because she has a broken arm. I asked if she had children.

—2. One died. And the other got married.

—What did he dic of?

—He committed suicide

—Oh! Then you are already dead.

—If I were! I live to live! But I have been through a lot! Life held only bitterness for me.

—why did your son commit suicide?

—Over a woman!

But he was crazy! When a woman doesn't want a man he gets another. Afterward, he ought to consider the woman. But when the children think about doing such a deed, they don't think of the suffering that it will give their mothers.

And did the woman marry somebody else?

—No. She is my cousin. She is from Bahia. She is single with kids from one and another man.

I suffered with my husband and with my mother-in-law. It is 24 years since my husband disappeared. I was pregnant with my youngest son. Neither of us knew that I was pregnant. The judge forced him to leave me because he beat me too much

—How old were you when you married?

—13. He left me when I was 19. In those days I was foolish—if I was smart like I am today! . . . He'd see! The authorities interfered because I was a minor.

—How old was your son when he committed suicide?

—22. And I made the youngest get married at that same age.

—You did right. I will also make my kids marry at that age because when I reach 40 the kids are grown up and don't tire you out much.

—And is your daughter-in-law good?

—She is very ill-natured

—A man came up and started to talk with her. The young fellow who helped me put the wardrobe on the cart helped me carry the fridge.

She gave coffee and milk to the kids. She filled a glass with milk for me. She gave me bread to take. I answered with my keenest thanks.

The man who came up asked her for milk of magnesia. She told him she had no medicine for belly aches i asked if she had anise?

—I do.

—It does the same thing.

I admired the order of her house. She told me that she suffered a lot when she worked as a maid. That she doesn't miss her women bosses.

—I say the same thing! i prefer collecting paper to being a maid because the employers are never satisfied.

The woman makes soap at home. she asked me if I wanted to buy a kerosene stove.

—Who do you take me for

And that ended that.

I carried the bottles to the cart. I bade her goodbye.

I told José Carlos that she is a Northerner.

—He looked at her for a long time and said:

—She is calm!

She smiled. I secured the fridge and came home. Senhor Rodolfo said hello.

I was pleased. This shows that he is not angry with me.

I got to the shantytown very tired.

I made a salad and soup for the kids. After I went to undo the fridge I planned to wash laundry but I got tired. i spent the afternoon writing. —Nobody bothered me.

When I went to fetch the fridge I met Aldo. And Vera invited him to our shack. —He promised to come and the poor, don't like to receive visits from rich people. He promised to bring a cake.

15 November 1958 The day loomed bright everywhere I directed my gaze everything clear. because today there is no smoke from the factories to leave the heavens gray. The people who are ambling about are meditating. They walk as if they were doing the stations of the cross. I got up and went to fetch water. After I went to wash the pigsty and take care of the pig. I separated the clothes to wash. I went shopping.

Rice, sugar, bread and butter I spent 50. And could carry the purchases inside my pocket.

i looked at the factory and saw the brazilian flag and its symbolic words—Order and progress! I thought: what would we do if order prevailed in the country! I put the bed linens in the sunshine. After, I lay down. And began to read. The children ate buttered bread. José Carlos and Vera went to the street market. I decided to make the beds. Ramiro came into the favela and I began to talk with him. He came to buy a guitar.

I went to the market—I was horrified with the prices. One heard the people complaining that the prices were an absurdity.

After Juscelino took office . . . whoever can, run for cover. I heard the poor women saying —What will become of us my God i always heard that one day the world would end . . . why doesn't it end today my God. The women who go to the market almost go berserk.

I took 40 cruzeiros. I exhibited the money in my hands. But I was collecting whatever I came upon on the ground. I bought liver, and papaya, and it goes up.

I got to the favela prepared a meal for the children. They enjoyed it. When I went to fetch water to wash the pigpen, I saw the children contemplating robbing a fellow who was coming along with a basket of fruits on his head.

The mothers saw and instigated their sons to pull off the watermelon. I thought: bad mothers! She who witnessed the offensive acts of her child and doesn't reprimand. When a mother has no culture she has intuition to correct her child. When the mother reveres her child's errors she is contributing to its degradation.

This morning I met up with Sergio. A big black guy, who lives here in the favela. i asked him why he left the Estrela do Norte bus station?

—He told me, that when he had worked for two years, senhor Morgado made a deal and fired him. That he gave him 13,000. That nowadays the bosses don't allow employees to stay on for years, and years in the shops. They wanted to keep him as an apprentice.

—He refused: —I told him: that in Getúlio's [Vargas] time, these fixed deals didn't exist.

—He agreed that the workers miss Getúlio. i think: why didn't the workers meet, and beat up Lacerda so he wouldn't put the beloved president out of the way?

If I were Getúlio, I would want to beat Lacerda with rubber truncheons. he is obnoxious. He whose tongue is bigger than his reason. I already heard a number of people say that Getúlio is missed.

Today it is hot. I bathed the kids. And they went to bed. When I went to the market I talked with the brother of Dona Carmen who has a shop on Carlos de Campos street that is a post office. We spoke of his genealogy. May everybody reach old age. How sublime it is to converse with polite people.

I am going to take a bath and lie down. I am not tired because I am tired by day. And at night I have poetry. i went to senhor Eduardo to buy ¹⁄₂ [liter] of oil, and a bottle of ink. A woman who lives near the emporium gave me, 1 basin and some scrap metal for me to sell. The woman who gave me the basin is Dona Diva.

17 November 1958 I got out of bed at 5 o'clock and went to fetch water. I fed the pig and went to buy bread, coffee, and soap. I have money because I sold 1 shirt and some pants to Adalberto. I made coffee. I gave the children a bath They went to school. And I went out with Vera. She went to the Cold Storage to beg a sausage. She got one: she was pleased. I went to Dona Julita. She gave me food coffee and papers. She was happy. What a noble woman! She doesn't know how to hate anybody. I was so tired. I complained to her.

She told me to go to Dona Juana's for she wants to give me something. I went. —She gave me sweets and sandwiches that were left over from the party. —I forgot to say that: in the morning Paulo went to called the Radio Patrol because Dona Juana and Lalau and a certain Alício stole a duck from him. And the feathers were scattered in the back garden.

—Deolinda said that she didn't eat it. Lalau said that he didn't eat it. And Dona Juana said that she was sleeping.

What depressing people. They drink so much that they don't have any idea what they are doing. How terrible it is to awaken

with the men of the law at our door. Dona Juana went off with the
policeman I said to senhor Antonio Venancio that now all the favelados will eat duck and afterward will say: that—it was Lalau. Lalau is
going to be an armadillo—because the anteater warms itself in the
sun resting on the back of the armadillo. When I went to collect
paper I was talking with Binidito's Juana who told me that she can't
stand Deolinda and her husband. When they drink, gutter language
takes the stage. That she is already tired of living in the favela. But
what can one do! if one has nowhere to go. I went with Juana to the
trolley stop. I met Rosalina who told me that Dona Maria the
Spaniard is going to hospitalize her daughter Maria José because she
continually has a spot on her lung. They say that the husband of
Sebastiana remained without work for many months poor
Sebastiana!

—I feel so sorry for these women with their problem husbands!

Ida and Clarisse are starting to prostitute themselves with 16-
year-old boys. It's a blast. More than 20 after them. There is a young
fellow who lives on the street of the health post. He is yellow and
skinny. he looks like a walking skeleton. His mother forces him to
stay in bed because he is ill and gets tired easily. He goes out with his
mother only to beg because his appearance moves people. —That
yellow son is her breadwinner. —Even he is after Ida and Clarisse.

So many young 15- and 16-year-olds have turned up here in
the favela that I am going to report them to the authorities to scare
them away from here—because here there are a lot of children.
Today I earned only 40 cruzeiros because I got sleepy.

The weather is changing. Could it be that the atmospheric
changes influence our organism? I didn't make lunch. I heated Dona
Julita's food. After that I lay down to sleep. But nobody can sleep in
the favela. When I returned I saw the girls at the Neusa candy factory all cleaned up. i thought: —they can say: we are always clean.
And me . . . I believe that I should say: I, I am always dirty! Clarisse
and Ida could work. They haven't yet turned 18 and are ill-fated
girls who began life in the mud—Ida is very lazy. She doesn't know
how to read because she didn't want to go to school. She has

another brother who is 10 who doesn't want to go to school. Here in the favela there are a number of children who don't want to go to school and their mothers don't force them I believe that mothers ought to observe their children to see their inclinations. With that rebellious energy. I found 1 ball in the garbage and gave it to my children to play. The vagrant men want to grab the ball from the children. The little boys throw stones at the awkward young men. And they want to hit the children. When they see me they calm down. because nobody wants to be included in my Strange Diary.

Today I am sad! God should give a happy soul to poets. I was lazy in bed. When I wanted coffee the children got it for me I asked for a comb José Carlos gave me one i had the impression that I was a congresswoman.

José Carlos asked me:

—Are you ill? because he isn't used to seeing me in bed. Vera began to cry I got up to see what she had. She was fighting with another little girl. I went to see if the pig had eaten the bananas, and I saw Juaquim fighting with his wife. Who can be classified as "Madame Useless." He told her we was going to beat her. She said that she didn't want the 2 daughters with their father. That he should take care of them. She held the children by their arms. There are some women here in the favela who grab their children to their breasts when they are arrested. Or when they receive a summons to go to the police station. they carry their children to serve as a shield. They began to fight with the children in the arms of the drunken mother who could not remain on her feet. During the struggle the children fell and I grabbed 2 little boys. The heartbeats of the two boys were rapid and were like tambourines in Carnival rhythm. —i thought: God shouldn't give sons to these snakelike women. With savage souls. The sons should always be jewels.

Pitita ran out with her husband behind her. The children watch these scenes with delight. pitita was seminude And the parts that women should hide were visible. She ran stopped and reached for a stone. She threw it at Juaquim. he ducked and the stone hit the wall. above Theresinha's head. i thought: she was born again.

Francisca Kiss began to say that Juaquim was no good. That he is a man only to make babies. I said to Dona Francisca that Juaquim gives money to pitita who spends it on whisky. She listened and wanted to argue with me. I told her that I was going to get her a place in Juquerí But if she attacked me I was going to slap her.

But, she is so weak She won't last long. Juaquim is already a candidate for widowerhood. She has no strength to fight. Her force is in her tongue. She only talks slang. I feel badly watching these spectacles. My fear was of the stone throwing. pitita is stupid she doesn't understand that it is the easiest thing to kill somebody. Leila shouted that pitita was fighting with Juaquim because he is sleeping with Iracema. Iracema is being fought over in the favela. She left her husband. She isn't used to working because her husband didn't let her. She thought that belonging to men was a happier condition.

What a mistake a woman commits who abandons a man, to be for the men. When Iracema was together with her husband she was fat. Now that she is whoring, she is fading. Leila said: this woman needs a beating! Leila in a fight is like gasoline in the stove—She goads and exchanges the spider for her web I saw the Bahian who talks dirty with Ida I went to tell him to leave my children in peace. He began to cuss me out. He is a Northerner, outlaw type i asked him where he lives—B Street Number 13. I went inside. I lit the stove and put water on to boil. I washed the pig and went to [the public phone to] call the police. I tried but the line was busy. I met up with an official car. I asked the driver if he could come into the favela to intimidate the poor people. That I was afraid of them throwing stones and hitting the children. —The driver told me that they were making an investigation and couldn't interfere in the goings-on of the district. When pitita was fighting I saw the Northerner who showed up here a few days ago. He and Ida behave scandalously in front of the children And when he sees my children playing ball he grabs the ball from the children. After he hit the children. I told him not to irritate my children.

—He said that my children are no good. That they are little

uneducated brats. But my sons are worth more than he is because they are literate I will finish what I was quoting:

—After I will come back to what I think of Bahia

The telephone didn't answer. I decided to go to the 12th [precinct] police station I got there I talked with the soldiers who received my complaint disgustedly. I saw Private Cardoso. I asked him to come. He looked at his watch. He said he would come, if the lieutenant ordered him to. The lieutenant ordered them to call the Radio patrol. But the Radio patrol didn't answer. Iracema was already registering a complaint. I left. I stood in the road waiting for the Radio patrol to appear. It began to rain. I told Darça to seek shelter because she was with a child. She told me: that she was looking for her son. When there is a fight here in the favela nobody stays inside I looked over that crowd that was watching the fight. it seems that in the favela there are more than 2,000 people. I wanted the Radio patrol to come to ask the guards to give that insolent Northerner a lesson —The top bandit He told me: Go call your husband. I want to see if he is more of a man than me But, from his pale color, color of wax. One sees that he suffered from a lot of hunger and has no strength for a fight. He is a type that needs to be recovered by a healthy diet—today, a healthy diet is a chimera, an unrealizable dream!

When there is a fight here in the favela everybody fights. Even he children. pitita was born a good person after she married she degenerated. She is the daughter of booze I think she is perverse. Over sexual stimulation mixed with alcohol. One notes that the child of an alcoholic is a slower learner. Their mentality is lethargic. —I am going to talk about Bahia. —The first capital of Brazil. It already is 458 years old. And in the meantime it is the state that didn't develop in culture. One or another stand out. The bahians who come to São Paulo the majority are semi literate. They are ridiculous and agitators. Some days I miss our favela from 1950—We only had 2 families from the north. And very well behaved. —Now! The favela is overflowing with northerners —And for the paulistas they are a different people.

Let us go back to pitita. When pitita fights everybody comes outside to watch. It is a pornographic show—She said:

—looking at her husband: —He . . . is a sucker! —And Duca asked her:

—What does he suck?

—She pointed and said: he . . . sucks my cunt. —The men smiled. And the children repeated. And smiling, and saying that they had seen Pitita's cunt, and that it was full of hair. And the little girls commented:

—Mine still has none!

The children began to say that pitita had lifted her dress. I came inside. I was already lying down and heard pitita's cavernous voice. It was a bitter afternoon in the favela. That's how the children of the favela learned that men suck women. They have no more doubt about these things. I feel sorry for these children who live in the dirtiest closet in the world and have uncouth teachers persons who perform these dirty acts and compete for the bad upbringing of the children. Analia. She is a promising substitute for Pitita. The student following in the steps of the teacher.

I was pleased: They came to tell me that policarpo's woman moved out.

—Nobody misses her. Policarpo put up three shacks here in the favela and sold them. he is an outsider who doesn't stay in one place. Whoever dislikes work doesn't find a place that's any good. He walked about saying he was off to Brasília. —I heard say that blacks can't get into Brasília. The time will come when the whites are going to burn the Blacks when they die so that they have no right to be buried. i sensed that the only thing that a white doesn't scorn is a black's vote. Only at election time is the black a citizen. I think that the Black of Brazil ought to be treated and taken for prehistoric. Because he represents the uncultured past of the whites— Sometimes I think: —The white states with arrogance that he is what he is, the superintellectual—Where does this superintellectuality come from? Whoever is an intellectual, is learned. And learned ones are not boastful. Prejudice is a manifestation of pride if the whites were wise they wouldn't have sold blacks. Leave the past alone! I thank God I wasn't a slave. I don't know the taste of the Whip. The only thing that enslaves me is the cost of living.

20 November 1958 I got out of bed at 5 o'clock and went for water. —What a line! That is the line from hell! I talked with dona Maria about Policarpo's wife. That she is a gossiper, and still finds followers.

I filled a big pot and came to make lunch—Today I didn't have coffee, and not even sugar. There was lungs and beans; that was left over from yesterday. I made rice and sent João to buy 7 worth of bread. A tiny piece of bread came back. I felt sorry when I saw the size of the bread. I gave them food. They changed clothes and I went out with Vera. —She went to the Incapre Cold Storage to beg a sausage there was a lot of paper in the streets because the garbage collector hadn't come by. I collected food for the pig. And the only street where I found more food was Araguaía street.

Dona Irene who lives on Pedro Vicente street 514 gave me newspapers and told me to button up my dress that I was like a clown.

—I told her that I had found the dress in the garbage and it didn't fit.

—Aren't you afraid of getting ill?

—If I die, I die late

She told me that Jesus said: —Avoid the airs, and I will relieve you of ill.

I told her: that the beggars beg food from door to door and don't know if the people who give them anything are sick

—Poor [people] have no scruples!

The poor have the stomach of an ostrich today only those who are rich can have fear.

—You are not as poor as you say: I have seen many people say that I am dressed as a poor person. If I had any cash I would

have my book published. because the ideal also is part of life. Dona
Irene is ignorant of the state of my soul. When I sensed that I was a
poet I became sad.

The day that senhor vili Aureli told me: Carolina, you are a
poetess, on that day I buried happiness that accompanied me just
like my shadow Up to that date my heart dressed itself in bright colors. After that it dressed in purple. —And now . . . in black. I think I
am black inside and out.

I arrived at the depot thinking about Dona Irene's words. That
she told me: If you die, your children are going to suffer. With you
they suffer but they have affection. i earned 50. I became happy and
reanimated.

I went to Dona Julita—She was at the market. I heated food
that her maid gave me. I talked with senhor João about the originals
that I had sent to the United States He asked me if I had gotten an
answer. That I should have sent the notebooks by sea mail. That it
was cheaper.

Dona Maria Améria gave me coffee—I didn't wait for D. Julita
to put the soup in my metal pan and I sailed off. —Vera got atro-
cious. A man put his hand on her head she began to cry. She ran to
reach me and a dog wanted to bite her. that was it. she cried twice
as hard. When I was near to the tiny bridge I met a portuguese
woman who told me to go to the Praça dos Esportes 70. to get some
papers that were there. At 10:30 I went.

The portuguese [woman] who gave me the paper told me that
she has known me for years. She told me that all poets go crazy. I
told her: that when I realized that I am a poetess I became sad
because the excess of imagination was too much. That I had my
brain examined in the Hospital das Clinicas That the examination
result showed that I was calm. That I greatly educated my brain.
That I did not let ideas overcome me. That the disrespect that
people have for poets made me sad. But now I am in the mature
state and don't get affected with the attentions of just anybody That
to those who please me, I am pleasing. Those who annoy me,
undergo hell with me. I told her that the whites of Brazil still enslave

the blacks. A Moral slavery—Intimidating the black with prison.
Most of all when the black makes a mistake and loses Moral force.
That I try not to err in order not to be dominated by the whites.
That I make the whites kneel before me. That I sensed, that working
I didn't have poetic ideas and for this reason I decided to work. but
I can't just sit around. That I tried different jobs. And did well collecting paper because I am always walking. That I wanted to be
included in Brazilian artistic circles But I couldn't stand the boastful-
ness of Brazil's semistars. That I say semistars because I think that an
artist needs culture. And to know how to deal with people to have a
public. An artist who has a public brings profit to a businessman.
That I prefer talking with a worker to talking with a Brazilian artist
workers are agreeable when they talk and artists are majestic. They
want to be idolized by the people. That I find the artists of Brazil
very affected. That I am an observer when I look at a person I
immediately form an opinion. In general dealings the worker . . . is
more pleasing I passed the Peixol factory to collect tomatoes: the
manager there now is friendly.

He doesn't want me to collect tomatoes that are on the ground
He gives me the ones from the box that are clean. There are some
japanese drivers who give me tomatoes. i felt that [if] people find
brotherhood life stops being a burden. I came home thinking of the
words of the portuguese woman in the praça dos esportes 70.

I told her that at night I'm not sleepy. That I get sleepy during
the day She told me that her husband is like that. That he sleeps by
day, and at night isn't sleepy. That he has been in bed for 7 years.
He, can sleep by day and I, can't.

—And . . . you must work I told her: you are good. She told
me that nobody is good as they should—be. I can't bear enigmatic
words. We spoke of Dona Angelina who was her maid. The portuguese woman told me that she has no sense. I answered that there
are a lot of people like that. That they age without showing any
sense. That Angelina put up a shack here in the favela to store her
furniture and never showed her face around here again. That she
ought to leave the place for a poor person. Vera is walking faster—

What a good girl my daughter is! She is so sensible. hearing her gives me pleasure She isn't fresh to anybody.

I got to the favela the kids were already home i made a meal for them Afterwards I put the tins and the scrap metal away and lay down i managed to sleep a little. João cleaned the oven he cleaned up the house. he made coffee—I was amazed because it is the first time that he shows any interest in the state of the shack. —He complained that his right leg hurts. I looked to heaven. it seems that we will have rain. I got up, had coffee and went to sweep the shack and the back yard and burn the garbage I saw some women looking toward the river. —I went over to see what was going on I had some onions that Biniditi's Juana gave me because I gave her some tomatoes. I sent Vera to put the tomatoes away and I went over to ask the women what was going on at the river?

—It's a child who can't get out of the water—I went to look, thinking: if it is a child I will cross the Tietê River to pull him out and if it is necessary to swim I'll go in the water. I ran to see what was up. It was a large jackfruit that floated with the current. I came back and went to write. João came in telling me that his leg hurt and he was crying. i asked senhor Luiz to have a look at him because he is a nurse he looked, and told me that it was nothing. for me to apply iodine—I sent José Carlos to buy it. i put water to heat to give João a bath because if it was necessary to take him to the hospital he would be ready. I thought José Carlos was taking his time i grabbed an umbrella and went after him cussing him out for being an arrogant worthless kid. For I was going to give him a beating i even grabbed a stick that I found.

I began to remember when I was a child. Wherever they sent me I went speedily. I went to the Bandeirantes pharmacy I met Dona Maria do Carioca and complained to her how sick I was of my children. That they were good for nothing—She confirmed that today's children are no good. That she worked for Syrians and earned 5 cruzeiros to scour the pots. I looked in the pharmacy and José Carlos wasn't there. I returned irritated. He was smiling at the door. He told me that he had been home a while that he ran back.

I thought that he had stopped to watch the fight of the common Northerner who beat up the semiparalytic old lady. Fernanda's mother—She is ill. But the Northerner is an animal and the worst that God put on this earth—Those with their mania for bravery deserve to be disqualified from any public respect. I heard Fernanda saying that she was going to call the Radio patrol. The Northerners when they come to São Paulo forgot to include a little education in their belongings, whether a northerner is polite or not, I try to keep my distance.

I will talk of José Carlos. —He bought iodine and told me that the man told him that he wouldn't sell 4 cruzeiros worth of iodine. He sold 6. that the prices go up—they go up—they go up

Even the children notice the commercial chicanery. The time will come when the poor people will ask: —What is a price list? I began to think. That it isn't my son who is worthless. I am the one who has no patience for waiting. i wiped the iodine on João. Vera pleaded with me not to beat João because he is sick. i sensed the nobleness of her soul. And the world needs noble souls. João slept. And José Carlos went to do his homework—He told me that he wants to study. to get a job because he wants to be well dressed. And he wants to marry a woman like Dona diva his teacher That his teacher is not lax. That she is not lazy. That she knows how to make use of time. That he doesn't want to marry a woman like Seu [familiar form of Sr. 'Mr.'] Chico's Dona Alice. because she is very lazy that Dona Alice is like a pig. That she eats, and sleeps. I began to read a newspaper and saw the want ads for Mechanical Draftsmen. I showed them to him. That there's work for mechanical draftsmen. —João began to cry. I went to see what was the matter. —His eyes were red. I decided to give him an aspirin and went out to buy one. As I went to the store I met the nocturnal crickets of the favela Leila, pitita, Analia and others—What disgust I have for people who have no aspirations. I went into the store, senhor Eduardo sold me Veranon [a medicine]. I spoke with senhor Luiz who prescribed a sulfa salve. I read the instructions on the package and thought that it would do the trick i administered it. The children slept and I went to write. When sleepiness came upon me I went to bed. I touched João's face he was sweating. I changed him. I dressed him in a pajama and I went to bed I was tired. I couldn't sleep i was thinking about what I had read that morning, that dr. Adhemar had allowed private businesses to increase their rates. That dr. Adhemar is the manager of high prices. I slept and dreamed. That I lived in a gold and silver palace. But my face was full of wrinkles and when people saw me they uttered a prayer! Such a lovely house, and such an ugly woman.

21 November 1958 I got up at 3 in the morning to write because I planned to go to the *Folhas** to talk with the reporter Audálio. I wrote until 5 o'clock. Afterward I went to fetch water. The [play-ground] birdcage that dr. Adhemar put here for the children to play in is broken because at night the drunkards pull it every which way. The night is a revelry that makes one sick. I made coffee and put beans on the stove to cool. I went to buy bread and butter. Today only José Carlos is going to class João is going to rest. I went out with Vera. She entered the Incapre Cold Storage to beg a sausage. she got two I met up with a portuguese woman who gave me some boards for me to pick up later

Today I have no luck. I collected so much paper and got nothing for it. Senhor Luiz began to tell me that I didn't wash his shirt. He is a mechanic whose garage is on Avenida Tiradentes It's that I didn't have money to buy soap.

He doesn't realize that a poor person has the same needs as others[.] i circled around there and went to senhor Rodolfo to get paper After I came home. I was so tired that I couldn't stay on my feet. I lay down. João gathered the cans and the scrap metal. I slept After I got up and made macaroni With beans for the kids.

I saw a lot of people at dona Lêila's shack. I went to see what was going on i asked Dona Camila what happened?

---

* *Folhas* indicates the office of the newspaper chain that included *Folha da Manhã*, a morning paper, and *Folha da Tarde,* an afternoon paper.

—It's the little girl who died

—What did she die of?

—I don't know!

i asked Lêila what happened with the little girl

—I took her to Santa Casa hospital and to dr. Zoôpe.

—i could tell that Lêila is lying. I saw that Lêila's eyes were wet. i thought: that is tears or she put water on her face. —I continued to think of Lêila's ill deed with this child who was only 5 months old I already mentioned that Lêila grabbed the little girl one day when she was 3 months old and threw her on the ground. And it was Adalberto who picked up the child. Another day she had a fight with her boyfriend and wanted to throw the child into the river Tietê.

—Nobody deceives God I have no idea what kind of soul this Lêila has. When she looks at her son it is with a cold eye lacking maternal warmth—she must be a witch. And another thing: whoever has children needs to work: because the child needs to eat. And Lêila doesn't work and the money that she gets, goes for beer.

I never saw Lêila's daughter eating bread with butter I don't see the little girl with a piece of fruit or a biscuit. Lêila already had 6 children. Dona Domingas looked after 3 of them. The 3 that remained died—I already said that kids of these woman don't grow up—they regress. they are the unfortunate who don't have adequate food or affection, and not even care The mistake of the judge was to give this child to the godmother. And the godmother gave it to Lêila. I heard that the little girl had measles. And the measles took care of her.

Could it be that Lêila who had 6 children still didn't learn how to take care of the child? —A child with measles can't get wet or stay in a breeze. Yesterday when I went out at night to buy medicine for João i met Lêila on her way to a night out. When a woman befriends her child she leans over the bed night after night to watch over it; until she sees it recovered. The mothers who feel no love for their children, are witch mothers.

—I went to the scrap metal depot to sell a little oakum. i got

36 cruzeiros—I went to the guine bakery and had 1 glass of milk I got home i bought 1 liter of milk for the children. I sent João for 1 liter of kerosene. I gave the kids supper and spanked Vera because she doesn't like to comb her hair. Sleepiness came upon me. i lay down. I woke to a big squabble near my window.

It was Ida and Analia. The scandalous couple of the favela. The argument began at Lêila's—They don't even hold any regard for the dead. Juaquim intervened pleading for respect for the corpse They went to quarrel in the street This here generation of the favela shows no Moral character. The majority are semiliterate.

—They didn't want to go to school. And their mothers didn't force them This morning I told senhor Juaquim the portuguese that Dona Mariquinha's daughter wasn't literate. —He said: They learn to fuck And they learn that without a school teacher.

I laughed and said:

—Portuguese . . . you are no good!

From my window I see Lêila's daughter in her coffin. It's a devil of disrespect at the wake—it seems almost like a party. In the 12 years that I live in the favela, I already saw 2 daughters of Lêila die. The Moon is marvelous. The evening is warm. that's why the favela is agitated. Some play the accordion. Radios. Others sing. They said a rosary for Lêila's daughter.

I said to Lêila: —Make an effort to raise your daughter so you aren't alone in your old age. The coffin is white

—I am going to bed. The noise is much louder i am going to bed Here anything is an excuse for a party.

24 November 1958 I got out of bed at 4 o'clock and went to fetch water. What a line! That Orlando Lopes messed up the favela. We had 2 spigots. Now there is only one. And it isn't enough for the people. I made coffee. i looked for money. only 5. i had 9. But 5 was João's and he took it—because what is his is his! I bought only 5 worth of bread They went to school.

The police came after Lalau because of the duck. It was 6

o'clock. What bad luck for Lalau who likes to get up at ten o'clock if the police were always severe—it would end the robberies. I like to see those who rob get themselves into a tight corner. if it created shame!

I went to Dona Julita's. She gave me a radio. And I sent it to be fixed. 1,500 for the job The radio is a Phillips. i thought about the differences of human nature—The Sheriff stole my radio. The so-and-so Sebastião Pereira the rogue who told me that when he is in a tight squeeze he changes his name. That the police are dupes. He robbed—and Dona Julita gave me one. i got 40. I got to the favela at 12 o'clock prepared the scrap metal to sell to senhor Manoel the owner of the scrap metal depot. I took two trips. I got 178.

I telephoned the newspapers to send some reporters to the favela to turn out the gypsies who are camped here—They throw excrement in the street. The shack where they are camped is like the headquarters of the flies They don't let the favela children play with their children because they don't like to mix. And they spend the day scaring the children.

—Those who live near the gypsies complain that they talk the whole night long. And don't let anybody sleep—They are violent The favelados are afraid of them i already warned them that with me it won't be so easy. They like to intimidate others. they like to be feared They are so dirty. The clothes and the teeth—The flies don't disgust them. They leave sweets exposed to the flies and after they eat them. Because their little girls go naked the bums of the favela sit near to their shack. Watching them—The thing is that if anybody attacks them the gypsies revolt But their nudity excites. it feels like I am already seeing a big argument of gypsies with the tough guys of the favela. Our bums are a thousand times better than the gypsies. Because they are relaxed they have no class.

I bought 12 of minced meat. I made minced meat with potatoes and rice. Senhor Manoel came here i drove him away because he perturbs me and I don't blend well with illiterates. They think that people not talking with them is due to . . .

26 November 1958 I got out of bed at 5 o'clock and went to fetch water. I looked at the place where the gypsies were camped. They only stayed 3 days. But that was enough to annoy us. They are undomesticable and disgusting. The place where they camped is so filthy and exudes a nasty smell. An unrecognizable odor. I made coffee and sent João to buy sugar. I fried some cornmeal cakes for my children. They ate and took the rest for break. I left Vera behind. Dona Irene on Pedro Vicente Street, 114 gave me two pieces of clothing for the children.

I am so sad. I am sick of the world! because life is insipid—In a few days we won't be able to eat anymore. —I don't have any faith in [President] Juscelino. And I don't like him because he lets my people suffer. He isn't a friend of the people, but I am. When I pass the workers I get irritated thinking that they could eat better. because they are young. because they are healthy. I went to Dona Julita. She gave me coffee food and meat I was pleased. May God help Dona Julita. I told her that I sent the radio to be fixed that the man charged 1,500. She found that expensive. I don't find it expensive because if I went to buy a new one [it would be more]. i got 50 cruzeiros. I bought 1 kilo of beans, a piece of watermelon and half a kilo of rice and the money vanished. I got home tired and went to lie down. I have an aching body.

28 November 1958 I got up at 5 o'clock and went to fetch water. How nice! Nobody was at the tap only me and Tiburcio's daughter who is always pregnant and nobody knows who her kids' father is. —She said that they are her father's children—incestuousness. Tiburcio already sold 10 shacks here in the favela. He bought Adalberto's shack for 1,000 and resold it for 7,000. Now Adalberto sleeps in the street. He exploits the incautious. I think that I already said this. I went to the Emporio to buy coffee, bread, sugar, and butter. The store was still shut. It only opened when Julio arrived.

I was horrified to see a Northerner buy 15 of cheese and 3 of sugar. He told that this keeps him going for a day. I made coffee and changed the children. João told me that Dona Maria do pinho's

son is after Vera to assault her. That he doesn't let him. I ran after
the boy and slapped him and pulled his ears. And I swore to kill
him if he bothers my girl I sent him to tell his mother that I hit
him—The boys went to school and I went out with Vera. She went
into the cold storage and begged a sausage.

I went to Avenida Tiradentes and got [scrap] cardboard. I went
to Dona Julita because I met up with her and she told me that she
had food. We ate lunch from what Dona Julita gave us and I didn't
spend a penny. i got 150. What a torment carrying the cardboard—A
number of people asked me if I am still writing. I say that I have no
time. When I arrive at the favela it was time. The shack was horrible
i made a meal for João and Vera. Afterward I went to senhor Manoel
to sell the cardboard and some scrap metal. I went into the guine
bakery, to buy bread and to drink a glass of Mineral water I waited
for her to make coffee

I told her that I was in a hurry—that I was going to do my
Diary.

—Well! Well! You live doing that Diary!

—It's that the reporters of the Newspapers tell me to write

—But they give you nothing!

—They are exploiting you!

—They say that they are going to give me a house.

—Wait sitting down. You will get tired standing. What they can
give you is 6 meters in Vila Formosa. And that won't last for centuries. Only for 5 years. When reporters promise they deliver.

Our talk was ended because senhor Manoel came in and
ordered coffee. I drank my coffee and left. i took the bread that I
bought—I went to buy wire to connect the light in the shack
because on the 7th I am going to bring the radio—I arrived at the
favela José Carlos came to complain that Silvia's children had fought
with them. Its that Dona Chiquinha Seamstress the northerner
vowed again that she is still going to throw boiling water with acid.
She already threw cold water on him one day. And I never spoke
with her again. These women need to get to know a jail cell to calm
themselves down a little.

I am so tired of listening. When will your book be published? There are days when I think: before this I would have learned to drink cane liquor. Now I have to continue with my life wasted to the end. But I have a lot of health. And alcohol weakens the human organism.

Today . . . I am happy!

29 November 1958 I got out of bed at 5 o'clock and went for water. I lit the stove and went to the store. It was closed. I stood around waiting for it to open. Other customers arrived I made a mistake. today I did not go to the emporium because there is stale bread and butter

I got João and Vera up. They washed and had breakfast. we went out. I took João along because he has no school today. I left José Carlos asleep because he went to bed at 11 o'clock at night. —They went into the Cold Storage and begged a sausage I went collecting paper and food for the pig. I went to senhor Rodolfo's, and combed many streets. I went to the shoemaker's. João was horrified when he saw how much paper I carry. —He went to see the radio. The man who is fixing it told me that it is a difficult job. I told him that if it couldn't be fixed I was going to buy a new one. He told me that the radio would be fixed. Now come the arguments. That I dread. I am upright about paying. I gave him 500 and owe 1000. After I see that the radio is working I'll give him the rest—I am not adverse to him. It's just that the radio is very old. And Vera wants a radio. i sold 115 worth of stuff. A vegetable vender threw out some green peppers i grabbed them and filled up a container. the sun is burning. When I got to the streetcar stop there was a man who sells guarana [soda]. He gave a glass to Vera and I bought 2 glasses for João and José Carlos. When I arrived at the favela it was 1:30. I looked over the shack. Inside and outside it is horrible And I am so tired. I am going to lie down a little. I lay down for 15 minutes After that I got up and began to make lunch.

Afterward I went out to do the shopping. I drank a glass of Mineral water I bought 20 of dried meat 1 kilo of rice. Half of sugar.

2 bars of soap and incense to kill insects. But the incense is no good. It doesn't kill the flies. It kills the hunger of the manufacturer who makes the stuff to extort money from the poor. —There are manufacturers who in the beginning make good products then afterward they relax. I burned the incense and it was counterproductive. I cussed out the incense manufacturer I believe that the poor ought to criticize the products that are no good—I felt reanimated.

I washed the dishes I bathed the kids. I changed the beds and went to the tap to get water to take a bath. It was 11 o'clock when I went to bed. I heard shouting voices I got up to see what was going on. There were 2 women fighting. I heard Lalau's voice. It's that he already got out of jail. He was jailed for 3 days because of paulo's duck I think that Lalau will never again want to eat his neighbor's duck.

30 November 1958 I got out of bed at 5 o'clock and went for water—What a line! When people get out of jail they are happy. When I manage to fill my can of water, I am happy. When I leave the tap behind I feel as if I am leaving hell. I saw a little boy fiddling with his foot. I went to see what he had.

—It was a splinter. I took out a needle from my dress and extracted the splinter from the boy's foot. The women were gossiping. Maria the mother of Amalia who sticks her nose into everything went for water. Peroxide to disinfect the boy's foot. And he went to show the splinter to his father. The little boy looked at me. What a look. —I thought: i have made yet another friend.

I carried water to soap up the clothes. I swept the shack and cleaned the beds. I washed Vera's head. I made lunch. I asked the boys to buy bread. They didn't go. Today we had no bread because the boys are lazy and didn't want to go to the streetcar stop. When I was at the tap I saw the vagabonds arrive—I just watch young people dissipating their health. They are 15 and 16 years old. And their mothers don't reprimand them. They don't question them they don't know what they did or where they have been. I was lying down. When Vera brought in a black woman who came in search of me And this black woman—I know for many years—She, has a son who was in jail in 1952 and she, every time she met me, pleaded:

—Dona Carolina, I want you to tell me if my son is going to stay a long time in jail or if he will get out soon

—Do you divine?

—Are you a visionary?

—When you look to heaven what do you see!

—Have you seen God?

—What does he look like?

—they say that you are a prophet?

I sensed confusion between prophet and poet. On these occasions I regret having divulged myself. And I in order to end her annoying questions answered her that:

—your son will be free after the first hearing.

The black woman [. . .] vanished. One day we met on Avenida Tiradentes she said to me:

—Dona Carolina! You were right! My son was freed at the first hearing.

But I told her that to make the old woman happy because mothers don't like to see their sons in dungeons. if I was right it was just a coincidence. —And today the black woman came after me to ask if her granddaughter was going to wed.

—I told her that she will.

I learned with the gypsies to say nice things that please the Spirit. I took the black woman to D. Cicilia. She invited me to her house. i promised to go. But I don't know when. I went to wash clothes thinking of the sad existence of D. Luiza with her partner senhor José the fishmonger. —What a man! That man inspires pity, it is expensive to read so well he buys 4 newspapers a day and is up to date about everything that goes on in the world he is like a diplomat—when he isn't drinking he is like a professor in his way of speaking—When he is drunk he takes pitita's place in pornography. This evening he talked from 12 to 6—nobody slept He threw a glass in Dona Luiza's face it hit the daughter in the face who went to call the police When the police arrived senhor José had vanished. The neighbor women are going to ask the inspector to take the fishmonger out of the favela—He is obscene Cario Capela from the parish church came to celebrate mass in the favela. The padre said: I like to be among these good people. When he said good people the favelados got frightened. they are not used to being treated with words of gas

i spent the afternoon conversing with senhor Luiz who talked about agriculture—That our politicians aren't interested in farming. That without farming, the agriculture in the Country will atrophy.

2 December 1958 I got out of bed at 5 o'clock and went to purgatory—The water line was enormous. I feel pity for the favelados. To get up at 3 o'clock to fetch water is common for Northerners. But, for the Paulistas this is a calvary. Two taps were already too few. then they took out the other one. I gave thanks to God when I filled the containers.

I made breakfast and went to wash the dishes João did his toilet and went to buy bread. I was going out but was so disheartened that I decided to stay home to rest. I made the beds. I swept the shack and went to the scrap-iron depot to sell some iron and a little oakum.

I took Vera. I got 16. I became nervous when I received the 16. I went into the guine bakery and bought half a dozen bananas because Vera wanted them and begged insistently. I smacked her She began to cry and a man who was in the bakery began to tease her, and he bought her sweets. and gave them to her. She was happy. And I was getting worried by the calm voice of that man. I went outside while he bought the sweets that Vera pointed to in the window. I thanked him and told him that when Vera wants something she is insistent. What I want to see is when she begins to work if it will be with tenacity. Vera began to speak telling me that it was good of me to pull her ears and her to cry because the man seeing her cry gave her sweets. I walked along home collecting manure for Dona Franca.

I arrived home and sent Vera to buy half a kilo of rice and I made rice, green pepper and meat. When the children arrived they ate lunch and we went to the blue Cross to take the cans to sell. After I left the Blue Cross I went to Dona Franca to deliver the manure. She gave us coffee, bread and bananas and 15 cruzeiros 5 for each child I went to Alfredo Maia street 511 to pick up some tins that a lady gave me. She told me she was a member of a Friends [group] and that she is going to give me a Christmas card for me to go there to get it since the presents will be distributed on the 21.

I took the kids to see the Radio. It is ready. But I need 1000 to pay for the repair. I was given some cardboard. On the return I put Vera into the cart and collected firewood. i stopped near to the Incapre Cold Storage to pick up coal. I got to the favela and saw the lazybones sitting in the shade. I looked with disgust at Cristiano. A type who came to live in the favela. I never spoke with that man. I don't appreciate his friendship with Vera.

I put away the loot that was in the cart. She was happy. João said that Dona Franca's house is very pretty. And that he is still going to live in a house like that. I got to the shantytown and went to talk with senhor Antonio. I was worried about Vera who came to tell me that the man had given her an apple. at every minute I was going to watch where she was going.

i took up my notebook to write. I wrote and talked with Antonio. When I saw senhor Manoel who was arriving. I said: we are in a bad way what is it that he is coming for here. I got up and went inside my shack. i sat down to write. João came to tell me that I was irritated with Senhor Manoel and that he had 1,000 I didn't believe it. Senhor Manoel came in and began to ask me if I had received the money for the book.

I don't know why the portuguese only thinks about money I got annoyed Vera and José Carlos began to argue—the worst thing in the world is to bring up kids. when they don't obey. I went out after her to see if she would stop crying. I came back in and began to write. I wrote only one word and got upset i stopped writing and went out screaming

—Vera! Vera! Vera! And she didn't answer i began to run

around the favela calling her. The children were fighting on A street. i went in the middle of the fight and called. and asked where Vera was. —She was not with the children. I began to think about that Cristiano guy. I called Vera and José Carlos called.

I went to look for her at the landfill where I saw that Cristiano. —[Vera] said: Mama! And I asked him

—Where were you?

—She came walking up quickly seeing Cristiano I asked him

—Was she with you?

—Not with me.

His rapid semilaconic answer led me to understand that she was with him

She said to me: Mother, the man grabbed me and was taking me over to the landfill.

—You shouldn't ever accompany a bum! Did he do anything to you?

—No. He said—that he was going to give me a doll that says papa and mama. —Is there a doll that says mama? He is going to give me one on Christmas day. This isn't going to stop here. I am going to register a complaint. For working this bum is no good! —He heard the little girl tell of his perverse actions. I entered the shack. I told senhor Manoel that the bum was taking Vera into a dark area and that I was going to call the Radio patrol. i asked for money, he gave me 10, I grabbed Vera and went out. I went to call Chico. It took a long time for them to answer. I called the press room to see if I could find Audálio. I wanted to ask him to get the bum out of the favela—Audálio wasn't there I called dr. Adhemar [the mayor]. the line was busy. I telephoned the Radio Patrol they attended me and told me to await the vehicle at the streetcar stop—I went to wait. The Radio patrol took a long time. I told Juaquim paraiba the depraved act of the bum. After I explained who he was he told me that the bum has the nickname Mineirinho.

—Mineiro . . . i thought: only in Minas [Gerais], do they have this type of man. who doesn't like to work—I'm from there and know that clan. Paraiba told me that I should telephone again. i asked him to lend me 2 cruzeiros. —He lent them to me and told me that if he saw Cristiano he would beat him up. That there is a girl who he wants who he pursues and for him to stay away from the girl. He said he can just imagine the empty head of Mineirinho. I had already spoken with his mother. Dona Francisca who told me that he was not in—I told her that I was going to report to the inspector

—She who already knows the prowess of her son didn't frighten.

—She didn't defend him like in these cases the mothers say that their sons are saints. —by her silence I gathered that her son, is not an article of the best material

From the streetcar stop I went to the police station and told the sergeant what happened. He called the Radio patrol and told me to wait he said into the telephone that it was the second phone call and that the little girl was only 5. We began to talk about this type of man. He told me that there are trials for depraved men. I got tired of waiting. The soldier Cardoso arrived and asked me

—Who hit you in the favela?

—I told him that a pervert was carrying Vera off to the woods

—And do you know him?

Yes. He doesn't have a job. His mother keeps him—a Son, who after he is grown up continues living at his mother's expense, —he is no good! Vera wanted to go to the Central police station. She said: lets go to the Central. There, they will settle everything in a minute. Cardoso was horrified. He said: that women begin to take an interest in men [when they are] around 12 and after. The Radio Patrol was taking a long time, the sergeant told me to go put Vera to bed.

—What a sergeant! A man and then some. Modest and very polite—I told him that I am going to punch Cristiano.

—In my birthplace my nickname is—Carolina the devil. and when I left my birthplace, nobody missed me. That Cristiano has a sugared mother. who wants to raise her son with words. i think, that a mother ought to raise her son with words when he, is obedient. When he is not obedient, give him the leather.

Cristiano is a piece of iron that needs fire and an anvil . . . well I must be the anvil in his life And my prayers to heaven grow and expand—just like the sea.

I returned to the favela. i went by the bar and returned the 2 cruzeiros to Juaquim [P]araiba. I was filled with anxiety with the desire to mince and remince Cristiano. [when] I got to the favela the rumor already had spread [and had] crossed the river and was winding through to Vila Guilherme. The human tongue is the king of information. it replaces the radio because, wherever there is no radio, the tongue also carries—so I don't know if we should say: blessed be the tongue, or damned be the tongue—I turned on the flame and heated up the food for the children.

Vera arrived and went to sleep. After I explained to her what perverts do with children she was horrified But, children this age see things as if they were asleep, they act like sleepwalkers. The man who takes advantage of a child takes the place of the lion. He becomes the king of the animals.

—I was so nervous that I got chills. two minutes later, I was warm. What I know to say is that we remain only a little while on this planet, or world. —But what a bitter period. so many things happen to concern us that we end up hating the world. why doesn't man give happiness instead of grief to his fellow man? And happiness with good deeds. The refined souls, the christian souls understand what I just related.

Cristiano's soul was crafted from rotten clay. From clay that stinks of sulphur. I told senhor Manoel that there was no Radio patrol. José Carlos began his homework it was 10 o'clock at night. Somebody knocked at the window. I went to see. It was the police—I went to show them Where the Dog's shack is. But a dog is more valuable than that disgusting man. They clapped. The dogs began to bark. i broke off a piece of the fence the soldier reprimanded me. Senhor Sebastian opened the window. And Dona Francisca also. The soldiers asked for her son.

—She said that he had put on his suit and left.

—We are going to search inside He is going to pay me for this! I want to teach him to respect innocents. —The soldier ordered me to shut my mouth—because you called us.

Senhor Sebastian opened the gate. And the dogs played their symphonies. We entered. Dona Francisca told us to enter i sensed that she was used to having visits from the authorities. She told us that her son has no sense. That she suffered so much with that son that she can't wait to die. The soldier asked her son's name.

—Cristiano Ranieri

—i thought: a black with an Italian last name.

—How old is he?

—20.

I asked her: —That Old man is 20?

—It's liquor that leaves him like that.

And I thought he was 40. The policemen told me to register a complaint at the 12th [precinct].

—But I'm not going to. because the day that he turns up I enter into action—with the hand of the pestle. I lay down. And didn't manage to sleep. I thought. And if I drank I would certainly sleep and would never sense Vera's absence. But once I understood that whoever has a child, cannot drink. —Children, are like a rudder that cannot be left alone.

3 December 1958 I left my bed at 5 o'clock and went to hell. to get water. —What a struggle! The water with Orlando's administration is horrible i got a little and came home to make breakfast and I left an empty can in the line. I don't know why Orlando cut off the water supply here in the favela. I made breakfast and went after water. Many people waiting their turn—paulo was seated when the black Lalau came up. The black man who walks with a bounce looks like he is rehearsing for carnival—he likes to show off. He told paulo that he had smacked him in the face. because he was drunk. And he kept on attacking paulo. The two hugged each other and fell. At the fall paulo hit his face on the ground and his nose began to bleed. I separated the two of them. paulo grabbed a stone.

And I said: don't throw the stone because if he threw the stone he could kill Lalau. Lalau is black. And he said I am a man! I loathe these types who say: i am a man! They have no Culture, no good-ness, no useful moral qualities, They don't persevere at work. they are terrible fathers and miserable mothers. Lalau even beats his mother-in-law. What I cited are the ingredients that make a man, a true man. But Lalau is scandalous, he is a pipsqueak who says: i am a man! The type of man that Lalau is [is] just like a cake that one begins to make, some ingredients are missing and the cook decides to bake it anyway and the result is no good. —Something turns out—and Lalau is a something

—Now about paulo he has some culture. He wasn't born for a favela. He isn't violent. —Me yes! It's that I know how to live in a favela. When it's necessary to be sensible I am sensible. When it's necessary to be crazy I am crazy.

i got the kids ready they went to school and I went out with Vera. Due to the late hour that she went to bed and to the fright that she had she was not feeling well. She said: today I could be dead! I didn't go to Dona Julita's because I was tired But still I worked until I got 100 cruzeiros.

I told the women in the depot that the pervert had been taking Vera away. I arrived home tired. But I had to make food for the kids. —The food was horrible and I had to give it to the pigs. I lay down to rest a little bit more But I didn't sleep for fear that Vera would go out. I decided to get up and went to talk with the girls And they began to say that Cristiano looks at them with a glance that puts fear into them. It's that he is always smiling at them. He disappeared from the favela. He likes to be alone near children. He isn't tall he might be 1 meter and 40 centimeters. He isn't fat, he is a candidate for tuberculosis. Rosalina came to ask me to lend her 60, cruzeiros, I did. After that I went to lie down: I had a headache and was hemorrhaging. —It was the scare from the pervert.

The favela people are horrified.

4 December 1958 I got out of bed at 5 o'clock and went to fetch
water. How horrible it is to stand in that line. I made breakfast and
went to shop. I bought bread, margarine and sugar. I changed the
children, gave them a breakfast meal they went to school and I went
out with Vera. Today she is more animated. She is walking faster.
She is singing.

I am upset with the bum scene. I went to D. Julita's I stopped
in at Dona Angelina's house she gave me sweets. because her son
has a birthday. She told me that she is happy with life because her
husband is very nice.

Dona Julita gave me food, and papers. I told her that I would
return there in the afternoon because I was going to pick up the
radio from the repair shop and I show it to her. —I told her that I
had snatched Vera from the arms of a pervert. —She was horrified
and told me to take care of Vera She told me some sordid tales of
perverts. I got back to the favela and changed my clothes to go to
the City. to receive money for Vera. I took José Carlos and vera

—What a mistake! José Carlos is the devil! He annoys me so
much in the streets that I almost go crazy—I gave him some smacks.
near to the post office, and pulled Vera's ears. for what! . . .

A woman who was walking next to me. Said to me:

—This isn't done! Where I come from they don't do these
things! The people there, are educated

—Where is your country, lady?

—Switzerland!

—If I were white I could say that I turned red.

—Oh! I have heard that the swiss are the most educated
people on the globe That you don't do ill to one another. That there
solidarity reigns.

She began to speak and I heard her with pleasure. because she
didn't speak nonsense. She told me that pulling the ears of a child
can harm them and the children can go deaf. That one should give a
mild punishment to a child. We spoke of the religions of the globe
I told her that white people have more chances in life than blacks.

—That the black person is always put aside She told me that this is a false belief That her maid is black and that she is perfectly pleased with her. She gave 5 cruzeiros to José Carlos to divide with Vera.

I took the streetcar. José Carlos and Vera were pleased because I bought them pastry. We descended São Caetano street and went to pick up the radio on Eduardo Chaves street. It was senhor Vicente de Paulo pedrosa who fixed the radio. his residence is on Avenida do Estado 1,227. I liked doing business with him He is like the lead that sticks when applied. He is polite. He fixed the radio. I showed the radio to Dona Guiomar of the Tiradentes cleaners—I told her that I had spoken with her husband that she had told me he was very good and asked why they had parted?

—He told me that Dona Guiomar didn't allow him to have fun with other women

—I told him that a man ought to love only one woman

—He told me that his heart is collective. That it is the same as the Americas Building. That there is only room for women.

They tell me that we shouldn't say that we don't like somebody. because we can come to need that person so I am undecided and don't know if I like Dona Guiomar's husband or not! She told me that she suffered so much with him that even her love disappeared like salt in water.

I told him that a reporter went to interview a lady who was celebrating her silver wedding anniversary. He said to her:

But you already spent 25 years with your husband! You must have wonderful memories. Can you relate to us some great emotion from your conjugal life? She thought and said: what I can tell you is: that in these 25 years of married life, I cried, 25 liters of tears.

The dry-cleaning employees smiled, and turned on my radio to see if it was working. One employee told me that he had a radio and was going to take it to the same man who fixed mine—I gave him the address of senhor Vicente de paula pedrosa.

I went to take the radio for Dona Julita to see. She liked the sound of the radio and praised the work of senhor Viçente and asked me for his address. to fix a radio that isn't working. senhor João pires told me that Carnival is coming and that I have a radio to hear the novelties and the homage to the Carnival King.

I told Dona Julita that a number of people want to buy radios—She smiled

I came up Eduardo Chaves street and told senhor Viçente de paula that he should go to Dona Julita's to see a radio that needed fixing He took down Dona Julita's address—I came to the favela When I arrived at the Cruz Azul I stopped to talk with the mother of Luiz Gonzaga. She began to speak of her miserable husband—listening to her I sensed that the union of both parts as times, carries one thousand and one sufferings for both.

She asked me to give her children advice. And I like her children so much that I will ask God that they may be precious.

Vera began to cry, she fell down and began to cry. A man who was standing near to the Cruz Azul began to please her so she wouldn't cry. It was José Carlos who made her fall down. She hurt her knee and her nose When I got to the streetcar stop I went into the bar to drink water The people look at me when I go by and say that I am courageous. because I stood up to the pervert and saved my daughter —I came to the conclusion that whoever lives in these sordid nuclei becomes transformed bit by bit. When I came to live in the favela, I was gentle. I liked to please. Nowadays I am worse than caustic soda. worse than a nettle.

I arrived at the favela I went to show the radio to Dona Nena. I turned it on at her house. I forgot to say that I went into the grocery and bought 1 kilo of sugar and . . .

This my Diary I wrote ten years Ago but I had no intention of popularizing myself I aimed to reveal my situation and the situation of my children that is the situation of the favelados.

Carolina Maria de Jesus

Carolina with an afflicted heart, due to the daily insipidity. Could it be that god will return to punish us and reprove us because of our errors, or will he forgive us with his go[od] . . . [Entry ends abruptly]

Carolina's first diary, *Quarto de Despejo,* was published in August 1960, making her an instant celebrity. She continued to write. These entries, written in the months following her departure from the Canindé favela, fall into the period described in her second diary, *Casa de Alvenaria,* which was edited by Dantas in exactly the same manner as *Quarto.* By now she is earning royalties and is living in the cinder-block house of her dreams in a lower-middle-class neighborhood in São Paulo. She is about to leave on a publicity trip to Uruguay, Argentina, and Chile.

1961

28 October 1961 I got up at 6 o'clock João went to class i gave him a note for the teacher to release him after class and gave another note to him to take to dr. Lélio de Castro Andrade [her publisher], to send me five thousand cruzeiros.

I stayed around waiting for his return: —A woman who wants me to lend her fifty thousand cruzeiros came to see me with her daughter, who is going to get married and wants to rent my shack when I move to the city. She complained about life saying that it is insipid I thought of Christ's words when he said: you are the salt of the earth. Too much salt makes the food indigestible. And what currently makes food indigestible are the prices of foodstuffs. She complains that her son is sick and the retirement institute doesn't give her decent assistance. I think. if the beloved Getúlio Vargas, was alive would Brazil be in such a mess[?] She complained that she doesn't eat well.

—But you need to eat meat!

—Who am I to buy meat! My future son-in-law eats in my house and it is a struggle to give him something to eat

5. Carolina's belongings being unloaded from the truck provided by the mayor's office in the process of moving her possessions into a temporary house before she was able to occupy her house in Alto de Santana. The truck had been stoned by angry residents as it departed the favela. *Photographer unknown.*

I invited the woman to go out with me, and I bought 1 kilo of meat and a piece of bacon and gave them to her. She was pleased I paid what I owed to the butcher, João brought the money.

I went to buy something in the market. The prices leave one depressed. The times are insipid. There is no chance, of living with little money—What sad people. Those who circulate in the market. Looking at the prices as if they were a spectacle. i spent the rest of the day writing—i bought fruit for the kids who stare at me as if I came from another planet

21 October 1961 I got up at 7 o'clock. I went to wash clothes [and] to clean the house. The children are plaguing me to go to the movies. I went to do the morning shopping. I am going to make macaroni. i asked João to sweep out the house.

—only if you pay me

—i grabbed the leather [belt] and gave him a swat, the worse thing is to beat somebody But, unfortunately, the mothers need to beat their children. I wasn't born to be an executioner. i prefer to please. i asked Ely [a friend, who for a time lived in her house] to help me put a plume on my dress because I am going to take it to Argentina. This morning when I went to buy meat, I talked with a man who said he was a fazenda [farm] owner in são juaquim da Barra, that the settlers prefer to live in the city rather than work in farming That he gives land and houses to whoever wants to plant and doesn't find anybody. I told him that I worked at farming. We didn't like the farms because the owners didn't let us plant. In the past the landowners let one plant, but nowadays they order the settler to buy And I recited the verses that I made up when I left the life on the farm. He listened and said that the verses were correct.

I told him that I am not against agrarian reform, but I would like the owner of unused land to give permission for whoever wanted to plant When the owner wanted it the land would be returned—i asked the landowner from são juaquim da Barra, if there are farms for sale in the interior?

—there are.

—don't you want to sell yours?

—No.

I said goodbye to the butcher and returned home to make lunch. The woman who wants fifty thousand cruzeiros came to visit me with her 14-year-old daughter.

i asked if the girl had a job?

—No she doesn't. She was working in a factory but left because she was too young. She wants to study to be a seamstress.

—because, I could not pay for her studies I sacrificed to buy her a machine that I am paying for.

—if you want I will help with the sewing course for your daughter, I offered

Well . . . I could not buy the materials. The one who could help me is my nephew who was the mayor of Santo Andre.

—Do you mean Osvealdo Gimenes?

—That's him. He is a scoundrel. He is the black sheep of our family. Once he started a shop and shortchanged his relatives, because he borrowed money from one and then another. I went one day to talk to him but the soldiers wouldn't let me enter. But God is great. He lost his mandate. And that disgusting man wanted to be president of Brazil.

—I thought: what a family, that one defames the others. In a family of ambitious members, those who get rich are hated by the others who stayed poor. I felt a dread for humanity.

While the woman was talking I was rinsing out the clothes. She said I swear! How hard you work! She said goodbye, i went to conclude my preparations for the trip. —At night a woman who sells in the market came to ask me to take her to the bar of senhor cariovaldo, that dona Marizette owed her four thousand cruzeiros. When we reached the city I showed her the bar and waited for her to return. I found it interesting that a little black girl was smoking a cigar. When she returned the woman told me that senhor Cariovaldo gave her the address of his house for her to charge his wife. that senhor Cariovaldo became disappointed. The worst thing I find is a Person to wait to be charged in order to pay. this is robbery

Some little black girls asked Are you Carolina Maria de Jesus?

—I am. why?

It's that on the 29th of this month there is going to be a dance sponsored by the 220 [an association] and other clubs. We are going on a procession to Aparecida do Norte.

I don't like dances. I like parties celebrating holidays and speeches. I told the blacks that I will be in são paulo, the 19th and if I can will attend the dance.

I can't be rude

We bade farewell to the black kids and went in search of a restaurant to Buy pizza for the daughter of the street vender who wants to be an actress. I advised her to not let the girl become an actress. She ought to learn a trade and get married. And be a decent wife. The world needs women who know how to care for children.

speaking of children saturday a teacher came to complain that

José Carlos had broken a flower in her back yard. That brazilians are poorly brought up because they study so little. That the best brought up children in the world are the French. That at the end of the year she is going to the United States. That brazilians are disorganized. She is harmony. She has a degree from Lebanon. i thought this teacher knows that children aren't just born with sense. When we returned form the city, we met senhor José, a collector of paper. He was pleased. we talked remembering the good times past. We talked about the dead Estefam who had a paper depot. His wife left him, he began to drink. I think about the perversity of women. And they were married and had children. I condemn friendships that don't develop roots.

I paid their fare. When I got home, I was exhausted. I wanted to write but sleepiness overtook me. I kept thinking about Luiz. Such an intelligent man. with aristocratic ways

30 October 1961 I got up at 6 o'clock. I will not sweep the house. I am going to write. Today I am a bit confused. I received a warning that something is going to upset me

I will not buy bread there is bread left over. I heated it up in the oven. I am not going to make lunch. there is left-over macaroni. I stayed remembering my times in the favela. Mondays I went to the houses of the rich to see if there was left-over macaroni. When it rains I think about the paper collectors. The depots don't accept wet paper.

I was writing when senhor Bertini arrived, an employee at the Editora Abraxas [a publishing house]. He came to invite me to go out with him to arrange my travel documents. I went to change and stopped writing saying to him if I could I would write day and night, The only thing that I like are books. I showed him my books. He asked if he could play my record I put it on and showed him the snapshots that I will take to Argentina.

He corrected an inscription that I made in a photograph Saying that it was prejudicial to me. It's that I wrote on the photograph, The Poor of Brazil are barefoot. He said that what people are interested in is hearing that I was a favela resident and loved books.

I thanked him for his sensible gestures. João returned and I suggested that he get Vera ready for class and heat the food. [I said,] if I have time I will go to the Registry to get a copy of your certificate. He ruined the certificate because he took it to the movies to pay half price. He needs the certificate for school—We took a taxi. We went to the Argentine Consulate

I asked if the argentine dancers went to Buenos Aires?

They did. They told us that you lent them money. I was satisfied, hearing this. It is proof that the argentines who sought me out are not robbers.

—It is beautiful to see a man who is poor, and honorable.

The photographs won't do for a travel visa. We went to take other photographs 5 x 5 the photographer is of german origin. Rodolfo Stein. I told him that the inventors of the photograph were two french brothers. Niepçe and Luiz Jaques Mandê [Joseph Nicéphore Niepce and his partner, Louis Jacques Mandé Daguerre]. —We spoke of the war. The photographer said that at the time of the war they arrest scientists and oblige them to reveal their chemical discoveries in order to use them in warfare. In my opinion, the man is crazy if nature destroys mankind why should men destroy themselves—We went to the vaccination clinic. Dr. Antonio Prado on the rua anhanguera attended me. I told him that I am going to Argentina When we left the clinic we headed for RCA Vitor I drove with senhor Bertini, to the office and we went to talk with senhor Roque, one of the directors. Carolina, do you know that I liked you a lot and now I don't like you anymore?

—why Fred?

—It's that you told that fellow who came to request employment here, that I asked you to lend me twenty-eight thousand cruzeiros and I didn't repay you And to Audálio. you lent thirty thousand cruzeiros.

—I didn't say that!

—I don't make trouble!

I gave shelter to that indolent white man who walks a lot, because he, asked me to. I felt sorry for the child and his pregnant wife. When a man is a man, he constructs a shack for his family but, he doesn't go about with his valise on his back. If he went to a white man's house to request help he wouldn't get anything. because the whites are not stupid. He said that he was at his aunt's house and she expelled him. He did this out of envy and evil to make my relationship with RCA Vitor and the magazine O Cruzeiro incompatible. thinking that I am earning a lot of money with you I swore nevermore to help anybody. Senhor Bertini went to talk about the records to get them ready without fail the 6th

I gave the RCA contract to Audálio to read, and keep for me.

I left RCA Vitor furious with Lauro for having entangled me with the people I work with. Audálio is educated, he sensed that Lauro is a scoundrel. He didn't learn a trade because he was a vagrant. When I got home I was soaked because it was raining.

There was food, I made beefsteaks and ate supper. Today I am sad the kids taking over. At ten o'clock Luiz, Arrived. With a common raincoat I was getting ready to go to bed. My children were pleased to see him they smiled. José Carlos went to tell him a joke. He smiled. A forced smile. I asked my kids to leave the room. they obeyed unwillingly. We were alone. I closed the door, and gave him an embrace and a kiss, as if he were mine.

He asked: Can you give me a manicure?

I descended the steps and went to heat water to cut his cuticles. He was scraping his nails with a scissor. —Oh Luiz! You are nuts! doing that you will ruin them. And I had so much work to make your nails beautiful. You are an ass!

—I admit it dona Carolina

I smiled and told him, then, I am going to give you a pair of gold instruments. Thank you for the present. After I painted his nails I asked: take off your jacket! so I can sew up the lining. He stripped and showed me the places that were unattached—I sewed them with black thread. i sensed that he wanted to say something to me. I stayed waiting impatiently.

he asked: —On what day was galvão here?

—I don't know. I put it in the diary and gave it to Audálio

—You put it in the diary?

—i did, but I stated that you are good, well mannered and helped me a lot.

—How did I help you?

—You got rid of the bums who were bothering me. The bums who wanted to take my kids to crime were intimidated by your presence.

—You ought to stay with the journalists

—And I am with the journalists. I have a lot of contracts with foreign publishers —why do you think I should stay with the journalists?

—because I am no longer coming back here.

What hate I felt for Luiz! love extended into hate i thought: if I could slice this man into little pieces! If I could turn him into a statue. I cussed him out in my mind. Dog. Commoner, ingrate, stupid. He will tramp on life, until he falls into an abyss.

he asked: When are you going to Argentina?

—I didn't answer

—Is Audálio going with you?

—I didn't answer

He knows, when I stop liking somebody I don't talk to them anymore

He took off his trousers for me to sew them and told me that I had to find a place for us to meet. [He said,] I won't come here anymore.

I was furious and said to him: I don't need a man. i can live without you i am a busy woman. I have a lot of say. I am a go-getter. We remained in silence.

i asked him if he wanted to use Ely's watch, on the trip to the North.

—I don't want it, because I don't like to use things that belong to others: Arms and watches, have to be my own.

I gave him his trousers to dress, and grabbed the key ring and told him to give me my keys.

He watched me take the keys from the ring There are a lot of types of scoundrels in the world. I have the impression that you pre-meditated everything And I said other hard things to him that I won't include in the Diary.

—Open the door for me, Carolina!

He descended the steps in front of me. I followed cussing him out in my mind.

I had left the keys in my room. i asked Ely to give me the key and I grabbed his trousers to look for it in the pockets. I found the key and opened the door. He went to say goodbye to Ely. When he extended his hand to me for farewell I gave him a big push, he landed outside and said Wow!

I quickly closed the door and went to sit down on the sofa. Ely, was frightened and asked:

—What was that all about Carolina?

We had an argument! And our fights grow roots.

Don't think that I will your embrace again need
My love on hatred feeds
from roots will seedlings breed.

Ely who was sleepy became lively again with the scene that she witnessed and asked

—What happened? You like this man so much you speak of him all day long The words of my mother came into my brain Never deceive yourself with men and you will be happy, living from your work.

I sat on the sofa cussing out Luiz.

I sensed that I don't hate this man. I don't love another man, because it is difficult [to find] a man with the culture that Luiz has.

But I am not going to moan I want to read, and write.

And life goes on.

31 October 1961 I got up at 6 o'clock. João went to school i quickly got a meal ready, I was changing when Frederico [P]enteado arrived.

He came to ask me if I will be in São Paulo on the 12 of November. to appear at the dance in the Maua palace. When I looked out of the window I saw dona Mercedes, and said to her:

You arrived at just the right moment. You can come up. She entered and vaulted up the steps and came into my room, I introduced her to Penteado, telling her[:] This man, is the director of the 720. A club of Black people. He is the one who gave me the title of Paulista citizen. [She said to me:] I have heard of you but didn't recognize you Penteado told me that he sent the photographs of me with the president of the Republic, and they will be ready on the 3rd. [I] asked for one to take to Argentina. He said that each photograph cost six hundred cruzeiros, there are four, I will pay two thousand four hundred cruzeiros. I found that expensive but now I am queen of the cash!

I changed and we went out. We went by bus. Penteado, paid the fare and we got down off near the Ultima-Hora newspaper office. I told him that Luiz had gone and wasn't coming back.

—He will return. said dona Mercedes.

I don't want him anymore! He begged me to have him, I didn't want to because an inferior man can't put up with my superiority—I move on thinking. I am like oysters that emerge [from their shells] and go speeding along. I don't sell my body When I accept a man it is because I like him. And I loved Luiz. We got off the bus and headed for the offices of Bali-Cola. Where the firm operates. I learned that Bali-Cola belongs to my Argentine publisher. Senhor Sahanvaller.

Senhor Bertini was awaiting me and said that I was late [I] explained that I had to get Vera ready for school and prepare lunch. Senhor Putáoras told me that his wife invited me to visit her. When I return from Argentina I promised to see her. It was raining when senhor Bertini said that he was thinking about me walking in the rain and that I was going to get ill. I have worked in farming. Rain water is distilled and isn't harmful.

We went to get the photographs and take them to the consulate. that was going to prepare my passport. Senhor consul wasn't there to put the stamp in the passport we left, we went to Manchete [a magazine] to ask Silva Netto about an article. He was leaving the elevator i bellowed:

Oh Silva Netto! I introduced him to senhor Bertini, as the representative of the Argentine publisher that was backing my trip for the launching of my book. —Silva Netto, gave us the address of the Manchete representative, who works at Radio El Mundo [a radio station]. to send an article from there back here. We went for coffee. Senhor Bertini took down the address of the Argentine correspondent. I took Silva Netto to lunch, he introduced us to a young girl who offered him some liquid to sweeten his coffee. He is on a diet. I told him about Chico Sá, of the O Dia newspaper, who decided to go on a diet, got sick and died we oughtn't to interfere in our organism.

We said goodbye and went to the Folha de São Paulo [a newspaper], We went by car. The receptionist telephone operator received us very kindly and connected to the copy room to ask permission for us . . . We went to talk with senhor Fred. I introduced senhor Bertini, who asked for an announcement of my trip to Argentina on the 6th. The reporter who attended us was senhor Carlos pizarro.

We left the offices of the Folhas [a syndicate]. we went to the Ultima Hora [a tabloid newspaper] offices. I was thinking of Gil passareli, who has my photograph with senhor Altino Arantes, i wanted it to take to Argentina Gil isn't in São Paulo, he went to Tambaú. At Ultima Hora, we spoke to Alik Kastaki. requesting Ultima Hora to announce that I am going to Argentina. When we left Ultima Hora, senhor Bertini asked me,

Who is this journalist?

—It is dona Alik Kostaki

—Ah! If I had known that it was her, I would have treated her with special respect She is a colossus! she is doing well. She is rich. She is a foreigner. She was born to be a journalist. And on and on, we got to the restaurant. Senhor Bertini ordered macaroni with chicken, and a dessert with whipped cream. we paid 700 cruzeiros. I was horrified. We are in an epoch in which some eat and others watch. Many people must see food as an abstract thing. Senhor Bertini, complained that I brought along dona Mercedes.

I got nervous because I don't want to mess things up with foreign publishers. I was complaining that I miss Luiz

—He'll return. You'll see. Said dona Mercedes.

If he returns I won't want him. I don't like enigmatic people. We argued. —Arguments reinforce friendships.

For me arguments atrophy friendships. We left the restaurant

we went to the Francisco Alves bookstore, to see dr. Lélio de Castro Andrade, he wasn't in. We couldn't wait we went to the consulate. To conclude the passport business. and I said goodbye to senhor Bertini, he wanted me to go back home by car But I had very little cash. I went to the offices of O Cruzeiro [a newspaper] and wrote a note for Taraks.

Taraks, lend me 500, cruzeiros, after I will pay you and I put the note in front of his eyes so he would see it.

—I don't have it. only when I am paid. Wait for Freitas he will give it to you. I sat down, and talked with a Black man with a goatee. I told him that my dream is to live in my birthplace, and give up literary life. It is a mess. When I was in the favela people looked down upon me. because nobody wants to befriend a favelado. They say they are robbers. But what is missing for the poor is food and affection. Now, so many people flatter me and annoy me

—The Black man said that the whites want to run the Blacks I told him that I won't allow a white to dominate me nobody puts either a saddle or a brake on me. I want to be as free as the sun. My favorite star. because it warms and I am always cold. for this reason I am the adoptive daughter of the sun. There are days when I think that if I were to choose a star to be my husband it would be the sun. I don't like wind. It is rude. It spreads everything about. The Black man went on to say that he is married to a white woman and she is against the Black race. When that article came out in O Cruzeiro, the nine Black muses were supplanting the white ones I thought: it's that the whites today are good and help the Blacks treating us with affection The Black man who heard me said that, living in the country I could write about the life of the peasants.

—I already wrote in verses and I recited the Settler and the Land Owner, I was reciting when Freitas, entered. I got up, walking toward him and saying,

Good afternoon senhor Freitinhas and I gave him a hug.

And asked Taroks if he knew! And I asked for a loan of 500 cruzeiros. He gave me 1,000. Audálio will pay you later. I explained to Freitas, why I had no money and I left the office. We entered a bar, I had a guarana [a soft drink].

Don't you want broth, dona Carolina? the waiter offered.

—Not today.

The broth is very tasty!

I smiled, and said: everything from here is tasty!

We left the bar, I asked dona Mercedes to accompany me to RCA Vitor I wanted to ask what day I will receive the payment for my Record. When senhor Basilio saw me, he asked if there were any letters for me.

—There are none.

A number of artists were there—with their sad expressions it appears that there is nothing for them? I asked Basilio to arrange some records for me to take he promised me he would. When we got to the door of the building I was talking with Charutinho—our darling Adoniram Barbosa. He complained to me that he asked Julio Nagib to record one of his compositions for Carnival and Julio Nagib refused. And he continued to talk about RCA Vitor. . . .

I was horrified with the points that Charutinho made who is not the first to complain about RCA Vitor. He asked me my opinion of the RCA Vitor organization. I am experienced at diverting uncomfortable issues. I altered my voice saying:

—Charutinho, my kids like your program.

Come visit me one day. and I gave him my address. I leave for Argentina on the 6th. I am going to see if I do a film there, if there is a chance of including Brazilian actors will you go? I'll go on the condition that I am the main actor.* I am doing the script. A black man who was with Charutinho told me that he is going to give me some records to take. I invited Charutinho to come to my house. He refused.

—I asked him and Oswaldo Malles, is he good to you?

—He is my father. You know that the journalist is good. The heart of a journalist, is covered in velvet. It has no thorns. Dona Mercedes, gave me a piece of plastic to put on my head, because it was raining. I refused. I watched the waters gathering on the ground, and thought of the favela when there are floods. I said goodbye to Charutinho, and invited dona Mercedes to come sleep at my place.

—I can't.

Or does the lady have a Luiz who sleeps with her?

—Nobody loves me. I am not Carolina Maria de Jesus. I took the bus near the Ultima Hora [office]. The line was long. And the peaceful poor people waiting their turn to board the trolley. One man cussed out the driver who asked him to put more gas in his car I thought: the man is going to pay but is being mistreated. I was writing. A man warned the employee of the gasoline station

—You are going to enter the Diary of Carolina she is watching you. The employee turned yellow. i thought: i am imposing mutual respect.

The line began to move i didn't get on the first bus i got on the second. When I got home I met dona Alba Borges who is going to care for my house while I am in Argentina. I found a note from Jorge Barbosa Elias, from paraná who invited me to go to the Cruzeiro to talk with him tomorrow at 2 in the afternoon.

I ate dinner and walked about the house. I made a bed for Alba, gave praise, and went to lie down. thinking about Luiz, who is traveling at one in the morning. He is going by airplane.

* Probably this is Charutinho speaking, but the context is ambivalent.

1 November 1961 I got up at 6 o'clock. I went to wash the clothes. Alba, and Ely were scraping the floor of the dining room. today I am nervous. I went shopping at the street market, I was horrified at the price of a kilo of beans. Fifty-five cruzeiros. Two kilos one hundred and ten. I was washing clothes when a lady rang the bell—I didn't want to answer it. —She said it was a message that she received by telephone.

I went to attend her.

—It is from panair of Brazil [airline], who called my house Saying that you have to arrange your ticket to Argentina

i begged the lady's pardon and told her that I had too many things to take care of. She said goodbye and I went to get ready to go to the city to take care of things at panair. i went to the copy desk to ask where the panair office was—Flávio pôrto, the new office director of Cruzeiro when he saw me said:

how pretty you are! Don't you want to take me to Argentina?

I smiled. I gave Freitas a hug. He explained to me where the place was. i left smiling. I got into the elevator and gave a hug to the elevator man and said to him. You are getting very fat. It's because you are continuously sitting down. I am going to put you to field labor. I went out of the elevator, i met the son of senhor Antonio, secretary of Dr. Assis Chateaubriand. i asked for Dona Tereza Beker.

She, is going to the United States to visit dr. Assis.

I went toward panair passed by the Folha de são paulo office. I spoke a few minutes with the cashier telling him:

the one who discovered me was senhor Wily Aureli, he was the one who told me Carolina, you are a poet. And I rebelled because I didn't want to be a poet. I cried so much, because it is horrible to have ideas, in the head that double instead of receding. I am grateful to Audálio, who helps me.

How much did Quarto de Despejo make[?]

We haven't calculated it. We are now making money from Europe

—And dividing it with Audálio?

I asked a number of journalists to help me, that the profits will be divided.

—Who were the journalists who you asked for help? —Matos pacheco, José Tavares, The deceased Castrinho The deceased Chico sá, and Mario de Oliveira. I was lucky with Audálio Dantas.

—Did you already buy a house?

—Yes. I want to see if I can buy a house for Audálio. With the money that comes from Europe. There are people who tell me so many things about Audálio, are they true?

I got to panaer [Panair], and worked out the ticket. I left senhor Bertini's calling card to finalize the ticket, he has to bring in the documents. I talked with the people there, telling them that I love books. When I die I want my grave in the shape of a book. i left the agency i returned home. I arrived sleepy i went to lie down thinking about the mother of Maria do Carmo, who wants a book to give as a present to a nun. I am not a fanatic for the church I am fanatic about books, and children who live hungry in the favela, i saw the children playing with the arms of a doll that they found in the garbage and heads without a body.

I came to the conclusion that if a poor person becomes rich, the soul continues poor. And if a rich person becomes poor the soul continues to be rich. And it became a mental dilemma.

There are people who tell me: you shouldn't concern yourself with the class who are hungry. The governments ought to think about this. The governments think about atomic bombs to destroy poor people. It gives the impression that governments don't like the poor. Yesterday I met Ruth de Souza [a black actress]. She saw me and was haughtily passing by i sensed that she didn't want to greet me. i approached her and told her that I am going to Argentina. For today . . . That's enough.

2 November 1961 I woke up at 2 in the morning to write. I am behind in my Diary. Today is the day of the dead [All Souls' Day]. I observe the hypocrisy of the living carrying flowers to the dead.

When a person is alive, they are mistreated and looked down upon. The society, that instead of calling it society, should be called moral rot excludes, and selects people wounding noble sensitivities. After they die they cry and praise them.

So many people died lacking means.

My house has the back yard of a cemetery. I watch the living visiting the dead decorating the areas with flowers and candles. Today I am going to stay home writing. Vera is going to play with the white girls, who receive her with disgust accepting her superficially. Like the living selecting and dividing the classes.

If a white boy enters my house, the mothers come running to remove their children as if they would be contaminated near us. There are times that I have the desire to send humanity to hell that . . . But today is the day of the dead. My children are cussing at me saying that I am always hugging and kissing men if they knew that I do this because I feel sorry for the Brazilians who struggle with the cost of living.

The people who pass by the saintly field complain about the cost of flowers.

I spent the day at home.

3 November 1961 I got up at 6 o'clock. Today João isn't going to class. Dona Alba, the young girl who is working for me said to me: when I was in Uberaba, my dream was to live with you.

I pay her six thousand cruzeiros a month to take care of my children and the house. She . . . occasionally is polite.

With relation to people there is a great possibility of deceiving ourselves. I am getting sick of people who shine like gold, but are really only foil. —Today I am nervous. Yesterday lightning struck near my house. it could hit me it could enter my house and kill me with my children. it seems as if poets don't have God to protect them.

I just had breakfast and left for the city. I went to panair to take care of my ticket. i asked the agent at panair to telephone senhor Bertini, letting him know that I was waiting for him in the office of the agency. I sat down, waiting for him. but, I am too nervous to stay seated. i went out to the office of Bali-cola i met senhor Bertini who was leaving for panair. I greeted him and we went to panair to Finish the passport. After that we went to the Diario [a newspaper] to see if the [photographs?] that they made with me [are] ready. they promised the [photographs?] for the—afternoon. The one in charge didn't work yesterday since it was a holiday. We left the Diario and went to the Livraria Francisco Alves [her publisher's bookstore]. senhor Bertini, wants to meet dr. Lélio de Castro Andrade.

But dr Lélio, wasn't there. The staff [people] said that he is ill. it seems that dr. Lélio, doesn't like to receive me. But I swore—I am going to give up literature. With the mix-ups that I faced with Quarto de Despejo, I was losing my love for literature. And senhor Bertini, the representative of Editora Abraxas, wanted my photograph with dr. Lélio. We left the Livraria i complained that I am going to leave literature aside. I am going to get a job. I don't adapt to being teledirected. With the money that I received from Europe I wanted to make the down payment on another house and rent out the one where I am living. With the rent I would pay the installments on the house. But dr. Lélio and Audálio interfered—they want to pay for the house all at once and that interferes with my plans. I warned senhor Bertini, that if I don't have money to buy food for my children I won't go to Argentina. He heard me indifferently. i thought: he doesn't yet know me. He doesn't realize that I am a descendant of the atomic bomb.

When we arrived at senhor Bertini's office, he gave me the photographs that we took for the passport. It's that I am going to have them copied because the photograph was pretty. He gave me the three hundred cruzeiros that I had lent him. I left, I went to the livraria Francisco Alves. Dr. Lélio, wasn't there. I stayed waiting for him. In the past he was the one who waited for me. Now it is me. But I don't cringe i try at least to carry out my duties. When a person begins to be confused I send them to hell. I am hard working and I make an effort that the people who deal with me have some advantage.

Barbosa Lessa entered and saw me. Of course. Because I was wearing a garish dress. He walked right in without looking at me.

I said to him: you are rich! You don't greet the poor. He turned and greeted me and hugged me. i spoke of the latest songs that I recorded at Fermata [Studio] and I sang some of them for him to hear

Looking at him I asked: What is the reason for your hair abandoning you is it disillusion for having entered into this way of life?

He looked at me and said: whoever takes on this way of life either loses his hair or his dignity.

I heaved a sigh commenting And I . . . I lost my illusions. This is even worse!

He went on, he was going to talk with dr. Lélio. I stayed there conjecturing. for me, dr. Lélio isn't in. And for the others he is. But I don't need them. I am losing interest in literature. I was thinking about the words of senhor Bertini who told me that I ought to take money if I want to have extra expenses. The Editor ought to arrange for advances. I got nervous, a man who works in the Livraria told me to be calm and be patient. i thought: despite my being explosive they want to illude me imagine if I were calm. I began to write:

Humanity

After getting acquainted with humanity
its perversity
its ambitions
I was aging
And disengaging
from its illusions
what prevails is badness
because goodness:
Nobody practices
Humanity ambitious
and avaricious
They want to get rich!

When I die . . .
I don't want to be reborn
It is horrible, to put up with humanity
That has a noble appearance
That covers up
its terrible qualities
I noted that humanity
Is perverse, is tyrannical
Self-seeking egoists
Who handle things politely
But all is hypocrisy
They are uncultivated, and trickers

A man came up How are you Carolina? are you selling a lot of books?

Ah! I answered brusquely. I am sick and tired of this confusion, and I read what I had just written. Humanity. He listened and asked This is your conclusion concerning humanity. And I am disillusioned in these surroundings. There are times when I want to collect paper.

The man heard me and said. There are people who are envious

—They are the simpletons who don't regard life's dramas. Christ had good luck and bad luck. Happiness and unhappiness are neighbors, vis-à-vis.

The man parted. i got tired of staying in the Bookstore i left. I went to have some coffee and told the employee of the Bookstore: if I don't have money to buy food for my children I won't go to Argentina and I left furious. A number of people invited me to live in Argentina. I was tired but I felt like walking, walking until I tired.

I decided to go to the judge to see if Vera's father left money. I met women cussing out their husbands. Complaining of wasting so much time here, and not finding money. The devil can carry off my husband—another commenting that the devil could carry off all men, they are so disgusting that these devils will not go to heaven

The other one commented. I would like to be the devil's secretary, to instigate him to mistreat these disgusting men who make
women suffer. Another who was listening said: and so many men
die in war still there are men who remain to hurt us—The line was
moving. Those women who got money were pleased and smiling.
Those who didn't left muttering. There was nothing for me. the
women were looking in wonder at me. Talking about the lawyers.
One complained that dona Olga Maria is in favor of her husband
and against her Another praised Dra. Zenêida, who is very good and
obliged her husband to settle his affairs in three days, She is against
men who abandon their children. That's what Dona Maria Arlinda
Silva dos Santos told me. She was pleased saying that she is
happy—She works by day and earns twelve thousand cruzeiros a
month and has only one son. they ask me, if I am happy?

—No. i am disgraced.

I think of life in one way and it dashes in the other direction.
At present I am becoming acquainted with men. There are those
who have beards and put on trousers. but they are scoundrels. God
should choose men. Honest men to be born with beards and the
bums without them. The men should honor their condition of man.
to be honest and walk with their heads erect.

—What do you do?

—I was a farmer, a maid, a scavenger of paper, and now I am
a writer. But the best time in my life was when I was a farmer. We
lived in the hinterland. there was solidarity among the land settlers.
Saturdays, we all helped out and at night there was a dance. there
was a widower who wanted to marry me. But I didn't want to
because he didn't trust me. I have no patience with the arguments
that couples incite. A home where peace and happiness reigns is
lovely. I wanted to walk without interruptions. I decided to visit the
nooks where I collected paper.

I went for lunch at Dona Angelina's house, at 15 Frei Antonio
Santana Galvão Street. I remembered past times. My brain was
peopled with illusions. I thought . . . I am going to write! I am going
to publish a book! I am going to buy a farm and plant flowers, raise

birds how beautiful is the crowing of the roosters. The cackling of ducks. The angola hens with their black-and-white feathers. I looked at number 17. Where dona Julita lived.

Senhor Angelo said: You got rich. And left us.

It's a lack of time. I answered running my eye around the house I asked: —What are we eating today? The girls were pleased to see me. They heated up soup, rice, and fried an egg for me.

I ate lunch, talked a bit and went to visit Veva. She, has a little girl. She is nine months old. The little girl is called Maria Luiza. She is darling—I felt pity for Veva. She is exhausted and sad. because she was visited by misfortune. We spoke of Dona Julita. of Glimôt, Veva's brother. He is pleased with the little girl.

—He is.

—Doesn't he mention your confused state?

—He says nothing.

But, he must suffer inside. Veva, was light-skinned, now she is dark, and complained about life to me. I have cried so much Carolina!

carolina, help me to be happy! You pity me!

You know, Carolina, I have cried so much. I didn't realize that the world was so perverse.

And where is your mother?

—She is working in Guarulhos in the factory of some relatives . . . My mother has worked so much! I thought of Dona Julita when she said . . . Veve needs to settle down.

I said goodbye and went to see Sandra. She is so pretty! she received me smiling her mother, wasn't home. I left and went to see the lady who has the rooming house. I went to the Bernardo institute to see Marlene. She was helping her mother. They smiled when they saw me. they asked how I was?

—More or less.

—Are you happy?

More or less.

They began to say that they saw me on television, with J. Silvestre, and on other programs.

Marlene told me that I looked at her mother and told her that she would marry a rich man. She answered me, if I marry a rich man I am going to help you. And [for] the rest it seems that Carolina is going to help me. I left Marlene's telling her that I had seen her father at the judge's. I entered the shoemaker's [place] to see Eduardinho, and his father who is the shoemaker and gave me paper. Today I am supersad I wanted to be in a deserted place, without noises. How horrible life is when inner peace is lacking

I have the impression that I am among millions of Judases—I don't like to be double-crossed. When I was a little girl, I thought will I be able to live as I like? buy pretty dresses, live in a red house, my favorite color—Now that I bought the house it wasn't possible to paint it red because the priests would say: Carolina is a communist I would like to have a red tombstone but the priests won't allow it because they want to order the poor around. The world to be good should be run by Jesus Christ, who is the superior spirit and has no ambition. They told me that the church has an organization called Metropolitano and it invests the alms in building construction to rent apartments why doesn't it use the money for the poor?

When somebody appears defending the poor, the church damns them—they excommunicated Fidel Castro. and I for writing this, already am a candidate for excommunication—We had noble priests who were interested in the education of the poor wanting even to teach the Indians. My head was heavy with ideas—I thought: today . . . I am going crazy! How horrible it is to have poetic thoughts. And this is why poets want to die. There are those who commit suicide supposing that they will find tranquility in the tomb—I went into the emporium of senhor Antonio, on the corner of rua Alfrêdo Maia and asked him if the house on the corner had already sold

—Not yet.

A lady asked me: —Do you know how much she wants for the house?

—I do. Twelve million. I thought: the woman who wants twelve million for her house, is eighty-five years old. Her muscles abandoned her. She is only skin and bones. She isn't going to live long enough to spend twelve millions.

those are the spirits who are tied to the world.
I have an anguished soul. And a profound disgust
From living in this mess
That is called the world.

Senhor Antonio went on telling the story of Carolina. A black woman who walked the streets, with a little girl, and collecting paper. I left, I went to see the owner of the Tiradentes dry-cleaning store.

I told her that I miss them, but I can't go to see them. I remembered: when she gave me soap, bread, macaroni, beans and shoes for Vera. Ah, now I remember the name of the owner of the dry-cleaning shop. It is dona Guiomar. I need to love those people. Those who helped me asked: are you going to seu Rodolfo?

—Yes. I miss him. There was a day when he was very irritated and I thought: those who are rich, don't need to be irritated. And I was mistaken: the life of the rich, is a hell. I going along Avenida Tiradentes, remembering me dirty with a sack on my back. bent over the cans of garbage. I was happy, when I found aluminum metal to sell to the scrap-metal place. I stopped to write in the streets. —I thought . . . if I could live writing forever . . . if I could live reading! I stopped at the shoemaker's to talk with the shoemaker remembering when seu Rodolfo Shenaufer, bought shoes for Vera. And she said: seu Rodolfo will go to heaven. I ran out, to show the shoes to the workers. When I opened the door to enter Senhor rodolfo, was just leaving. We smiled and embraced.

You disappeared! You are rich. Rich! word that I find disgusting to hear! When I see a little piece of a candy devoured by ants I think: this piece of candy is like me. after I published Quarto de Despejo.

How is life?
—I am in hell!

Nothing turned out as I wanted. And I don't like being bossed around. They manage what I earn. i wanted to rent the house where I live and buy another in my taste. With the rent of the house I would pay the installments. but, I have to obey if I had a higher-education diploma I would be respected. But I only have two years of school. I am semiliterate.

I complained of my bitterness to senhor rodolfo Sheraufer. He told me: well I told you: that you would be happy if you went on collecting paper. You are among the rich . . . whoever can't fake it there, cannot win.

—I stood reflecting mentally—fake it.

Senhor Rodolfo gave me a bottle of wine saying relieve your deception in this wine.

i smiled, and turned about to see again the corners of the workshop from which I used to collect paper and conversed with the employees of senhor rodolfo Sheraufer. Looking at those men, with their dirty and stained clothes I thought. These are clean men. They live with the products of their labor. They are not scoundrels. They are not men with dual personalities. The workers are the most honest men in the world.

I asked senhor Rodolfo permission to telephone. He acceded.

I called Cruzeiro telling the journalist Carlos de Frêitas that I won't go to Argentina, because I don't have money to buy food for my kids. I would have an extra expense and the money isn't enough Frêitas, advised me not to go. that I will spend a lot. I hung up the telephone and asked for dr. Souza.

He is ill. that's what senhor Rodolfo told me. I plan to go visit him. I wanted to return home but it was raining. I looked at Senhor Rodolfo and said to him. You are gaining weight, you need to lose a little weight. You ought to work more—He smiled saying, dona Carolina, you are not my friend. i already work so much.

i asked. And has your daughter graduated?

—If all goes well, she graduates this year.

it stopped raining I left When I was awaiting the bus the rain started up again. A young man offered me his umbrella i waited with him. When the Vila guilherme bus appeared he got on the majority of the workers were standing under the tree grove. I stood in the rain remembering when I worked in agriculture sometimes we didn't have time to get to cover and we wet ourselves through. A good period of time. I didn't know the world that is inhabited by human worms.

Today I am sad. It's that I am not living as I wanted. I wanted to buy another house and leave the district where I am living. When the bus arrived I was soaked. But I am not afraid of rain. Rain is natural. Things that are natural are not harmful. The rain water is distilled. When it goes into the heavens the impurities remain here on earth. And we ought to be like that also. Our defects are buried with us.

A black man, wished to give me his place. I refused. My dress was heavy with the rain. When I got home I thought: I am going to . . . I entered and planted a flower seedling that dona Juana gave me. The woman of the night. João opened the door for me—I went to take a bath. i got out of the bath with a headache. i thought: what torture the human body suffers.

i felt hungry, cold, aching, nostalgic, and restless. I felt thirsty, aimless, this black dream that distorts man. Man is false. He is petty. And I had a desire to die. But death doesn't come when we call it. But one day it must come . . . João had the radio on, i asked him to turn it off. No. Ely and I want to hear charutinho.

It is six o'clock. Charutinho's program comes on at ten.

João said. Wow, mother! You have some personality! I got up nervous grabbed the radio, flung it to the floor and broke it because João doesn't respect me. He doesn't obey me. Ely da Cruz turns him against me. I offered Ely hospitality, in my house, but I regret it—I was only sorry to have broken my radio. But there are people who we have to be violent to in order to respect us. And the blacks are terrible children.

I have trouble breathing. João looked at me with his hardest glare. Only José Carlos regards me softly. I sent João to buy a piece of paper and I wrote an article for the Ultima Hora newspaper. João took it there. I gave him fifty cruzeiros to pay the fare. The displeasure that I feel is because I lived in a favela they think of me as a tramp. I am not . . .

[*4 November 1961*] I got up at 6 o'clock. I went to write. thinking I am not going to Argentina because I don't have money to buy food for my kids. My situation is deplorable. There is a nun who is asking for my book. The religious people are always requesting something. Who wants to buy? I am not a fanatic for the church. My fanaticism is for children who are hungry. João didn't go to class. he went to the bank to withdraw two thousand cruzeiros for the expenses at the market. While I waited for João, I wrote.

João arrived and gave me the money. I went to the street market to shop. The prices are jumping over each other. it is already difficult for the poor to reach them. When I go to the market I get sad thinking about the humanity that is condemned to die of hunger. I made my purchases and joked with the venders and returned home. Dona Alba prepared lunch After I ate lunch I went to write. At four o'clock dr. José Roberto pena, reporter of the Ultima Hora came to do an article. I complained to him about life. and told him that I am not going to Argentina anymore because I don't have money to buy food for my kids. My life is confusing. I was unpacking the valises. I showed him the books that I bought and those that I am writing. He looked around the house saying:

How I would like to have such a house.

i asked him when he will marry me. He said that life doesn't allow for a man to think about marriage. At night senhor Pytágoras arrived to tell me that I won't be going to Argentina due to the general strike. I told him that I am not going because I don't have anything to leave my kids to eat. My life is so confused. My life became insipid There are those who want to marry me and come requesting money.

God set me free. Whoever writes needs peace and I don't have any. I said to Audálio that I didn't want to go to Argentina.

—You have to go . . . He ordered me. There are times when I

become semiconscious, living the period of infancy, when I ate unripe guava. Green mango. green mangoes are bitter. I see my mother washing clothes there in the house of senhor José Saturino. And me playing with Eliantho. With a slingshot in my hand. It was with a slingshot that David killed goliath. Long ago there was only one giant and he could be killed. Today times have changed. We have the wholesalers, who have no pity for anybody. They don't see the poor complaining of hunger. the worst giant of these times.

Senhor Pytágoras said: you are going to Argentina. you didn't tell me that you needed money for food.

I told senhor Bertini.

—But Bertini is not the bureau chief.

i thought: what's happened to my life. I must die.

You come to my office, Monday or Tuesday. there are days when you are positive, today you are negative. And he smiled.

I began to feel a chill. i felt my pressure going down. I need to leave this world.

Senhor pytágoras said that he needed to see his wife who was out of the house all day. that they worked a lot. I accompanied senhor pytágoras to the door looking at the turkey hen on the wrapper of Bali-cola. He was happy, smiling i thought: what a contrast with my life. He happy, me sad. I remembered my poetry, the aged and the youth.

—He left and I told him that I wrote an article in ultima-Hora telling people why I wasn't going to Argentina I am horrified at my current life, I entered and sat down reflecting I am already tired of this confusion. we sat and talked. Dona Alba, told about some young people from Uberaba who decided to do a serenade in the cemetery and didn't realize that the gravediggers were working at night. They sang. After they sang, the gravediggers applauded. The singers ran away dropping their instruments and breaking them.

I went to lie down. I didn't fall asleep.

5 November 1961 Today is sunday. I am tired and sad thinking about my life that is as confused as a puzzle. i spent the day at home. Dona Alba made lunch. I was dizzy i went to lie down. i am already sick of life. I gave money to José Carlos for the movies. I was lying down reading when the reporters of Ultima Hora arrived to photograph me for Manchete. Today I am worried about my life. It is not evolving as I desired. we think about life one way, and life runs the other. I complained to the journalists that I wasn't born to be teledirected. I went to find Vera for us to go to bed.

6 November 1961 i was sick at night dreaming that i was wandering around a cemetery looking for a place to bury myself. My coffin was glass. I saw my body through the glass adorned with colored glass flowers. I looked at the plots and didn't like any of them. I woke up to the voices of the kids who were going to class. I got up hastily to get João ready, since he is in the fourth grade. I plead with him to study and earn his diploma so he can enter the Liceu de Artes e Oficio [a vocational school] to learn a trade He wants to be a mechanical draftsman. Today I should be going to go to Argentina. I am not going due to the strike. But I would like to go because of the strike. I wanted to write about the hardships of the Argentines. The cause of the peoples' discontent. Is it the cost of living? Is it political pressure? What is the cause of the discontent of the classes? In my opinion if lands were free The people would be reanimated. Working on their own account they could construct houses and marry. Nowadays a man cannot marry because he has to live on a salary that offers no benefit to anybody. I am going to spend the day at home because I am sick and have difficulty breathing. I went to the pharmacy to buy some medicine I gave up because of the price.

There are times when I want to die! Then I think of the kids who are not old enough to work. One child is expensive for his parents. When they grow up and are good people the parents have a recompense.

The journalists of Ultima Hora came to find out if I am going to Argentina. I am not going because of the strike. They photographed me and left. I was cold I went to sit in the garden, to heat my body because the sun, is hot. I sat thinking about my life that is the same as a building that we build up and then it collapses. When I was a child I asked my mother if the world was pleasant?

—She didn't answer me. I looked to the sky with the clouds revolving lazily in space. I didn't suffer hunger and thought: the world is beautiful. One day, I asked my mother.

—Mother, am I people or animal?

—She didn't answer. And she smiled. My mother spoke, very little. A rare thing, among women. With the passage of time I observed the world and its confused actions. What horrified me was to see a soldier kill a man. The soldier smiled satisfied. saying: I have a target at hand, he didn't tremble. I asked my mother if the man has the right to kill a man?

—She didn't answer.

i felt that it was up to me to observe the world. One day I saw a woman crying, and I was horrified. I thought that only children wept. Senhor Rodolfo sheraufer gave me a bottle of wine. I am drinking it to reanimate myself because I am cold. I spent the day at home.

Nothing more exists for me
In nothing find I beauty
Nothing as sad then can there be
as plain old melancholy.

i spent the day at home. Some ladies came to visit me, I didn't receive them because I have a headache. I am sick of living. I think about Belinda Lee, who didn't enjoy life. She tried to kill herself and died in an accident. What was her inner grief? for the unfortunate life is too long.

I went to collect paper, to be photographed and I stumbled. The reporter said: you are out of shape.

In the house of a poet, happiness passes. But it doesn't stay.

I lay down during the day and dreamed that a man was running after me with a knife. I ran and jumped a fence looking for a place to hide and I woke up sweating and I told José Carlos that I dreamt about a man running after me with a knife.

—José Carlos said: give me his address and I will go fight him.

When I become sad, my children tell me anecdotes to cheer me up. It's that they ignore my melancholy, the cancer of the soul. It is incurable. When illusion *suffers,* the charm of life disappears.

When I infiltrated literature
I dreamed of an adventure
My soul was full
I didn't foresee the commotion
When I published Quarto de Despejo
I realized my desire.
What a life. What happiness . . .
And now . . . Casa de Alvenaria.
Another book circulates
My sadnesses duplicate.
Those who come to ask for aid
To fulfill their desires solely
i think: publications should I have made . . .
of 'quarto de despejo' only.
In the beginning came admiration
My name circulated about the Nation.
There emerged a writer favelafied.
Called: Carolina Maria de Jesus.
And the works that she produces
Left humanity stupefied

At first I became confused.
it seems that I was imprisoned
In an ivory container.
I was sought after
I was exalted.
As a cherub

After they began to envy me.
They said: you should give
your possessions, to an asylum
Those who spoke to me that way
Didn't think.
About my children.

The women of high society.
Said: practice charity.
Giving clothes to the poor.
But the funds from high society
Are not aimed at charity
It is for the Prados [an elite family] and for playing cards
And so, I became disillusioned
My ideal was retracting
just like a body aging.

I was getting wrinkled, wrinkled. . . .
petals of roses, wilting, drying up
And . . . I am dying!

In the graveyard silent and gray
I will rest my bones one day. . . .
I don't suffer any illusion
because the writer from the shantytown
Was the rose by petals shunned.

So many thorns in my heart.
They say I am ambitious
that I am not charitable.
They count me among the usurers
Why don't they blame the industrialists
Who treat the workers like animals?
—The workers . . .

7 November 1961 Today I am sad. Sadness came to spend the end
of the year with me. I thought that she had forgotten me. They say

she persecutes poets. Sadness is mean. Happiness doesn't like her. They are irreconcilable foes. Happiness is young. It is pretty. it only likes children and the children are always smiling. Sadness is a wrinkled old hag. It enters homes without an invitation.

Today I am cold. Inside and outside. I was seated in the sun writing and I implored, Oh God! I need a voice!

José Carlos who was at the upstairs window said: I am here dona Carolina! I looked at the window and laughed. When I am sad he pleases me and says "sing mama!" Sing the waltz you composed . . . I'll help you!

All I can say is: that the women who have small children in these times don't know how to smile, because the prices of basic foodstuffs make us cry. —if land was free there would be abundance the men who migrated to the city would plant crops and marry. When people understand that land has to be free. There, there will be a new garden of Eden.

I went do to the morning shopping [and] a driver took me to Ultima Hora and I read my article. I read it several times trying to understand what I wrote. I believe I should explain to people why I didn't go to Argentina. The strike, the lack of money for my kids The children, are the shadow of mothers. A son is the favorite boarder of a mother's thoughts.

i spent the day reading, and rereading what I had written. I am going to finish my novel Diabolic Woman.* if I could live only from writing . . . but my life is derived . . .

There are times when I think that I am equal to the clock, always running! if the clock stops, man makes it run again

There are times when I think: why is it that I didn't stay in the interior planting crops? But the lands belong to the fazendeiros [ranchers]. And one has to plant only what they want. But that's how life is for whoever passes through this world money is scarce. one spends fifty cruzeiros on bread per day.

---

* This novel was never published.

the children wanted bread. i made it of cornmeal cake and dona Alba made a lentil soup—I was in the kitchen when the bell rang. Ely went to answer and returned saying it was a journalist and told her to enter. She went to the kitchen and said to me:

You don't know me. But I know you. I am from the Jornal do Brasil [a Rio newspaper] and I came to talk to you.

—Talk about what? i asked apprehensively

—about the article that you wrote today for Ultima Hora—It what you published all true?

—Yes

I answer with a tired voice as if I had been in the world for a hundred years for me the world is the same as a prison, in which I am crazy to leave and cannot since the bars are my children.

—Was it you who wrote that letter to Ultima-Hora?

—It was.

—They don't make you write it?

—No.

—What motivated you to write such a confusing letter?

—seven things.

1 Sadness

2 Disillusionment

3 I got sick of living and want to die

4 Deception. I seem to be amidst ferocious beasts. But the most ferocious is the worm.

5 I wasn't born to be teledirected the worst thing there is, is for people to see, and be pulled in a halter as if one couldn't see, or as if I was . . .

6 I wanted to rent this house and move out of here.

7 What bothers me are the requests for loans. And I can't lend.

She heard me in silence and the photographer photographed me.

—Don't you have a love affair?

—No.

—Do you believe in the ingratitude of love?

—Of man for woman yes. Of woman to man no. The woman is more faithful than the man.

—Why do you speak that way? you had an amorous experience[?]

—No. but I read in the books and I read amorous facts that newspapers publish.

—She smiled commenting: Nobody defines a topic without profoundly knowing the topic, or living the drama.

—No. I don't believe that. why?

—because the newspaper O dia from Rio published an article that you practice *macumba* [voodoo].

I didn't smile, and I didn't find what [she said about] the O Dia article amusing. They could publish some excerpts from my book Quarto de despejo to remind the politicians that the poor can't stand the cost of living, and the children need good food and the lands must be free for the poor to plant and have abundance. I told her that I don't believe in macumba. That I pity the practitioners. because what they spend on macumba could buy meat to feed themselves.

She insisted that I say that I had a love affair.

—I love no one. I am capable of liking a person but I don't let love overpower me. I forget people quickly. In the letter that I sent to Ultima Hora I don't mention love. I mentioned that my money finished, and I again return to the garbage.

She answered that she had not read the article because she doesn't like to write already knowing the problem. But seeing that you are a intelligent woman, how is it that you wrote that letter, and sought out a newspaper! A newspaper that is discredited by everybody . . . why did you choose Ultima Hora?

—because they visit me when I am sick

The photographer said to me: She is the Silvia donato who won the Esso prize for reporting

—Ah! Is it you? [I said]. you were widely talked about here in São Paulo!

The photographer confirmed what I said.

Looking her over I told her that I am returning to primitivism. We go back to soup and cornmeal cake. She cut a piece of the cake and ate it. saying that it was tasty and the photographer also ate some and asked:

—Did Carolina make this?

Dona Alba said: yes. The photographer gave me the address of the São Paulo branch, Rua sete de Abril and the telephone in rio

I invited her to see my house. She found it pretty and asked me:

why isn't your house fully furnished?

—I am not vain

We went upstairs. She found it comfortable and asked. How much did you get from the theater play?

—Nothing yet

Ah! You recorded a record

—I did. Do you want to see it?

I put the record on the victrola She listened and asked:

—Did you receive the royalties?

—No, ma'am.

—Who handles your business affairs?

—I leave it to them.

—And if they deceive you?

—No problem. They know that I am explosive. i was vaccinated with the atomic bomb.

So the book, quarto de despejo, resulted in a play and a record?

Her glance wandered about the room. I watched her and said: don't you want to live here with me? You are talkative and so am I. we can make a pair.

She regarded me seriously She looked at her watch saying that she was taking the plane at eleven o'clock at night for Rio.

—Your book, Casa de Alvenaria. What is it?

—It is a diary. My life in the city

You could talk of love, but you don't wish to . . .

I never loved. If I live with a man I treat him well. but, I don't love him. if I live with someone, and this someone abandons me, I soon forget him. My concern is my children. A child is a very delicate thing.

the photographer, withdrew saying: You and Silvia stay here. And tell everything to her. You women understand.

—you can stay, because I have nothing to say. My friendships with men are platonic

—How did you have these children? They are yours aren't they?

—Yes. I got them by way of adventures. Unfortunately everybody learns to reflect when mature.

—Don't you have a love? You give the impression that there is an amorous relation in your life.

—I love nobody.

the photographer looked at me and said: With all your charm. I don't believe it.

—Thank you for your kindness

Dona Silvia, thought and asked me: Carolina, is your problem sexual? With so many male journalists besieging you . . . I pretended not to understand the question and said to her. of course we returned to primitivism. The cornmeal soup, the cornmeal cake. I consider this lapse of living in a cinder-block house a dream . . .

What are you going to give Silvia? asked the photographer. A souvenir. I ordered Ely to fetch two bound books and I autographed them giving them to them. the photographer said: A writer doesn't offer a book like this to anybody. we must buy it, then you autograph it.

—These books I reserved for journalists. because it is you who motivate a writer.

They left. I accompanied them to the gate. Dona Silvia gave me a kiss. I looked at the white station wagon with Jornal do Brasil written on the sides. The driver waited inside the car. They got in and departed. I went inside the house thinking that my letter had nothing to transform it into sensationalism. I was confused. I had the impression that my head was growing bigger, growing bigger and then getting smaller—it seems that my brains are turning around inside my head. I looked upwards, seeking heaven, but I saw the plaster on the living room ceiling and understood that heaven is so far away . . . and a person who is alive, doesn't go to heaven. And those who already died, don't come back to tell us if they are in heaven. José Carlos said: you should have said that you love Luiz!

I forgot, my boy!

8 November 1961 Today is the local street market. I wake to the voices of the venders. speaking of markets the prices in the markets are so high that one has the impression that foodstuffs came from Sputnik in outer space. I was horrified. The price of potatoes 60 cruzeiros. João went to class, I gave him a note to give the teacher to let him leave at 10 o'clock and he took a note for dr. Lelio de Castro Andrade, asking for ten thousand cruzeiros I let him know that I warned the manager of the Abraxas Publisher: if I don't manage to get money to buy food I won't go to Argentina They are very economical. I wandered about the street fair and bought a kilo of rice. I don't buy anything in my street market. because I am Carolina Maria de Jesus—they say I became rich. I went to buy two sacks of flour to make dish cloths.

—How much is each one?

Forty-five

He looked me in the face and opened his eyes.

—Are you dona Carolina?

—I am!

—Author of Quarto de despejo?

—I am.

—Ah . . . then the sack costs ninety. —How many are you going to take?

I stared at the owner of the stand and didn't reply. i left furious thinking of death. I believe that only with death will I have spiritual tranquility.

Afterward I think. No. I ought to live. Writers ought to recognize the qualities and the defects of humanity. My thoughts resounded inside my brain they seemed like waves bashing against each other. I go back to thinking about the past. When I didn't have any money I earned alms. those who looked at me looked with pity. And nowadays those who look at me look. Look with envy and anger commenting. She became rich! I have the impression that my life has two faces. One of copper—the other of gold. Or that I was an oak tree full of leaves and now . . . the leaves are turning yellow and becoming loose until reduced to powder. It is horrible to go out in the street and hear the people say: Look at Carolina! and they comment as if I was from another planet. But I can't curse . . . if I could return to the past I would change my build just like one fixes a dress. I would like to give myself a new form. There are times when I think: I would like to be a fool. By being intelligent I entice enmities because I don't let anybody make a fool of me. But if I were a fool, an idiot doesn't understand anything. But . . .

God! have mercy.
protect the unfortunate poetess
You gave me so much intelligence . . .
That . . . it makes me a martyr!

I was thinking. My God if dr. Lélio, doesn't send money, I will pick up the discards from the street market and make a soup.

José Carlos came in with a sack of paper and said: A truck was passing, and the sack of sugar burst and a little sugar fell out and I picked it up and brought it for you.

I can continue picking up what I find in the garbage

Are we going back to eating from the garbage?

I don't know my son

Our life is like a hot-air balloon that rises and afterwards burns and is finished.

José Carlos looked at me and said: I think that I will take you to a doctor, for him to take an x-ray of your head to see if it is functioning right. —You are going to be crazy

He left and returned asking. Buy a belt for me.

But the belt that he uses, still is good. He left saying: I am going to see if I find João, if he didn't bring money I am going to pick up scrap metal—dona alba made lunch I was eating. Ely arrived saying that there is a strike in the city. João arrived with money and told me that dr. Lélio said for me to go there. But I am so disillusioned . . .

i need to refurbish my soul with happiness. I went to pay the butcher, and the bakery. The butcher feels pleased when he sees me. I feel happy because nowadays I am received with crude looks. I ate lunch and went to buy shoes for João. The shoemaker wrapped up two pairs. I returned the other telling him that if I rob something, I can't sleep.

I have a well-formed character.

He grabbed the shoes and thanked me. We conversed. I told him that I like his work. it is well done. He said he was a gaúcho. He has been in são paulo for thirteen years. We spoke of the price of a child. It is the price of a suit. nowadays whoever raises a child is a hero. I left João's shoes to be fixed and returned to my house in the shantytown.

With the news that I am poor, nobody bothers me—I spent the rest of the day at home. At night I went to the city to see what there was in the newspapers. we went by bus.

the driver asked me: Are you the author of the book?

—I am. Have you read the book?

—Not yet. But I will read it. I promised to give him a copy and we got off. We went to Ultima Hora. I wanted to know if [the article] had come out in the Jornal do Brasil. It hadn't. But it had come out in Manchete. It is the article that I did. And the journalist Guimarães gave it to me to read. I thanked him and we left the office. I am sad. i left my house to see if I found happiness we wandered about the streets. I wanted to see the film Jeca Tatú, with Mazzaropi. We didn't find the film. We went into a bar to have a drink. But I wanted to refresh my soul. Audálio said: You have nothing to complain about life. You have everything. That you stuck in my mind.

And the others? The workers who have children . . . and can't feed them decently. I have the impression that I am a thousand meter statue, Observing the suffering of humanity. Brazil is going to be a wonderful country when lands are free. The agrarian reform was he hope of the people. It was on paper only. But the people need reality. We went home.

11 November 1961 i spent saturday doing the shopping to leave with my children. i bought foodstuffs in the emporium because the prices in the street market were beyond the reach of the poor. I am packing my valise. I should travel on the 13th.

12 November 1961 Today is Sunday. I received an invitation to go to the dance of the 220 [Association], but, it won't be possible. i am exhausted. i need to read some books and write some articles to publish in Argentina . . . I don't like dances—I prefer spending the evening reading. Books . . . fascinate me. I was created in the world Without maternal guidance. But the books guided my steps to avoid the abysms that we meet in life. Blessed are the hours that I spend reading. I reached the conclusion that it is the poor who ought to read because the book, is the compass that will direct man in the future. i spent the morning writing.

Dona Alba made lunch. I went to buy a chicken [but] didn't find one. Today I feel cold. There is no sun in sight i went to write in bed. I stayed beneath the covers until I get warm. after, I sat up in bed, and write. Dona alba went to visit her sister. I washed clothes and went to lie down. Senhor Pytágoras came to tell me that he received a telegram from Argentina saying that I should travel on the 15th, Wednesday. We spoke of my article. I swore not to write sensationalist things because then I have no peace.

Senhor Pytágoras said that I should be teledirected because as a writer I can't go after a publisher and that I should obey Audálio. That I owe everything to him. i thought: if Audálio hears this he will blow up like the frog who wanted to be the size of a bull. But I don't have the temperament to be teledirected. My temperament is like the breeze.

I read the poetry that I wrote for seu Pytágoras to hear.

Mystery

So many times one entrusts friendship
to a vile type with no character
Destitute of any worth
Who makes us cry, and suffer.
But, who is able to understand.
The mystery of love.

Sometimes an honest man
Is not our favorite
We don't feel fondness for him
And we love a scoundrel
Whoever doesn't honor the suit that he wears.
Rubbish

He thought it beautiful and requested a copy. I gave him one. He said that that's how it is. That it is the opposite types who unite. I told him that I like a civility, supercorrect, more polite than me, the journalists, and even himself. He brought respect to my house, sent off the vagabonds and I named the advantages I had with Luiz. He advised me to write to Luiz to ask him to return. But my affection for Luiz is already vanishing.

I have my reasons for forgetting him. I think about Luiz all day long. I became used to him. I am irritated because he doesn't want to ever come back . . . He knows how to live with me. With him I was living. I shined his shoes so he wouldn't dirty his hands. I washed his suits so he didn't have to pay the dry cleaner. I came to the conclusion that men are more ungrateful than women . . .

Senhor Pytágoras named his brothers. They are Plato [and] pericles. The names of ancient philosophers. He said goodbye I gave him a book. I forgot to say what he taught me: That I ought to tell the argentine favelados that all poor people ought to read and learn a profession love work be polite and not to lie. Whoever knows how to read prospers in any place.

Vera went to the movies with José Carlos. She was happy, saying: I wanted to have food, house and clothes. And God gave me all of these. The day that I meet god I am going to tell him many thanks because he is better to me than my own father. Who ought to have given me all of this I don't find it funny to say . . . father! i prefer to say Audálio, mother paulo Dantas, ronaldo Taraks senhor Francisco, senator, and dona Luiza.

I said to senhor Pytágoras, that my children cursed me when we lived in the shantytown, I went hunting for paper. When we returned I found my kids talking about me. I listened to them. God liberate me from having a mother like that: i wanted to have a white mother. because the whites live in the cinder-block houses. The blacks live in the shacks. Blacks ought not to have offspring because they can't even feed them.

When she gets home she will make polenta. I don't like polenta. If kids cursed useless parents, they should struggle and work. I showed my books to senhor Pytágoras and told him, I read every day. At night dona rosa Esfaciotti came to visit me and invite us to the movies. She is pleased because she came out in Manchete. She wants to know if her book will be published. We'll see. She came to thank me for my motivation. It is the era of the book. I am pleased to see Brazil embracing culture. I played my record for her to hear She loved the waltz. I read her poetry—The mystery. She listened and said: that poetry is real. I didn't want to go out anymore . . . she told me about her cousins. One had a son but he doesn't like to work. And whoever has kids needs to work.

I told her that luiz left. And we spoke of his superior education. I changed and we went to the city we went by Ultima Hora. Dona rosa wanted to thank Magalhaes for the report he did in Manchetti [*Manchete*]. She was so elegant. It was pleasing to watch her. I told Reno Pajella that I travel on the 15th and showed him the article from the Jornal do Brasil and I read him my interview with Silvia donato, when she put down Ultima Hora.

He listened to me and said: —You create confusion and afterward say that we are the ones who are no good. I found his answer sensible.

He asked for the telegram from Argentina. I promised it for tomorrow. I asked Reno: when are you going to decide to gain weight? he smiled saying that he doesn't want to gain weight.

We left Ultima Hora and went to the paissandú Cinema. At 11 o'clock we left the cinema. I arrived home sleepy.

14 November 1961 I got up at 6 o'clock. I woke up João to go to class. I went to buy matches, salt and milk. There is leftover bread from yesterday. João went to buy yogurt for me. Dona Alba arrived at 7 o'clock saying that I am good for her, she doesn't like to take advantage. I received a visit from the journalist Alexandre Germano from Ultima Hora who came to find out if I am going to Argentina on the 15th. I wrote an article for Ultima-Hora and a note to senhor Pytágoras and gave them to Ely, to take and to telephone senhor Pytágoras. But I gave them to Alexandre and told him that we have to make an effort to elevate culture. We have to imitate Socrates He smiled and left. Ely went with them to Ultima Hora. I gave Ely money to pay the light bill. I went to lie down for a while. I am thinking about my trip to Argentina. I was writing when Vera, went to attend the bell and scampered up the stairs telling me that a man from Channel 5 wanted to speak to me.

He is told to come up. I receive visits in my bedroom. I continue seated, writing. It was senhor Lombardi who came to invite me to the program, nothing more than two minutes for me to clarify what's what with my publishers and talk about the article that I wrote. I told him that I cannot go because of the trip that I am taking on the 15th. I gave him the telephone number of senhor Pytágoras, to confirm if I am going or not.

i spent the rest of the day reading and writing.

At times men are agreeable
are gentle, and worthy
But women, are imbeciles
They love: what is inferior

14 November 1961 I got up at 6 o'clock and went shopping. João went to class. There is no water. Dona Alda made lunch. I slept during the day. I awoke to the voice of the Japanese neighbor reprimanding her children I went to see if mine were included.

They were.

—What's going on?

The Japanese woman said: it's that they ring my bell and then run away children and the devil are the same.

—Do you know the devil?

—No. She answered, laughing, that one hears tell that the devil is horrible. I thought: if humanity thought before speaking it would not talk nonsense.

When my children saw me, they headed for home. I was stupefied. It was their first gesture of elegance. The water returned and I went to wash clothes. I went to the pharmacy to buy perfumes.

Ely took the radio to be fixed, and returned saying that it was already ready I paid 400.

At night senhor Pytágoras, came to tell me that we have to leave at 5 o'clock in the morning. He picked up the suitcase to see if there was too much weight. He asked me to take something out. He left. I took a bath and went to bed.

15 November 1961 I awoke at 3 o'clock in the morning. I opened the window. The sky was dark. It is raining. i went to arrange the bedclothes to warm my daughter. I saw that the fleas had bitten her i killed some of them. I turned on the radio, to radio Bandeirantes to hear the time. I went to look at the clock, it was 3:15. I decided to write a little, and read some parts of the novel that I am writing. I am already concluding it. it seems that I went overboard in the love scenes. At four o'clock I changed and awaited the arrival of senhor pytágoras to take me to campinas. The night watchman passed by and saw the open window; he stopped in the street and whistled. I opened the window and told him that I am going to travel.

Is the house going to be vacant?

No, but it is best to keep watch.

All right, then, until your return.

I was finishing up the provisions. I awoke Ely to make break-fast. I gave ten thousand cruzeiros to Ely to buy fruit for the kids. The street venders were arriving. I went to greet them they were the japanese, they smiled and asked me:

—Do you like to get up early?

I am travelling to Argentina.

—How nice. If I could travel . . . well, then, until your return! and one of the japanese gave me a hug saying:

—It's nice, isn't it?

I went to see if senhor Pytágoras was arriving. I went in and sat down, thinking about the kids who are going to be alone, because children without their mother's presence are alone. João woke up with the radio that was tuned to the program on tangos—Senhor Pytágoras arrived with senhor Gualter De Luiz.

As soon as I saw the station wagon I roared: hello! João and Ely, were already carrying the valises. I received the records that senhor Pytágoras brought and put them in the handbag and off we sailed. I was thinking about the children. Today is a holiday. Very few people in the streets We arrived easily at the city. The bus was already there. We put the baggage on the bus, and went to find a newsstand. I bought Ultima Hora. I was horrified when I read that Baby [P]ignatari [a famous playboy] is going to get a divorce. Don't these couples know how to love? Could it be that they don't miss each other? Or don't they have hearts?

How wonderful are the couples who celebrate their silver wed-ding anniversary. Surrounded by their grandchildren.

The bus was to leave at 11 o'clock.

Senhor pytágoras, bade us goodbye and left. in the bus was a japanese, who spoke with an english accent—I asked him if he spoke English.

He said he did.

—Where did you study?

—In japan.

—Do you speak portuguese?

—Yes. I have been in Brazil for three years

—Your name?

Takashi Ebizuka.

we paid for the tickets but the driver said that we were going to leave at 11 o'clock. Senhor Gualter De Luiz went to tell senhor pytágoras, that the bus was going to be delayed. I waited for him, went out for a sandwich, and talked with the owner of the bar who said that he likes to read but he doesn't have time. i sensed that he wanted to please me, because when we like something, we make time.

I paid for the sandwich and left hastily wandering my eyes over the flowers that adorned the garden in the praça da Republica [the principal public square]. I was thinking that the world is beautiful. When will mankind understand that the world is a retreat for adoration and veneration? In the heavens there are stars, the sun and the moon. In the gardens there are flowers with varied colors. And in the homes there are children. And the children need bread. Adults have the duty to think about heir children. When I got to the office of panair Senhor Gualter De Luiz still was away. I went in and sat down. The manager looked at me and smiled. A smile of contentment. It appears that the man does now know melancholy. We started talking about the situation of the country. Criticizing our currency that is very weak. He revealed his plan—if he were a politician he wouldn't allow people to become superrich. The person who gains unlimited wealth becomes an egoist. He would distance himself from the poor people since he wants to be a politician he wants to enslave mankind. i would impose a law not to let poor people spend unnecessarily. Everything imported would have to be rationed. I thought: the person who acts this way sacrifices the poor. i asked him his name he said he is called Ronaldo. He went on saying that he would reform the government, eliminating the bad politicians.

Senhor Gualter de Luiz arrived and we left in the station wagon driving to Campinas The day was warm. The trip went without any abnormalities. I contemplated the marvelous scenery with the groves adorned with flowers. And the abandoned lands without any cultivation. I think about the foodstuffs that man could have if he loved the land when it was planted. After the mother, land is man's best friend that gives us our daily bread.

I was talking with senhor Gualter, who told me that senhor pytágoras is a decent man, correct and humane. That he is happy in the firm. That he admires him a lot and hasn't yet met dr. Luciano Sahonvaler. When we arrived at the airport the sun was hidden. The site where the airport is located is pretty. I was the target of stares. And a number of people asked for autographs. I acceded in good spirits because today I am happy. I was greeted by some argentines who asked if I am carrying my feather [carnival] dress? I answered that I was. A young man gave me his address to look him up in Buenos Aires, or call him—Ulises Bruno Capello. Another gentleman told me that the argentines have been awaiting my arrival since the 6th . . . Thank God, he said, that I will have the pleasure of seeing you in my country.

They carried two guitars with them, commenting that they are cheaper here, and they showed them to me. the airplane that they were going to take was ready for departure. They [were] saying: until this afternoon in Buenos Aires. The passengers were scurrying away, and others gathered around me. Some teachers greeted me and said that they teach rural workers. One is a professor in Campinas—Maria do Carmo. She teaches business.

—What savings do you think that the agricultural settler can make if what he already earns is so paltry?

—She told me that there are a number of ways to economize. Are you happy in this circle that you are a part of?

—No.

—why?

—No one in this group is sincere.

—why?

Now that [my book] has prospered they are reluctant to pay what they make with the book, so I am becoming discontent. I am a bystander. I feel that if I complain I will not be attended. The only thing that I win will be enmities.

The professor told me that all writers complain. In that case I will renounce literature sadly because I like literature. And life! And life is life, with its downs. I recited for the teachers. They listened and I told them that we the favelados are the agricultural settlers who are tired of being exploited and we abandon the lands and their owners. i felt that landowners indirectly contribute to implant the favelas in the large cities. They said goodbye. Senhor Gualter invited me to have lunch. I ordered risoto because the other dishes were complicated. We spoke over lunch criticizing the woman who castrated her husband. What perversity. She could have divorced him. We spoke of the woman's infidelity. I don't approve. Man is not an object that derides himself and throws himself to the lion.

After lunch I took a walk around the airport. It has fruit and poinsettia trees with their red flowers, my favorite color. Silva Netto arrived and said he went to meet a politician. He was accompanied by his brother and a lady said that she planned to go with me to Argentina but it wasn't possible. The airplane arrived. I embarked with difficulty since some wanted autographs. I found it amusing listening to a man talking in german: we have the honor of having a black lady on the plane. The germans who heard me looked at me. I responded to their glances With my hard and cold look. The journalists interviewed me and photographed me. Senhor Gualter accompanied me to the airplane arranging a place for me. He was pleased because I wrote some verses for dr. Adhemar and gave them to him to take to his wife, who is an Adhemarista [an adherent of Adhemar].

On the plane I was greeted by the stewardesses who howled

—Welcome dona Carolina!

I gave Audálio's telephone number to senhor Gualter to call tomorrow. —My companions in the row were two men, Armando pagano, and Eduardo Espinosa. Agreeable and cultured. we listened to viennese waltzes. i thought about requesting them to play the tango but . . . I was embarrassed. The airplane didn't shake. I felt like I was in a living room. I was seated next to the president of the Bolivian sporting federation who was returning from a European excursion, the player Senhor Eduardo Espinosa. The president and senhor Armando pagano, who had a book in his language, told me that I should continue writing. —Write the truth to enlighten the people.

[In broken Spanish]: There are things that cannot be written about. Some things need to be forgiven.*

He listened to me. I thought. he is going to criticize my spanish, poorly pronounced.

[In Carolina's Spanish]: —Conscious mistakes you have to will to the ears of the poor.

The young people in the plane treated me amiably. The stewardesses [were] most gentle, asking about Audálio. Is he old?

I answered that he is not. He is a man who looks like a little boy. He is very small.

—Is it true that you are his lover?

—No. Only his friend why?

—because people say that he is very good for you. And the men when they are good for a woman it is due to interest

When we arrived at the airport I was staring through the glass window at the fabulous Rio [de] la plata. The river is navigable. I thought: [this is] The river that I read about in geography and now I am seeing it. I remembered when I was a little girl I said to my mother that the book says that the world is large. I thought that the world was only My country. Or only as far as the eye could see. I

---

* Carolina writes: "Existe algo que non se peude escreber. Tienes caso que es preciso per donale."

recognized dona Beatriz Braide de Sohavaler and the wife of the
publisher Dr. Idel Luciano Sahavaler. I was happy. I wasn't tired.
While we awaited permission to leave the aircraft I was gazing at
the argentine sky. It was blue adorned with white clouds. I didn't
see flying birds. With the stentorian oases of the airplanes the birds
stay distant they go to the countryside. I thought of the swallows
who abandoned Campinas. Even the birds feel horror at progress.
The swallows fled from the airplanes and man in the future will flee
the atomic bomb.

The players who were in the airplane spoke of pelé. He is rich.
He sold the story of his life for twenty million. The man commented
that pelé was born under a golden star. He was lucky to be born in
Brazil. And the brazilians are not egoists. They love each other and
value their compatriots. They are sincere when they like somebody.
Brazilians don't look at one's skin color. Pelé ought to say: thank
God! I was born in Brazil. They liked [President] Janio [Quadros].
Janio didn't understand that he was born in a humane country. He
was ungrateful. When we received the command to leave the airplane the players were the first to descend. I got in between them
and descended with the handbag, and my red sweater. The photographers were waiting for me and photographed me. Dona Beatriz
was with him. The soccer players, stopped to gaze at me and one
said:

Isn't it what I told you? Whoever is born in Brazil is born with
the mark of happiness. Don't you see this woman, they took her out
of the garbage bins.

I greeted dona Beatriz and asked for dr. Luciano Sahovaler. He
couldn't enter. I retreated to the side in front of the airplane for an
interview with the journalists, and the staff of the airport asked the
journalists to photograph me with them. The photographers refused.
I felt sorry for the staff of the airport who honored me by being
photographed with them because it is beautiful, to see men working. Work is the proof of integrity. I didn't want to insist with the
photographers. I am not in my own country and I want to leave
good impressions, to please Audálio. There are times when I think:

can it be that Audálio likes me? I like him, his wife, and his son. Wishing them happiness. It is here in Argentina that I felt Audálio's worth. I smiled when I heard an argentine journalist say that in Brazil there is a God called Audálio Dantas, for me the man who did a good deed is a God. The person who translated my words was the journalist Haydêe Jofre Barroso.

I was born in Brazil We lived in Copacabana. I go yearly to Brazil.

—For Carnival? I asked.

—It is beautiful. She answered me with an indolent voice.

There is a bridge and the airport lies beneath it. The people who were at the gates of the bridge waved handkerchiefs at me. I looked all around for a black person and didn't see any. we passed through customs to examine the valises and the photographers were taking pictures from behind the glass. senhor Sohavaler was outside among the people. When we left I went to greet him. What a notable man. he has a serene appearance. he seems to have an inner calm. I am envious of calm people. We got into dr. Sohavaler's car. The journalists followed in another car. The airport is far away from the city. The photographers took pictures of me reading inside the car. I was gazing at the trees, green of Argentina. It is a brilliant green and looks like the land contains iodine. the city is flat. there are no peaks. it is a valley where the view doesn't rise. It was warm. The traffic is slower than in Brazil. You don't see anybody running to get across the broad streets. We got to the Hotel. The Lion Hotel. Comfortable inside. A went to my room, #407. What an apartment . . . magnificent. With silver mirrors and bookcases. Two ample rooms with colored upholstered chairs. One must see the place to appreciate it—I had the impression that I was A queen.

I received a visit from a journalist of *La prensa* [a Buenos Aires daily newspaper], Oscar henrique Villardes and the photographer Jorge Miller. after we went to have dinner in the restaurant 9 July—Don Quixote or Avenida Carlos pelegrine. The Avenue is 140 meters wide. Senhor Sohovaler's car broke down. What torture to fix it.

I was horrified at the quantity of people who eat in restaurants. It is not the wealthy class. It is the middle class.

I was the subject of stares. What I found interesting was the night beginning at 9 o'clock. We had a television program that was postponed—i ate meat. A delicious meat . . . And I thought of poor people who need meat.

We returned to the Lion Hotel and I went to bed thinking about the kids. Dona Beatriz looked over my dresses.

16 November 1961 I got up at 3 o'clock. I looked to the left side for Vera. i didn't find her and remembered that I am in Buenos Aires. So far from my kids. I thought of João and said: João wake up to go to class! And I put my telepathic powers into play. I wanted to turn on the light to write but the Lion Hotel regulations don't allow it. I stayed in bed waiting [for] the time signal. I didn't hear the chimes. I got up, washed and went to write. At seven o'clock I called for breakfast, and went on writing . . . At ten o'clock I received a phone call from a journalist telling me that he was coming to interview me. I called Dr Luciano and he told me that he would return in ten minutes.

Dona Beatriz went to talk with the journalists and I went on writing. She took a copy of my book for them to see. When I went downstairs I was taken to a large room with a big table in the middle surrounded by a number of chairs. They showed me to a chair at the head of the table next to a chronicler who read some passages from my book. Senhor Bernardo Ezequiel Koremblit described my book saying that there are orthographic mistakes. But there is accuracy in that I was relating and touching on a problem that afflicts the entire continent—the cost of living that affects the proletarian classes. That it is the powerful leaders of nations, the causers of the disorganization. They are owners of industries The avaricious wholesalers who in their unrestrained ambition don't turn their eyes to the humble creatures who need their daily bread. That humanity evolved in culture but remained inhumane. He lauded the intelligence of Audálio Dantas in perceiving in my words when he visited são paulo that I am an intellectual who was waiting for a chance to reveal herself. To senhor Audálio Dantas, our brother, my esteem for his gentility demonstrating that he is a journalist who mixes with the poor. At the conclusion of the presentation, I went to sit next to the journalists, to answer their questions There were so many that it was not possible for me to take down their names. They asked me:

What are the brazilians going to do to wipe out the favelas?

—The extinction of the shantytowns has to be done by means of an agrarian reform, because we the shantytown dwellers are the peasants who work the land. When the land owners didn't let us plant anymore we the peasants emigrated to the city. The fazendeiro unconsciously implanted the favelas in the large cities

Q—What do you plan to do with your life?

A—Write and bring up my kids

Q—What is your opinion of Janio's resignation?

A—I predicted that senhor Janio wouldn't complete his term of office. He is an actor, not a patriot. He is a metamorphized man. He wants a place in history.

Q—Who is the best politician in Brazil?

A—Dr. Adhemar de Barros. But the poor didn't understand his worth. But the poor are already disillusioned and await a Messiah. The world needs a Messiah, Carolina, answered a man who was listening to me. The reception hall was full of men and women. Dona Carmen Silva, the Brazilian writer, translated. She humorously said:

—Do you know Carolina, I write but I am obscure. I am going to take advantage of your publicity to get well known.

A journalist asked dona Carmen Silva what Carolina symbolizes for her.

A—She symbolized a grenade is exploding against hunger.

Q—Carolina what is your opinion of the world?

A—Inhumane. It is the unseemly acts of bad politicians that contribute to enfeeble the beautiful minds of the young people of today. A politician is obliged to be a good moral, administrative model to be imitated.

Q—Is there racial prejudice in Brazil?

A—No. The Blacks in Brazil don't know that they are Blacks because the white people don't mention our color. The white people in brazil are very good and offer opportunities for Blacks to improve themselves.

Q—Are there people of color in politics?

A—Yes. The black Brazilian has freedom to choose what he wants. Nothing hampers him.

Q—Do you read many books?

A—I do. And I read El hombre mediocre [*The Mediocre Man*] by José Inginieiros [Ingenieros]. They say that he wrote his own biography. I defended the notable portenho [Buenos Aires] writer, because I admire his intelligence in observing the social classes of the world. He knew how to define people and their qualities.

How I would like to meet José Ingenieros?

What do your children want to be?

João José, the eldest, wants to be a mechanical draftsman. José Carlos wants to be a doctor. Vera Eunice wants to be a pianist and a teacher.

Q—Does she write?

A—She wants to write. She writes beautifully. The other day she wrote that women should change their clothes and not their husbands.

Dona Carmen translated and everybody laughed.

Q—If you could be born again, would you want the life you had?

A—Yes, and the luck to meet another Audálio Dantas because without him none of this would have happened. He is the key to all of this.

I received flowers, a bouquet of carnations and flowers from the Brazilian Embassy, where dona Carmen Silva is on the staff.

Q—What do you think of Fidel Castro?

A—I read nothing about senhor Fidel Castro. I only hear women say that he is very handsome!

Q—And of Frandizi [Arturo Frondizi]?

A—I hear tell that he is an extraordinary person. That his intelligence is as vast as outer space.

Dona Carmen Silva smiled commenting: you are quick, eh, Carolina!

Nobody makes a fool out of you I thought: I can't criticize the politicians of my country because they are mistaken. What I observed in the argentines is their taste for art. The women are capricious and neat. They don't have bad breath. I saw no children begging in the streets. The houses are comfortable inside they are decorated tastefully. The floor boards are joined and are two palms long. It is hot. They use light linen clothes. I didn't see any drunken men in the streets. I saw no Blacks.

I asked one man: Sahovaler, are there no Blacks in Argentina?

A—There is prejudice here

A—There is no prejudice. But here it is very cold in the winter, and the Blacks don't like the cold. They emigrated to Cuba, and to Montevideo.

When the press conference ended we left. I returned to my magnificent apartment and wrote. My picture comes out every day in the newspapers. I am happy. . . .

By 1962, Carolina had virtually stopped receiving royalties except from abroad for *Quarto de Despejo,*, and these were not large amounts. *Casa de Alvenaria* was published in Argentina but neither in English nor in French. She would never again publish anything that would sell. People still considered her bizarre and treated her badly. Her white neighbors were astonished when she took driving lessons, because they could not imagine a black woman driving. Secretly, she was preparing to give up her house and to move her family to the outskirts of the city where they could live in peace.

1962

21 September 1962 I woke up at 6 o'clock to prepare the kids who are going to school. Vera is studying mathematics. She says she is going to be a teacher. Today I am unwell. I am going to make a soup. And a soup is very expensive. The house is dirty. I can't afford to pay a maid.

When Vera returned from class she went to the shop to buy cabbage and meat.

Senhor Verdi came to visit me and said that I am going to have lunch with Janio [Quadros, the former president] on Tuesday. Vera went to fetch the neighbor's daughter and gave her food. the little girl suffers from rickets. Her stepmother mistreats her too much. And my children nicknamed the girl "Cinderella." I told senhor Verdi that the law ought to intervene and remove the child—How the children of drunkard women suffer. Senhor Verdi told me that there is more suffering in the North: That the [state] governments are inhuman.

It is that Brazil is immense for me humanity is still [too far] in the embryo to realize that the government is responsible for all the disorganization in the country. Everyone needs to cooperate in the

6. Carolina during her publicity tour for *Quarto de Despejo*. The photograph may have been taken in Rio Grande do Sul, Argentina, or Chile, 1961. *Photographer unknown.*

progress of the country. Senhor Verdi ate my soup for lunch and said goodbye. I walked him to the corner; the children get ready to go to class. I received a visit from the woman who sells in the market she came to see me. I owe her 14,000 cruzeiros. i bought clothes for the kids. The children use up a lot of clothes. A child costs an extraordinary amount for a parent. So it is necessary that the son when he becomes an adult is a decent man for the parents to have a reward for their efforts.

Children should not go astray. While we are children we have to be guided by our parents. It is the only period when parents have tranquility of Spirit. What I observe is that The men after reaching adulthood deviate from the social norms. There are those who will rob. And the man who is known as a thief is shunned by the public.

On the 17th I went to the federal police. I am taking out a new identity card and I spoke with the official, Amorôso Netto. It's that I went to consult Interpol about the chance of transferring to Brazil a young Chilean with his mother to work on my land. He said that Brazil will be his second *patria*. Senhor Amorôso Netto said that it would not be an impediment. And we spoke of delinquency in Brazil, A country where there is a vast, undeveloped rural area. So many people have farms and want a couple to take care of the land and don't manage.

It's that men today want to stay in the city enjoying the false pleasures that the city offers. It is terrible to live under congested conditions. People should be relocated on the periphery of the cities to ease crowding. [But] nobody wants to live where there is no electricity.

Another thing that I note is that the Russians [and] the syrians who come to Brazil don't go to work in farming. They go into commerce. They are uneducated types who think that having money is the solution. If I were a man I would prefer to live in the countryside to plant. But today's man I don't know if he is weak or if he is lazy, in the police department we spoke of the moral punishment of the past. The police chased a robber through the streets and the children went hooting: Thief. Chicken thief! And the children went beating tins and lids. A real treat for the children who didn't realize the drama in which they were taking part.

I thought—What is it to be a thief? But the moral punishment of the present day is one hundred times worse—The press that publishes the photograph of a thief. Yet as bad as it seems, Brazil is still the best place. We have shelters for underage children we are not inhuman. In Buenos Aires, the wealthy don't like the poor. In Chile, rich people predominate. I didn't see any shelter for underage children in Santiago. It is terrible to see children begging in the streets. I think about the chaos of these times. People exterminating each other. The revolution in Argentina. I noted the inner hatreds among them. After all it is the white man [who] rules the world.

Cleide asked for Vera's notebook to copy the lesson because Vera writes more quickly. Vera did not want to lend it to her because Cleide's mother forbade her to come to my house. Vera told her to ask the white girls for a notebook. And Vera is not to enter Cleide's house anymore. Humanity's pride is foolish. Everybody dies. When God said: Love one another, he already foresaw racial segregation.

The children went to school I went to drive. I am taking lessons to drive a car. I want to see if I buy a car. I want to live in [P]arelheiros. I am at the Santana Auto School. I am enjoying driving. I already know a number of neighborhoods. Those who write need to have a car. I am becoming acquainted with the city. The Blacks become startled when they see me driving. They exclaim: Look at the Black woman who is going to buy a car.

If the Black in Brazil still didn't develop it is because he has a huge complex. And those who earn well don't know how to organize themselves. I don't have a complex. My instructor is senhor Gabriel. He doesn't drink alcohol and doesn't smoke. I like to hang around at the driving school. The students are decent and pleasant. If I go back to writing my Diary [for publication] it's that the poor people are requesting it.

In the morning I was sad. In the afternoon I was becoming happy. I want to be well organized. I had a urine exam taken. They told me I have nephritis. in the human body there are many confusions. An organ that gets weak. I received a letter from Eva Vastari [a Finnish writer].

22 September 1962 Today I am feeling well. Vera went to her mathematics class. I cleaned the house. I am going to have a visit from Eva Vastari. I made lunch. Rice beans and jerked beef and salad. I am only going to buy meat once a week. 'til when! the cost of living [goes down]—The kids went to school. João will leave at 3 o'clock to go to the Francisco Alves bookstore to take a letter to Dr. Lélio. I went to drive. I came home in the driving school car. I went to the pharmacy. Vili the pharmacist is horrified at me not having gone to a doctor. if I die, I die. Nobody is eternal. Today I am happy. The neighbors are amazed at me driving. It is an enormous responsibility. One can't be careless. yes . . . life today isn't easy. And can it be that it will get worse?

In Argentina there is revolution. What foolishness to destroy one's own country. And they are civilized.

It is raining in São Paulo. I am calmer. I am becoming less foolish. A Black came to sell deodorant. What an intelligent Black man! he could be a writer. He told me that he is a mystic. I don't know what that is. He told me that Christ was a mystic. I am going to read in the Dictionary what it is to be a mystic. The man became pleased when I told him that I am Carolina Maria de Jesus.

—So it is you! I am going to tell my wife that I had coffee in the house of Carolina Maria de Jesus. He sold me a disinfectant for the wardrobe for 40 cruzeiros and took his leave.

The neighborhood women who saw me driving the car are stupefied and talking. for them I am a phenomenon. Today I didn't receive any visitors. I am going to go to bed at 6 o'clock in the afternoon. Vera has a deep cough. I was ill during the night. With pains in my kidney. What torment when I go to the street market. The venders say that I am rich. And I become irritated. It is horrible to live in these times when the poor only think about money.

I reached the conclusion that Brazil is not a country to be born a poet. The mental torture that the people inflict on me is terrible. I have to curse the people who speak to me of money. João went to withdraw 5,000 from the bank. he paid the light bill and bought a bottle of medicine for me. I am beginning to become ill.

I can't eat salt.

23 September 1962 Today is Sunday. I don't like to go out of my house on Sundays. I am going to stay home to wash clothes and to iron. It is raining and the children use up a lot of clothes. I bought a chicken for 450. How absurd. Today I am happy. The children are calmer. They fear becoming orphans. And orphans in Brazil suffer because here it is every one for himself.

At night, senhor Verdi and his wife came to visit me. What a cultured man. He visits me twice a week. The neighbors say he is more attentive to me than Audálio. Senhor Verdi's wife made a cake. And we spent a pleasant afternoon. How good would be the world, if everyone was cultured. The children went to the movies.

Vera stopped playing with Cleide because Cleide's mother forbade her from entering my house. The worst neighbor is the bourgeois turned rich. Unfortunately our bourgeoisie don't stand out. Those who buy a little house and a television become haughty and petulant. I was waiting for a writer who was introduced to me by paulo Dantas, who is going to write a book, Carolina and Her Loves.* He is coming to interview me to start his book. The men who I loved couldn't put up with me hinting that I am superior. They made a mistake—I am not superior—I [simply] do not shirk work.

And I take on any kind of work. I am noting the differences in the men of today. They fight for a salary raise. It's that all of them want to remain in the city, relishing the false pleasures. What I observe in the city is human disregard. some kill others to rob them. Forgetting that a person who kills another becomes a defendant before the judge. He has to face the earthly judge and the celestial judge. The man who wants to live from killing to earn a living is a crazy man. He is a smart man. Even as a crook he is very valuable. When we are ill is when we value the human being. When I went out in the afternoon to go to driving class I felt a pain in my kidney and I went to the office of Dr. Furlan, on the Voluntarios da patria street. there were a number of people waiting for the arrival of the doctor, who is the mechanic of the human body. A woman arrived writhing. I was the second to be examined. i gave up my place to the woman who was moaning. After she was examined the woman went directly to the hospital. she was to be operated on at nineteen hours. As she left she thanked me. When I went to be examined, dr. Furlan told me that I have pyelitis. That I must rest for 6 days. I told him that I did a urine exam and I will send him the result. that is

---

* This book, if it was ever written, was never published.

with senhor Verdi who was going to arrange for me [to see] a doctor. i paid one thousand cruzeiros for the consultation, and gave a two-hundred[-cruzeiro] tip to the nurse.

In the waiting room the women were discussing the stupid crime that happened in Campinas. The young man was killed by a masked man. Can it be that the man who kills to rob is sure he is a man? He is a man only in fame. An infantile man who grows up and does not mature. God told man to feed himself by the sweat of his brow! Women don't kill to rob because the woman knows the work that it takes to raise a human being.

I said goodbye to the women thinking: if I die, nobody buys eternal life. i passed by the pharmacy and bought the injections and took one of them. 140, each ampoule. I bought 6 and paid 8400. I took a taxi and returned home. João went to buy the Albamicina G U. pills. I gave him 400. He returned saying that the medicine costs 1,150. I didn't have the money. Vera went to ask Dona Elza Rêis for 2,000. She lent it to me. João went to buy the medicine. he returned cursing the pharmacist Thief, miserable! He scratched his head saying: how those who are poor do suffer! I took the medicine and lay down.

I couldn't sleep for the pain in my kidneys. I told the doctor that tomorrow I am having lunch with Janio. He is purged of the guilt of his resignation because senhor Brochado da Rocha defended him. So Janio is not guilty. He is a victim. My children are fearful. They say: if mommy dies . . . João went to the city to talk to . . .

24 September 1962 I woke up the children at 6 o'clock to prepare the room. The Finnish journalist Eva Vastari, is arriving from Rio I invited her to spend a few days in my house. She is going to translate my book into Finnish. The children are busy dashing from one side to the other. At 3 o'clock Eva arrived. I was lying down with a pain in my right kidney We talked. At nine o'clock senhor Verdi dos Santos and his wife arrived. I told him that I could not go with him to the meeting with Senhor Janio Quadros. Dr Furlan told me that I need to rest. Senhor Verdi said that it was already arranged and it was not possible to postpone the interview. I got up thinking about the thorns that glory reserves for us. I rose, changed, and went out with senhor Verdi. i asked senhor Verdi's wife to make lunch and kill the chicken. I went out with senhor Verdi. I went to senhor Villi's pharmacy and took an injection. He asked me: where are you going?

—I am going to have lunch with Janio. Those who were going to have lunch were me Janio, Busola and the ex-minister Brochado da Rocha. But senhor Brochado da Rocha got ill.

We headed for the praça da Sé. Senhor João Rocha was supposed to accompany us. He wasn't there. i bought a magazine. A number of people came up to greet me and to ask if I am writing. And what is my next book.

I answer: that I have written many books and don't know which one will be published. That is up to Paulo Dantas. Senhor Verdi didn't want to wait for senhor João Rocha. we went on. I was horrified at today's electoral campaign. Lots of music—Lots of propaganda. The times when I dread Brazil. The [festivities of the] month of June, because of the fireworks and rockets and the balloons.The month of Carnival with its songs and exoticisms. I went along talking with senhor Verdi. we moved swiftly up Avenida Brigadeiro Luiz Antonio. I was gazing at the poor women who directed the Social Service Center and need to ask the government for help. In other countries it is the social workers who seek out the poor. Sad undernourished women. It is a shame in a country so wealthy, [there are] poor maladjusted people. It's that if a person doesn't study they don't know how to live or to organize their life. The maladjusted people have too much imagination. There are times when I think: it doesn't matter if I write about social maladjustment if nobody fixes the world. Poor people are still on level-B.

When we arrived at the meeting held by ex-president Janio Quadros, I was stupefied at the number of people. some [were] writing, others [were] begging. Others wandering about. I heard a murmur, Look Carolina! I was climbing up the steps. a lady was accompanying me. she was speaking about my book Quarto de despêjo [*sic*]. Janio's secretary received me. The photographers circled about. I decided to write A text for Janio-what moved me was the oration of senhor Brochado da Rocha, saying that senhor Janio Quadros resigned [from the presidency] to remain honest. That being the case, we ought to reelect him again because the country needs honest men. For this honest gesture I give my congratulations to senhor Janio Quadros. And I ask him to continue honest because honesty raises a person's character. And we need an honest man and one of character in the government of São Paulo. Not a little man who performs boyish tricks.

Senhor Janio emerged. What a handsome man! He was well dressed and happy. A number of people wanted to be photographed with him. He said: wait, Carolina, afterward and I will take a photograph with you. I was terrified and asked him: —And with all this chaos you still gained weight?

—I did Carolina!

I thought the protector of Janio is his father's Ghost.

I moved closer to Janio to be photographed. He embraced me. With Janio's contact I felt good inside. I thought: I am in the arms of a man.

And I decided to vote for Janio. He said: Thank you Carolina! I said goodbye and left. And the voice of Janio remained exploding in my brain just like an echo—Thank you Carolina! When Janio pronounced my name, I had the impression that he was signing a pledge with me. And I thought: Janio is the Linconl [Lincoln] of Brazil. I and senhor Verdi went to the Bus station to pick up Eva Vastari's baggage. We took a motor cab. A number of people looked at me as if I were from another planet. we stopped at the Auto-School. I told senhor Andre that I can't attend classes for now.

I am going to rest for 6 days. I already went to speak with Janio, and tomorrow I will be in the newspaper A Hora. I got in the car and drove to my house. The wife of senhor Verdi had already prepared lunch. But what a lunch! I went to lie down thinking: I am already becoming an old tired lady also with this life so agitated! It is an invitation for me to go to heaven, an invitation for me to go to hell. They think that I run on engine power. i paid the taxi. We removed eva Vastari's baggage and that was the 24 of September 1962. I couldn't get to sleep because of the kidney pain.

25 September 1962   At 6 o'clock I woke up the children. João went to the city. Yesterday I left a message for Dr. Lélio asking for an advance of 10,000. João went to see if Audálio had withdrawn the money from Yugoslavia. Audálio said that it will take two weeks. He sent me this message: "Carolina: the chaos around receiving the money from Czechoslovakia continues that a payment order must come from Rio and will still take some two weeks. At the moment I have nothing. You would have to turn to Lélio. Any new developments I will let you know. Regards! Audálio"

Dr. Lélio gave the money. I repaid the 2,000 that Dona Elza Reis lent me. José Carlos went to buy the newspaper. . . . The article with Janio came out. I spent the day lying down. Eva Vastari went out. She went to speak with Dantas if there was a chance of doing a translation of Quarto de despejo. In the afternoon Eva returned saying that she is not going to translate because no request came from Finland.

I am feeling ill.

Eva brought a newspaper announcing that ex-minister Brochado da Rocha died. What mental torture they inflicted on him in the Ministry. to govern a country the good will of everybody is needed. It gives the impression that our politicians are pirates. Those who ought to be congressmen in a country should be wealthy men who can work some hours for the country and not receive any payment. What leaves me horrified is that the sons of Syrians, the sons of Jews, all want to be congressmen. They are the only race who think they deserve being included because they become affluent. I am thinking. why is it that a man has such gigantic ambition? for me man only has worth as a child. They are born so pure. And as they are growing up their character is turning rotten. And the world is needing firm ethics. Senhor Verdi said that if Jesus returns to judge mankind, even the pope will be judged!

26 September 1962 i spent the day in bed. I have a pain in my kidneys. I can't walk. The newspapers are announcing the death of senhor Brochado da Rocha. And the rumors generate confusion. Saying that there will be no school. Today is market day. I am not going out—João is doing the shopping.

The woman who sells in the fair who I owe money came to visit me. In the afternoon I got up and wrote a letter to Professor Mendonza [her host in Chile on her book tour] and I went to have injections. The market venders are commenting that they saw me in the newspaper with Janio. Dona Eva Vastari went out. She said that she was going to arrange articles to write. I am moving on to [eat] fruit. At night senhor Verdi came to visit me and asked me to lend him my typewriter to write an article against David Nasser [a journalist] for writing against Janio Quadros. He said that Hora will publish it. Eva Vastari typed the article. Senhor Verdi was furious with David Nasser. Eva said that senhor Verdi will lose. That when we enter a fight we ought to enter with the conviction that we are going to win.

I am eating so much. I am on a restricted diet. [My] life is reaching an end. i made supper for the children. The house is filthy!

27 September 1962 Today I don't feel well. I didn't manage to sleep. . . . I got up and was spinning around. I am finding the day sad. The Neighbor came to visit me commenting on the death of senhor Brochado da Rocha. I went for an injection. My arms are full of stabs and aching. I went to talk with Dona Elza and show her the article with Janio. She liked it. I bought the newspaper to read senhor Verdi's report [but] it didn't come out. The children went to school. João went to take a letter to Dr. Lélio. He [João] and José Carlos quarreled and broke a window pane. My God! How children cost their parents. I washed the stairs and the bathroom.

28 September 1962 Today I got up at 6 o'clock. We forgot the open tap and the water flooded the parlor. What a frenzy. The children joined up to take out the water. Pail broom and squeegee went into action. Dona Eva Vastari was horrified, thinking that I was washing the house. Conclusion: we spent a day without water.

Today I am content. I prepared lunch for the children. Vera went to class and came home saying she is going to be flunked because she doesn't know her mathematics. Dona Eva Vastari teaches her. Eduardo de Oliveira came to invite me to go to a cele- bration of the promulgation of the Free Womb law.* In the name of the First World Congress of Black culture, in the large auditorium graciously offered by the Folhas de São Paulo newspaper group. I ought to thank the illustrious journalists of the Folhas for granting us their elegant auditorium.

I am sick. But . . . I will go. I like to be among Blacks. And I hope that the Blacks in the future may be cultured. And that all may be educated.

29 September 1962 I didn't manage to sleep because of the pain in my kidneys. I couldn't move. Pain and pain. It has a priority in the human body. It attacks us. I planned to stay in bed. João went to the Banco de Credito Real de Minas Gerais to withdraw 5,000 cruzeiros. This week I spend a lot buying medicine and fruits. And they sell the fruits for an astronomical price. A papaya costs 100 cruzeiros.

I was lying down. But how awful it is to stay inactive in bed with the house dirty. The children fear having to do the housework. When I am healthy, I can do everything in an instant. And Vera keeps looking at me, the other day she said:

In a brief second
My mother housecleans
can she be wind
can she have wings

---

* One of a series of late-nineteenth-century laws that led to emancipation of slaves in 1888.

I laughed because I perceived she had composed a quatrain for me. The arm and thought are the wings of man. It is necessary to work. And I always was a workhorse. I always cultivated elevated thoughts. I like to achieve everything with my own efforts. I think that [when] a person is perfect their physique has the chance of winning. But it is necessary to be bold. I like people who work quickly. . . .

João works quickly.

José Carlos is slower and irritates me. When I ask José Carlos to work I end up arguing with him. And today we argued. I got up and ran after him [and] he went into the street. Vera was washing. I went to examine it [but] it wasn't to my liking. I took out the poorly washed items and left some so as not to wound the sensibility of my daughter. I was washing, teaching her that we ought to rinse the clothes a number of times in water. I tell Vera that the woman who doesn't know how to work in the home will be a useless housewife. After washing the clothes I went to the street market to shop. I bought fruits and fish. I am happy. Eva Vastari went to the city to talk with her Finnish compatriots to commission articles.

In the market the venders and the poor were content. i thought: they resigned themselves to the prices thank God the suicides are declining in Brazil. Better days are coming for everybody. I walked through the market. João went after me and gave me the medicines. I was pleased. He said that the prices downtown are cheaper. That the injection cost 900. He carried the bag for me. I went into the pharmacy To see if Villi got the medicines for me. He said they were coming in the afternoon. I returned home thinking: I don't want to die and leave my children here in this neighborhood.

When I returned I was happy and went to prepare lunch when senhor Araujo entered with the sewing machine that I asked him for. He buys the parts and readies the machines. He is a cultured Northerner. A decent and correct man. I told him that I am sick and am not going into the city. But Monday I will have gotten the money. The price of the machine [is] 22,000 in cash. He ate fruits.

Everybody who enters my house has permission to eat. I am not stingy. He who eats has health. I prepared the lunch the kids ate. Vera went to class. I went to lie down and turned on the radio to hear the drama program. It was the play Maria Cachucha. Someone knocked at the door. I looked out and saw an ugly blond little girl with a flat nose. A type who could be used as a scarecrow. Due to washing so many clothes my kidney was aching. And I wanted a bit of peace.

João said: answer it mother!

i thought: they are little bourgeoisies who come to bother me. I opened the window and the ugly one began to speak: they told me that you robbed my dog. I closed the window and went to lie down again concentrating on the drama. Eva Vastari arrived saying that she spent fabulous amounts buying films, to photograph Finnish industry. And that she couldn't buy anything for my children. They knocked at the door. I told her it wasn't necessary to concern herself. I am thinking about the money that I must get to pay for the [sewing] machine. But I know that Jesus protects me. I am, his adopted daughter. Before making a business deal I think: I beg you to help me.

They continued banging on the door and Eva Vastari went to open to window to see what was going on. And she said to me: Come see, Dona Carolina? I went to see. The ugly toothless little girl was with a policeman who demanded that I give over the dog. And requested permission to enter and see if the dog was in my back yard. I told them that my word is my bond. If they wanted to see my house only with a judicial order because if you don't find the dog, I can open an investigation and charge damages because I never robbed anything Those who rob are people of weak Spirit and I, am strong. My commonplace Neighbor Levi brother of Fabio paulino, A man who doesn't like women, went to the policemen and said that he heard a dog whining in my backyard.

—At what time did you hear it? asked the policeman.

—At nine o'clock Affirmed Levi the child molester

—It's a lie, because levi works in the city and leaves his house at seven in the morning

And I spoke loudly not for exhibitionism It's because I have a stentorian voice. Now that I am no longer hungry.

I cursed levi. Big white one! Macaroni without sauce.

Levi the child molester gave me a meek glance! I dread effeminate men. I like male men. It is horrible, when the effeminate men argue with women they don't give us any peace. And they have no shame. they like people to know that they are child abusers.

The curious were turning up. Eva Vastari said: here there is no dog. When I arrived Dona Carolina was sleeping and the children were not at home. But Levi the child abuser affirmed that the dog was in my house. The policeman told me to be courteous in my answers. I went to see if there was a dog I found nothing. The pain in my kidneys had returned. Eva grabbed the camera and pretended that she was taking a picture. The ugly little white girl with the flat nose turned her back. And the lazybones ran away.

I got nervous I went to the pharmacy to buy a tranquilizer. And Edgar and pedro the neighbor of arguments went to telephone the radio patrol. I complained to Villi the pharmacist that I dread this neighborhood. i bought the tranquilizers and felt better. I bought paper with the intention of relating this incident to the Diário da Noite newspaper. I told the police that they hate me because I demanded payment of the thirty thousand cruzeiros that fabio owes me. And they don't like to pay anybody. It is proved that when a person doesn't do what he says and waits to be charged it is proof that he is a cheat. Levi went to call his brother who is a carpenter. And the obnoxious Fabio appeared. Ready to beat me up. And is that how Fabio repays me the favor that I did him? i am the creditor of the house. Fabio is white! There is an old proverb that the Black who doesn't shit when he enters, shits when he leaves. And Fabio is white and is shitting on the favors that I did him.

I began an article relating the facts. But I was in a hurry. I ought to go to the Free womb celebration. I went to get ready. João went to the movies and José carlos stayed with Vera. In the bus I met up with a journalist from the Diários and we spoke about Paulo Dantas, who is gentle in his speech. But he knows how to control. i thought about saying that paulo is drizzle. And I am thunder. I told him that here in the neighborhood everything that happens they accuse my children. When there is a broken window there in hell they will say that it was my children who broke it.

But the human tongue is a worm that man carries with him. Our poet Fagundes Varela wrote that arms are the human tongue.

—can it be that the poet was the victim of the human tongue! . . .

I introduced Eva Vastari as a Finnish journalist. I asked the journalist from the *Diários* if he had children?

—Eight

He was with his wife. A simple woman. She didn't use makeup. And when we arrived at the praça do correio he paid the fare.

Here I register my thanks.

—I think: when I was a shantytown dweller and needed to get to the city, I went on foot since I had no money to pay for transport. And now that I can pay. I meet somebody who pays for me.

I and Eva Vastari looked for a taxi. we found one near the Cine Bandeirante and we went to the folhas. When I enter the Folhas I joke with the journalists.

—The good life! sitting down, Living the life of Lords. There are those who are afraid of journalists. But for me the journalist is a person just like any other. Eduardo de Oliveira received me and said: I am pleased you are here.

Of course I must appear at the celebrations of the Blacks. Luiz gama [a mulatto abolitionist] did not look down upon Blacks.

Henrique Oras

Jose do patrocinio

Ataulfo Alves.

When the Black is an intellectual he tries to protect the class.

When the program started senhorita Ana Florência de Jesus handled the presentations. She was inviting people to take part in the judging. A journalist from the Folhas appeared representing the

Folhas. I was included to take part at the Table of Honor. The Chorus from the department of Education sang the National anthem. The welcoming speech was given by senhorita Ana Flôrencia de jesus. A speech on the Free womb [Law] by Dr. Francisco Lucrecio— He said that a human being who doesn't have an enlightened mind, doesn't have a chance of living with comfort. That slavery arrived at an inconvenient period for the Black. That we should . . . Transform the Black into a dynamic and decent being. That it was the poets movement that contributed to the freedom of the Black. After emancipation the Black didn't have the right to live like a citizen. They didn't educate the Blacks. They said: The black doesn't need to learn the law. It's that Brazil was dominated by the portuguese and the portuguese who came to Brazil were exiles. The pirates. And the wealthy portuguese sent their children to study in [the University of] Coimbra. If they had educated the Blacks the Blacks would be more advanced. More developed.

Counselor Luiz Hugo Levigoi spoke. Jewish. That powerful men shouldn't be egoists. That we ought to follow the example of Jesus Christ—I was amazed. Hearing a Jew cite the name of Christ like a preacher for humanity. The chorus sang selections by senhor Aricó Junior. A good conductor. The poet Eduardo de Oliveira composed a hymn 13 of May [Abolition Day]. And Eduardo wants to record it for the congress.

Senhorita Ana Florência de Jesus said that the Blacks need Culture—She was applauded—Culture is the bass string of humanity.

The commemoration was an incentive. It is beautiful to see our Blacks awakening! When the celebration ended we said goodbye— A journalist from the Folhas took us in his car to my house. He told us he is a doctor. And he advised me to rest. That Pyelitis turns into Nephritis. Eva told him that I work a lot. The doctor said that a Housewife doesn't rest.

30 September 1962 Today is Sunday. i spent the day washing clothes we bought newspapers. The Folhas and the Estado de são paulo. The Fôlhas announced the meeting of Blacks That they are covering the First Congress of Black Culture. The Fôlhas mention my presence. The children went to the cinema. Eva Vastari and I stayed at home.

i made lunch. I made risotto and breaded beef. I washed so many clothes and ironed that I had pains in my arms. Dr. Furlan said that I ought to rest. And it was the week that I most argued and walked, and got tired and the illness went away.

Today I am happy.

Later I am going to explain my arguments with Fabio.

1 October 1962 I got up at 2 o'clock to write because I wasn't sleepy. I woke up the children to go to school. Vera is studying mathematics with Miss Dorotéia. It's that Vera's teacher began to teach her to divide in recent months. And tells the class that she will not pass. She leaves the child with a complex. And Eva Vastari promised her: if you pass I will give you a doll. And Vera comments: Each teacher teaches me a different way. And there is confusion in my head mother!

I tell her: to calm her down: You aren't to blame for not knowing how to divide—the guilty one is the teacher. And Vera comments: Cleide is going to criticize me, mommy!

—Don't worry about criticisms my child. It is the function of the human tongue to wound and to disillusion.

I washed the clothes And ironed them. João went to typing class. I was washing the clothes when I heard a newspaper boy pass by shouting: Two female students disappeared from their homes in an unexpected and unusual way. I ran out scared. Telling their respective mothers that they were going to school they left carrying a change of clothes in their bags instead of books and notebooks. Threatening notes demand a ransom in cash for the return of the little girls. panic in two families and difficult work for the police.

Let's go to the facts.

The newspaper has a photograph of the minor Maria Auxiliadora. She is my neighbor. She lives at Francisco Biriba Street

466. 15 years old. Period of transition. Period of the mistakes of adolescents showing their inclinations. Maria Auxiliadora pereira. She was studying typing in the Imirim Culture Center. With my son Joâo. Joâo my son told me that she skipped class a lot. And she didn't apply herself to her studies.

She is a black girl with wealthy parents. She was well dressed and has a maid. She is a Black noblewoman. Her father is decent. Her mother is an emancipated Black—At times she came to write letters on my typewriter. And I told her: —be decent so you can manage to get married.

She smiled. The smile of *la gioconda* [Da Vinci's *Mona Lisa*] She spoke little. She wasn't suffering from hunger. She had no reason to run away from home. These young people left one University and enter another that is the world. If the girls become pregnant and are embarrassed to seek out their parents their end is delinquency, the shantytowns and the huts. And the mistake is a scar that leaves its effect on public opinion.

What horrifies me is the poor character of men who know how to trick a young woman and afterward leave her suffering in the world.

—When will men stop being perverse? Until when? are men going to overpopulate the world with prostitutes?

—Until when?

The uncultured man is the one who practices these antisocial acts. And spreads disgrace in the universe.

The women commented that Maria Auxiliadora pereira knows what she is doing because she is already studying at University level. But in the United States, students disappear. . . . And they are strangled. Today it is Maria Auxiliadora pereira who is being talked about. for me the big city is a theater and this is one of its scenes. Dramatic scenes Robberies, etc. And speaking of robbery, every day the newspapers publish that somebody robbed.

When are these bandits going to feel shame? —With so much to do in Brazil nobody needs to rob. Those who rob deserve moral punishment. They ought to organize a protest demonstration with the thieves in the streets and placards saying: this man is a thief. The man who robs is a weak man.

Vagrant Etc. Write everything that is humiliating to see if the thieves could be eliminated from the country. It gives the impression that people are losing shame. They don't have fear of criticism.

Another thing that I will fix: Men who marry and afterward abandon their wives—It gives the impression that the man is childish because the children see a doll in the store window and find it pretty. When they get one they play with the doll a few days, after they start getting annoyed—and at last they discard the doll. And the worst of all this is that the man leaves the women with the children to raise. it's because of this that I didn't marry because it is terrible for a woman to be superior and to have to obey an inferior type. I dread men who carry on projecting themselves: I am going to do this! I am going to do that and they do nothing because they are men who fill their time with words.

The man is the owner of the world! he ought to fill his time with action. Courage. This is the way to achieve progress and become the example for those who follow. Men cannot be irresponsible.

My children discussed the disappearance of the school girls. Let's talk about educators. The teacher needs to enlighten the mind of her student she explained that all the acts we practice have consequences. . . . At the Barão Homem de Mello school a policeman appeared and explained: the students shouldn't go off with men. That the man is dangerous. I don't know if this speech by the policeman was timely because the child will think that man is a monster. He ought to clarify that children should not be afraid of a man, when the man is their father, their uncle, and their teacher. There are those who say that the schoolgirls fled with boyfriends. When we plant a tree, we wait for its fruits. And the schoolchildren began life erring and the mistakes are the forecasts of the future.

Eva Vastari arrived. I was washing clothes and dishes. I was tired and wanted to lie down a little. she brought paper from the factory. She went to do an article on Finnish factories. When I was in the favela I didn't know that this country called Finland existed. I listened to her talk about the beauty of the factory.

She went to change clothes and went out to do the shopping. she went to buy fruits, bread, and ice cream. I am in Aliki Kostaki's column. I ought to appear at the book-signing evening. And the journalist Aliki Kostaki wants to organize autograph afternoons. João went to the city to speak with Audálio. They are going to the bank to withdraw the money that came from Czechoslovakia. Now I want to employ my money sensibly.

I want to build a house in Parelheiros and plant crops. It is necessary for us the women we ought to return to farming because men today only want to live in the city.

We women are becoming superior. . . .

There will be a time when women will not marry if men continue to be futile—Eva returned with purchases. . . . We had ice cream [and] I went to ready myself to go out. João returned saying that I should be at Dona Aliki's party at seven thirty. I am thinking: it was I who called people's attention to the book. I think I ought to say:

—Congratulations Carolina. When I like something I want everybody to like it.

And I adore books. I want everybody to adore them for me, the book is the greatest jewel in the world.

João came with the address for the evening autograph session. I am sick but I will go. My appearance is in homage to the books. I had no stockings I went to purchase a pair. I bought on credit to pay later. The women were discussing the disappearance of the two girls. I told them that I was going to a party and I dashed out. In two minutes I was home. Dona Eva Vastari was horrified at my quick change. I went to the pharmacy to buy nail polish remover to clean my nails. José Carlos was in the street. I forced him to enter. I am forceful with my children. When I say it's a, It is a! When I say It is B, It is B. And they obey me. . . .

Everything matters with me. Today I am happy with a desire to

sing. I don't sing because I am tired. At six o'clock I went out with
Eva Vastari. She is a well-bred woman. She does not try my
patience. I thought she was a useless high-class lady, but she isn't.
She knows how to work, she knows how to cook wash iron. And
she irons better than me. We were chatting in the bus. Eva carried
her camera. When we arrived in the city we went to the post office.
And we spoke about the Argentine publisher. He wanted me to visit
Mexico. i refused because I was tired. The wife of the Argentine
publisher is a lawyer. we left the post office and went to 7 of April
street. I felt unwell and we went to a restaurant in front of the
Diários. I ordered a chicken soup with rice. Eva ordered fruits.
When we were finishing dinner Audálio appeared at our table. He
greeted me first. And I shook his hands. He smiled saying. You,
took my hand today! —I thought. I shouldn't take these hands. I
should kiss them because it was these hands that labored for me. I
owe everything that I am to Audálio My children have their daily
bread, they have a roof over their heads. I didn't marry. But I had
the luck to find this man who supplanted the men who crossed my
path. I am not ungrateful. A boy approached selling carnations. And
offered them to Audálio.

   —Buy flowers for the ladies.
   —How much?
   —One hundred cruzeiros each
   Audálio protested that the price was too high.
   And the boy said that carnations are very expensive.
   But Audálio was happy. And he bought two carnations. I
thanked him. Audálio paid for my meal. And we spoke of Miller
who collaborated in the marketing of quarto de despejo. And who
took care of the contracts with Europe. Audálio said that he doesn't
know how to negotiate and explained that he receives a certain
amount when money arrives from abroad. I am not ambitious. And
Miller is efficient.
   I was anxious to autograph. I said goodbye to Audálio and
seeing Miller who was eating his supper I went to greet him. —he

asked me if I was going to Aliki Kostaki's party because your name is in the papers.

Audálio asked me if I was cured.

—I am recovered.

We said goodbye. I heard the band of the civil guard playing and we went over to the place. When we were approaching I heard voices. —Look Carolina! She is a supporter of Janio! My glance moved about rapidly like lightening. I waved at the civil guard and we entered. Aliki Kostaki was at the door receiving the guests. She gave me an embrace. I introduced her to Eva Vastari and stayed there looking at her dress. How beautiful. It was Denner who made her dress. And he promised to give me a dress.

I circulated about greeting the writers. I didn't find my booth. I continued to circulate And I was photographed with the writers. One of them was Marcos Rey. I feel sorry for him. He complained with an embittered voice that he was fired from the Ultima-Hora newspaper. Marcos Rey is cultured and doesn't write banalities. He is a well-adjusted man. He gave me his new book, Entre sem bater [Knock without entering]. Flipping through the book I sensed that it is good. It was published by Autores Reunidos Publishers. It was published serially in the Ultima-Hora newspaper. It's in the fourth edition. Marcos Rey is the author of Café na cama [Breakfast in bed]. The book that competed with my quarto de despejo. I was circulating.

dona Aliki Kostaki showed me my booth. I was going to be the neighbor of Jorge Amado [Brazil's most popular novelist]. that's what I said to Dona Eva Vastari. I was looking for Jorge when I was wrapped in an embrace. It was him. I sensed the nobility of his character. He doesn't hold grudges. It's that I had a misunderstanding with Jorge. Unfairly.

It's that I was from the favela. And favelados don't try to verify facts and appeal by means of violence. When I went to autograph my book in Rio, I autographed only 50 books. I thought that it was Jorge Amado who set the quota.

When I was in Jorge Amado's arms I thought: if I could remain in the arms of this man for centuries and centuries! . . . He is clean. He doesn't smell of cigarettes. he has the perfume of the newly born. purity. I adore well-groomed men Who care for their bodies. The photographers surrounded us. And I went to my booth. I thought of George [*sic*], a man who has been in literature for 30 years. He deserves to win a street with his name. George Amado Street. Streets are guidelines. And George Amado is One guideline of a man.

My sponsor was senhor[a] Jonhn [*sic*] Herbert. She is a beautiful young Well-Dressed youth. She was wearing a black blouse with black flowers. The gorgeous dresses were designed by Dener [*sic*]— I asked the price 50,000. i thought: Dener wants to become a profiteer. He wants to buy a rocket to go to the moon.

I sensed that Dona Eva Vastari didn't think much of my sponsor. She treated him coldly. I became concerned. She who is always so gentle. I managed to sell some books. Dr Lélio approached. With his wife. And I introduced him as my publisher. And I told him that I already earned a lot of money with him—I was well compensated for Quarto de despejo. Paulo Dantas was with his wife. I didn't see Dr. José Tavares de Miranda. I didn't see Arápuan. I didn't see Cid Franco. I didn't see Dorian Matos pacheco, Mauricio Loureiro Gama Silva Netto wasn't there. Ruth de Souza [a black actress] went to my booth. I told her that I am going to see her film Assalto ao trem pagador [Assault on the train ticket taker]. The reviews are favorable. I forced myself to be pleasant.

My dream was to meet the poet Oliveira Ribeiro Neto. He was my neighbor. i managed to buy a book from him. Os Bens de Deus!

I told him that I like his verses. That poets are the ministers of the angels. The Book has 201 pages. it was published by Livraria Martins. . . .

A samba school [of black dancers] circulated about the hall. And the soldiers in full gala dress walked through the hall. Audálio, Miller, Tarak Carlos de Frêitas from O Cruzeiro didn't appear. José pinto, Ronaldo de Moraes and others. Finishing the autographs, we were leaving. A black woman who is a supporter of Janio went to congratulate me for writing the article for Janio. A Finnish woman appeared at my stand and bought a book. I invited her to come to my house that a Finnish journalist is writing a book and is going to publish it in Finland. Eduardo de Oliveira was present. He said that he autographed 80 books. And he accompanied us to the bar on 7 de abril Street. Dr. Lélio and his wife were there. And dr. Lélio wished to pay for my coffee. I found 5 cruzeiros and paid for the coffee. Aliki Kasloki asked me if I was pleased with my sponsor. She is cultured. Recently married. I pleaded with her not to separate from her husband that they ought to make silver and golden wedding anniversaries. And have many children and grandchildren. They are rich in the hard times that we are going through only the rich can have children. because it is only the rich who can buy something to eat.

Dr. Lélio invited me to his house. I told him that I can't because I am having lunch with Janio. I showed him the invitation: There are those who say that Janio has a mania for Resigning that Brazil will do anything for him. And Getúlio [Vargas]? he had power at hand. And he lost his life. Senhor Tancredo Neves didn't manage his ministry—he resigned. Auro de Maura Andrade, refused to be the prime minister. And the heartfelt Brochado da Rocha who lost his life to mental exhaustion. At the time of dying for one's country, the gaúchos are the ones who die. I heard say that they attacked the exalted Senhor Brochado and he turned resentful.

This is the work of the crows. Until when are we to have black crows in politics. I was moving around the bar when the fabulous poet Paulo Bonfim entered. Accompanied by some young women and he gave me a hug. I pleaded with him: paulo! paulo . . . For the love of God don't hug me! I heard that your wife is very jealous and forbids you from talking to women, That you are afraid of her.

His wife was there and said: Just imagine me . . . being jealous of Paulo. He goes where he pleases. Who was it who said that?

—I will consult my Diary.

The young girls who were with paulo smiled. And paulo said to his wife—Did you see, darling, how famous you are for being savage? They said goodbye.

some chileans arrived and asked, —How is Professor Mendonza.*

—He is fine. He is very cultured. I don't know and didn't think that the press was going to involve itself in Our friendship.

—He is a journalist and understands the people of the press. I like him. Audálio asked me, —How is your friendship with Jorge?

—It is going well.

And Audálio said: I have the impression that Jorge is a decent person.

I detest hypocrisy. When Jorge was in São paulo, Audálio didn't wish to receive him, he didn't come to my house to greet him.

—The one who likes George is me.

I said to the wife of Jorge Amado that the Chilean is Cultured, educated and decent.

And he sends me money.

Zelia Amado complained that I was unjust with Jorge. That he aids beginning writers. He is the patriarch of literature. I shed so many tears. I told her that I was nervous because I was very hungry. when my organism began to receive proteins it rebelled. I didn't eat butter, I didn't eat beans I am still under treatment all the organs are weak. I am eating fruits to get some vitamins. Those who go hungry are neurotic. When Jesus prayed asking, Don't leave us without our daily bread, he was foreseeing these times. We said goodbye to Eduardo de Oliveira and headed for our house. we stopped in a bar. After we left and took a taxi.

When we arrived home it was raining. And the streets are being repaired. The car could not leave us at the door we intended to dash up Bento pereira street but the car had no drive [a broken transmission] and could blow out a tire. We walked on foot. And arrived home. I ate supper and went to bed and immediately fell asleep. . . .

---

* Chilean literature professor Jorge Mendoza, who befriended Carolina during her trip to Chile and acted as her host. He visited her in Brazil.

Carolina has decided to flee the city and move to rustic Parelheiros on the outskirts of São Paulo. She is distancing herself from her mentors. She refers to Dantas, whom earlier she thanked for bringing her a better life, as "Mr. Dantas." She feels cheated because of the small amounts in royalties she is receiving, and she must sell her typewriter to buy food for her children. Hunger and want have returned to her life. Her bitterness is deepening.

1963

8 January 1963 I am still nauseated. I took a laxative of castor oil. I went downtown. Dutra arranged for senhor Virgilio to build my house. Senhor José who sold me the land is helping me out. he asked senhor Virgilio to draw up a payment contract. When I returned to the city I went to the office of senhor Romiglio Giacampol, to receive the money from Germany. I learned that senhor Audálio Dantas had received 200 marks in advance. But senhor Audálio Dantas didn't divide this with me. this is why he refuses to make a rendering of the accounts. I received from the translation Rights 64,129 cruzeiros as first payment from Germany. little. for the number of books that sold.

9 December 1963 i spent the night thinking that I have nothing for the children to eat and they went to sleep hungry. If God had warned me that I would be unhappy I would not have left the favela. In the favela I begged. And thought that I was miserable. I was wrong. but erring is typical of mankind. I remember when I was preparing to leave the favela I said:

Thank God I am going to live among high-class people!

And Adalberto said to me in his drunken voice—You are going to live among people of a high class.

And here I am fulfilling my great dream that was to be a writer. Oh Dream! That the greatest victim[s] are my children. I told João what senhor Luiz said. That Vera cried last year because she didn't receive a toy.

Tomorrow I am going to sell the typewriter to buy food for my kids. José Carlos, has no shoes. They say that I am a fool. That I let Audálio exploit me. I am not a fool. I am honest. And I don't like conflict. When I met Dantas, . . . he insisted that I write quarto de despejo.

I asked: I write the book and you get me out of the favela But I don't want to stay in the city. I want to live on a farm, because around 1970, it will be difficult for the poor to live here in são paulo. In 1970, the poor of Brazil [will have] died of hunger. but Audálio, he didn't take me away from the favela. He took out my book because the book was going to make him money. They published the book the 19 of August and I stayed in the shantytown taking a beating from the angered favelados. I lacked knowledge. who moved away from the favela were senhor Antonio Soeiro Cabral and the Jews. And senhor Antonio [S]oeiro Cabral shook his head saying: poor Carolina! But I was too thrilled to understand all of that.

It was the fulfillment of my dream. Food and a cinder-block house. What confusion in my mind with those warnings. The first to warn me was Renato from the Gazeta [a newspaper]. He told me that I was being exploited. That I was going to wear out

—I thought: He says this because he is jealous. Jurema Finanur warned me. Barboza Lessa and others. Now that I am hungry again is when I understand the warnings. The warnings are the seeds that are planted at one time to be harvested later. It wasn't possible for me to sleep thinking that I have no soap to wash clothes. And I don't have money to buy bread.

The barber Dutra in the city told me that I should be receiving 200 thousand cruzeiros a month. But the reports from Russia say

that in the capitalist countries The poor work to maintain the bourgeoisie, types who emerge from the middle class.

That's life. And the most inhuman class to live amongst, it is
the human class that with the passage of time is deteriorating.

And it is now in fashion. To kill and not be punished. They
killed Dana [Dona?] de Tefé to steal her money. And the worst of all
this is that the one accused of having killed the Lady is a lawyer.
The man who studied to defend the human class are semi-
intellectual types. who pass their exams for protection. He doesn't
study to be honest. They study to learn to rob. It's for this reason
that I live among the human class but, I don't mix much with this
class because it is dangerous.

On 22 November 1963 they killed the president of the United
States. He is the fourth president of the United States to be assassinated. A disgusting recurrence for the North Americans. The world
adored Kennedy because he was good. He was not a four-legged
human type. He was not stupid. The worst is that all the ills come
from whites who from ancient times think that they are the owners
of the world.

And how many unfortunates suffered in the world of the
whites Jesus Christ was crucified. Socrates died poisoned. Ke[n]nedy
died assassinated. John the Baptist decapitated. Joan of Arc was
burned. And me? How will I die? i think that I will die murdered
because the swindlers who handle my books are not leveling with
me. And I despise them because I don't have a great love of material things. I am Black And the Blacks have limited ambition. I got
out of bed at 5 o'clock daylight time. I listen to the steps of happy
women going out for bread. I don't envy them because my day will
come! If God wills! I go in search of happiness. And I will find it

I took in a little puppy who spent the night whimpering. Could
it be cold, or hunger?

What horrifies me is finding out that my daughter complains in
the neighbors' houses that we are hungry. Don't embarrass me
because I work for white men. I can only say one thing: after I
moved away from the favela I became a racist. blacks dancing with

whites don't get the rhythm right, dancing to this music that is called life. If Dr. Lélio and Audálio were intellectuals, they would help me construct the house in parelheiros. But the whites when they have money, they like to be flattered. I am a poetess, I won't flatter anybody.

But Brazil is a portuguesed [*sic*] country. And the portuguese like to be flattered. And people today, more intellectualized want rights and not alms. I spent the morning writing in order not to think of the difficulties that it is difficult for me to transpose. But, I am strong. And the strong don't shy away. But, will I manage to struggle with the cost of living? I am horrified listening to Dr. Lélio de Castro Andrade say that Nobody lives from authors' rights. What torture. to wake up in the morning with nothing to eat. It is the rerun of the favela. Only that now there is no more dona Julita.

I turned on the radio to hear the news. on bandeirantes [a radio station] at eight thirty, I went out with the typewriter to sell it in order to buy food for my kids. I sold it to the merchant who I bought it from, who was horrified, when I told him that I have nothing at home for my kids to eat. He is Hungarian, he commented that writers are exploited by the publishers that the writer dies in misery. That the most inferior class of men are the publishers.

I listened in silence because, I didn't know. The only thing that I know, is that I liked books a lot and wanted to write. The book was my idol. But I am not sad. It is known that the bourgeois class exploits the poor. Only the poor the favelados don't exploit anybody. They exploit the garbage cans.

I showed the merchant the Russian magazine Ogoniok that has an article about me, and I told him that the book is being translated into Russian and that I am going to be invited to autograph it in Russia, that the Russians want to meet me. That the Russian reporter knows that I am hungry. But I will not go because I am already disillusioned with literature. I don't see any just reward.

He told me that I am right and he was thinking. The people who entered seeing me sell the typewriter, were horrified. I met an acquaintance from the favela who was pleased to see me saying:

Carolina, you are in heaven! I told him that I wasn't. That the publisher is a person who wants to oblige the writer to kneel at his feet.

—And I, I only kneel at the feet of Christ because I love Christ.

And the neighbor from the favela said that he was building a house. I sensed that the pride of the person who lives in são paulo is to have a house. He was accompanied by his adopted son, A boy who was going to be tossed into the Tietê river by his own mother. he dashed out dressed only in underpants and grabbed the child from the arms of his monster mother and said that he was going to raise him. And the evil mother answered him with sarcasm: you can raise this shit. A women deprived of maternal love is inhuman. What I hope is that the boy may turn out well in order for his benefactor to be rewarded.

The favela neighbor said goodbye,walking away like a man who is fulfilled in life.

I stayed talking with the owner of the shop who cursed the damned mania of men who make wars. That war ruined Hungary. The clerk went to get money for me. A number of people came into the shop and remained guessing. But I am immunized. I already got accustomed to life's revolts. The clerk came with the money, and gave me 10 thousand cruzeiros. I hastily left and went to get a [tutoring] lesson for João at Don Bôsco. And I showed the article that was in the Russian magazine. That my book Quarto de despejo is to be translated in Russia and I will have an autograph afternoon in Stalin's country. The girls looked over the magazine saying that Ogoniok magazine has no advertising. It's that there it is a socialist country.

I ambled about the waiting room and my gaze was directed to the teachers' room and my eye met the glance of a teacher who headed for the secretary's office and sat down. i was speaking about the cost of living that is oppressing the poor and the fathers of the country still wish to earn 100 million per year.

That way, there will not be any money left to construct schools for the poor people. Will the Brazilian poor be eternally illiterate?

That the inscription on our Flag [Order and Progress] does not hold true in the country, that Brazil needs a Salazar [the Portuguese dictator]. In spite of Salazar not appreciating me I like his politics because he is an austere politician. I heard tell that everything there is on a standard price list.

The teacher who heard me said: So are you the famous Carolina Maria de Jesus? —What are you writing now?

—I am disillusioned with literature. It is very tiring. And there is so much entanglement that my ideals are growing weak. If I had a husband who was competent to take care of my books, I would write but to write with others doesn't work. I looked at the clothes of the portuguese teacher, well pressed. As if he were an actor who was going to perform.

he asked me—why is it that Salazar doesn't like you?

—He didn't consent to my book being published in portugal.

—And the teacher told me that I ought to write Salazar to undo this confusion.

But I am mutilated and sad. I fought and didn't manage to get what I so much desired that is to have a house on a farm because I love the countryside. I appreciate the trees. I like to be in contact with the earth. A young girl came up complaining that her shoe had come apart. I told her that I was going to find a shoemaker to mend it. And I left.

What is unpleasant is to have to walk down the steps because the elevator doesn't work. I looked for the Rapida shoemaker and gave him the shoes. And the shoemaker was handing over shoes to the white women i protested. Well. The man delivers their shoes first because, they are white and I am Black. . . . I continued saying that it used to be that way. if a Black entered a bar to order coffee or to drink cane whisky they became furious if a white man was served first. as much as I spoke nobody paid me any mind.

I told them at the end of next year, that I am going to Russia. That they are translating my book. And I showed the Russian magazine Oganiok. Then all of them began to talk with me at the same time. What a torment to answer all of them at once. But, I was pleased because I saw Brazilians smiling. When a lighter-skinned man went out I gave him a tap on the back telling him that he looks Russian. One man told me he saw me on television.

I received the shoe and asked how much.

—Nothing.

Oh! But is madame waiting? I pressed him.

—It's nothing I already said!

I thanked him and hurried out.

I went into the building where the school is located and entered the elevator. But the elevator doesn't stop at the floors. It goes up and down. I had to climb up on foot and I gave the young girl her shoe.

—How much did you pay?

Nothing!

And I remembered what is written in the Bible. Give for nothing what you received for nothing because God, doesn't appreciate the ambitious. i took João's homework assignment and went out down the stairs and thinking that I ought to get home as quickly as possible to buy bread for João. How horrible to see a son who is hungry. It's a time when a woman is disgusted to be a woman. When I got to the bus stop I was pleased to see the bus. I joked with the receiver of the fare saying to him:

—A good life! You are rich!

He smiled I paid and went to sit down in the front.

I was sitting next to a handsome man who was reading a newspaper. Glancing I saw that it was the Folha de São Paulo, and reported that Admiral Silvio Kech [Heck] was in jail for 30 days for criticizing President João Goulart. Saying that Brazil has no president. This is the impression of the majority. The young man who was reading the Folha de São Paulo agreed with the Admiral i sensed that he wanted to speak with me. I told him that my book is awaited in Russia. And I showed him the magazine.

He mentioned the Osasco crime. The strangling of the young woman, Maria Edina, 21 years old who was murdered by an unknown person. Large cities are depots of the bad and the good.

Unfortunately we see people but we don't see their conscience. I think that if people had a human and a social sense the world would perhaps be more hospitable for us. The young man seated next to me complained of his wife who said to him:

I hope that when you travel by airplane God allows it to crash.

I was horrified because in general, women don't want their husbands to leave this world. But there are women who get annoyed with their husbands after they marry. The women who act like this, are those with mediocre minds. What a clean man. He doesn't have bad habits. i thought: If I could always be seated next to this man! I noted that he was a magnificent man. He told me that he is not proud, it's that he is a northerner from paraiba. I showed him the article in the Russian magazine. He told me that he read my book and did I earn a lot of money? I answered that the book earned a lot of money, it wasn't me who got rich, that I suffer much more since leaving the favela in the favela everybody knew that I was poor and gave me alms. But nowadays, with the publishing of the book, the poor people say that I got rich.

He looked at me compassionately saying: Here in this country I work like the devil so the beautiful people can eat. We spoke about the cost of living that is oppressing the poor people the struggle for life, it began in the favela, and is reaching the middle class. . . .

15 December 1963   Today I am ironing clothes and washing them. I made lunch for the children. I gave João 200 cruzeiros to go to the movies. And 100 to José Carlos. I was washing the dishes when the Black fellow Luiz Carlos Rocha arrived. he came to take me to the dance that is going to take place at Vila Matilde. I told him that I wouldn't be able to attend.

But, I already told everybody that you are coming.

—In that case, I ought to go so you won't be ashamed in front of the people.

I was feeling ill and wanted to lie down. But I went to take a bath, shut the door and delivered the key to dona Elza Reis, asking her to give it to my son José Carlos. She admired my outfit. We took the bus. At anhagabaú we took another one. 3 hours on the bus. It gives the impression that são paulo is a city without end. When we arrived at Vila Matilde I admired the progress of the neighborhood. The next district over is Vila Galvão.

Luiz Carlos Rocha's house is well kept in contrast to mine. The furniture is good quality. And there is so much to eat. And they dress well. In Luiz Carlos's house, there is what I would like to have: happiness. I spoke with Luiz's aunt, who is a shirt maker. And to her husband who was a policeman and afterward was dismissed due to an intrigue. Later his innocence was proven and they asked him to return. If he returns he will be compensated with a million. But, he doesn't wish to return. I appreciate people with opinions. They offered me many things to eat. Chicken and cakes that gave me the impression that I was reliving a scene from A Thousand and One Nights. [They were] well- dressed, wearing expensive neck- laces. they spoke of politicians, who want to earn fabulous sums of money The quantities that the politicians want to earn ought to be used for school construction for the children of the towns. That the politicians pretend that they like the poor people. That the philan- thropy of the politicians is false.

They spoke about my book. That it was Audálio who became rich. These are opinions, that predominate in the minds of the people. I was anxious to return. Luiz's mother went to change her clothes. She is the mother of four sons. —They went for a taxi to take us to the dance. At seven o'clock we left. I paid for the cab because nobody had any change. Luiz told us that I should stay waiting at the door. He went to find the princesses and the queen [of the ball]. When the young girls arrived I went in front. And we were applauded. I saw more than 2 thousand eyes staring at me. It's only that I was no longer that naive Carolina from the favela. I don't believe in anything anymore. We headed for the stage. Luiz intro- duced us. We crowned the princesses and the queen who were

Edith dos Santos, maria Rosa pereira, Rosa Ignacio. each one was accompanied by an escort. I crowned the queen and they went to dance a waltz. After, I cut the cake. What a gigantic cake.

The dance began after I recited my poetry—Noivos—again. I was giving out autographs. And I was speaking with the intellectuals who were present. I was given two bouquets of flowers. I didn't dance. I am discontent with the world. I am in the Autumn of my life. Watching the young people dance I remembered my youth so far in the past. When I found the world to be always pink. But life offers each of us a fraction of suffering. the hall was decorated. with colored balls. They danced to records. At two o'clock the dance was over. What a torment to find transportation. The night was warm. The dance ended without incident. finally we decided to take a taxi in the streets. men were fighting. When I arrived home it was four o'clock.

I was godmother of the second anniversary of The Avalon Club.* I thank them for their attentions to me.

I was sleepy.

16 December 1963 I got up tired at 8 o'clock. I can't stay up all night. I have to sleep so my literary thoughts will predominate. i made lunch for the children and divided the flowers with Dona Elza Reis. i spent the afternoon preparing old clothes. Tomorrow we go to parelheiros. I will weed the corn and water the vegetables. i plan to spend the rest of my days planting at the farm because by 1970 the city of são paulo, will be unbearable for the poor person to live with the cost of living. I am horrified at the number of mortalities at the end of this year. The newspapers say that hunger is the secretary of death.

18 [December 1963] We got up at 7 o'clock preparing ourselves to go to parelheiros. José Carlos, didn't want to go. I cursed him—Dog! you ought to start a union of the lazybones and you will be the

---

* A social club for blacks.

director. I said that João was going along with we and the house was to be closed. Then José Carlos decided to accompany me.

We took clothes and blankets. In Santo Amaro I bought bacon, and meat at the butcher shop 1001. And I told the owner that I am going to live in parelheiros. We were lucky. Just as we were leaving the parelheiros bus arrived and we got on. When I arrived at the farm I saw the electricity wires i thought: it is possible to move-but to my house in the country. We went on for 500 meters. I am happy when I see the house. It is unfinished. The windows are missing. i asked for the hoe from the wife of Senhor Orlando and I went to weed the tomatoes. I seasoned the meat. I cooked the bacon and made macaroni soup.

At night José Carlos slept on the floor. Complaining that he is used to a cotton mattress. What delicious silence. There is no radio. Only the croaking of the toads. What a refreshing sleep. I don't hear those strange voices.

—Carolina is rich!

That Black man, who wants to rent my house has my preference because he was the first to ask for it. I told him to go to the real estate agency since I will only rent the house through an agency. If he didn't call at the agency. . . .

Early in 1964 the armed forces overthrew the constitutionally elected government of Brazil and installed a dictatorship that would last well beyond Carolina's death in 1977. By 1966 she was living in Parelheiros under difficult conditions. Sometimes she had to take her old sack and travel by bus back to the neighborhood of the Canindé favela and scavenge again for refuse to sell. A newspaper published photographs of her collecting garbage but no one came to her assistance even though the story was reported abroad as well as throughout Brazil. Eventually she was able to stay in her house because her two sons were old enough to work. But life remained harsh.

1966

6 September 1966 I woke up at 5 A.M. I made coffee for Vera who goes to school in some other neighborhood. She goes by bus every day and it is 14 km. away from here. I tried to start cooking beans but the wood was wet and it was impossible to [make a] fire. I asked José Carlos to do it for me but he declined saying that it would be too difficult to make it. I cursed him. Nowadays men think everything is too difficult. We started an argument and I left home without having coffee.

I went to Santo Amaro from where I took a bus to Liberdade. I went to Liberdade to go to the bookstore to buy two books for Vera. I asked Sr. Tomaz for the books—Questionário de história e geografia and Questionário de portugues,* by Carolina Rennó Ribeiro. He told me the bookstore had the books. I went to the Brasileiro de Descontos Bank where the invoices from the house in Santana I sold, are deposited. I withdrew the money I needed to buy the books. I passed by the [Largo de] São Francisco [district]

* Social studies and Portuguese textbooks.

where there are used-book bookstores. The seller, a black man, told me he heard from some students that I was a rich woman and that the article [revealing that she was poor again] released by the newspaper O Diário da Noite of 24 June 1966 along with its photographs was printed to sell more papers.

I answered him that the students should go visit me in my house to see the actual living conditions of a miserable writer.

—Do they believe my book gave me a lot of money?

The only thing I know for sure is that the international publishing houses were demanded not to give me a dime. I complained to the book seller by explaining to him that the world is still a black world for the blacks, and that the only good living condition for blacks is in the favela or thrown in the streets. Though it has been almost a hundred years after the abolition, blacks are not free yet. There is a lack of financial independence for blacks. There is no black entrepreneur and a black person is always a socially marginal person. It is so lamentable that blacks had an underdeveloped past to a level that permitted whites to imprison black people in their own land in order to sell them as if they were animals.

We, blacks, are always classified as inferior, we are human merchandise that is never considered during the share of the profits. The illiterate black has to endure injustice whereas the educated black rebels. I talked to this black seller about pungent things that I learned from Dr. Ernesto Miller, a man who spoke six languages and who was responsible for setting up the international publishing contracts for my book. I told him that I was still alive because I found refuge in agriculture by planting manioc. I bought two fairy-tale books in order to reread my childhood days' stories. These stories reminded me of the pleasant large courtyard where I used to spend time together with my mother. At this time I thought the world was beautiful.

I paid 3,000 cruzeiros for the books and I said goodbye. I was walking in the streets and I was thinking: Why do blacks have to be so unhappy? What is our future going to be here, in this country? How would it be if Brazilian whites decide to copy the North American whites' prejudice in relation to blacks?

Here in Brazil the only strata of the population that doesn't like blacks is the mulatto people. The mulatto prefers to marry a stupid white rather than a black woman. And there are blacks who suffer because of this attitude. We, black women, are not to be blamed because we were dispersed all over the world.

During the colonization period, the prevailers needed arms to work on their lands. They couldn't dominate the natives. Only Europeans knew about the existence of blacks and they were responsible for the use of blacks [as slaves] in the world. We are the innocent victims of the incommensurable ambition shared by the people who are the owners of the world. . . .

Nowadays black women are able to study through high school. However, it is much more expensive to be a lawyer, engineer, dentist or physician. In the old days a black person would be already happy if he could have an elementary-school graduation diploma. Now they can get to high school. I bought the tickets. When I was leaving the place I saw Dona Carmen, the nurse responsible for vaccination. We chatted about the actors Manuel Durães, Edith Morais, Celina Amaral, Carlos Diriari and his original laughter. When he doesn't show up in the theater my daughter Vera becomes nervous because, according to her, his appearance in it is the piece's strength.

Dona Carmen asked me for an autograph to give to her son. I gave it to her. I told her about the predicaments I went through in the literature profession. By this time if I hadn't been observant I'd be dead today and my children would be by themselves.

A man recognized me and told me he was a garbage collector who used to work close to the favela where I lived and he used to see me writing. He moved from garbage collector to inspector! I congratulated him for his upward professional move. I said goodbye.

Cars were passing by and I was waiting for a chance to cross the street. Another man recognized me. He wanted to talk about Jacinto, we chatted, I excused myself and got on the bus. In the bus, I started reading the fairy-tale books. The woman [who] sat by me said:

—Carolina, are you reading fairy tales?

—They remind me of the years between 1928 and 1950. Those were peaceful days when we could live more calmly. People were less cultivated but they lived better. Brazil was a country whose main resource was agriculture and its main raw materials were cocoa from Bahia, sisal, and coffee. I remember the healthy court-yard! People were not neurotics nor even [worried about] the infamous inflation that is responsible for all social rebellion and dis-integration. Food prices were indexed, and retailers enforced the laws. An inspector was respected as an authority. In the old times they used to call *bola,* a piece of poisoned meat that a bad person would give to fool and kill a dog. Nowadays we call *bola* the cor-rupted money the inspectors collect from people in exchange for his favors. In the old times poor people were able to have a humane life. It was not usual to see poor people sleeping in the streets as it is now. Everybody had a chance to get married and have a home. Even children's literature was healthier than it is today. The only thing I know is that this industrial Brazil brought more difficulties than prosperity for the people. It brought more poverty for the poor. When a poor person buys a piece of land to build his house he will be in debt for the rest of his life and he will die paying for it. After the woman I was talking to got off the bus I tranquilly came back to my reading till I got to Santo Amaro.

I went to the newspaper Gazeta de Santo Amaro to look for my poetry notebook that I had lent to Dona Maria do Carmo. Quarto de Despejo will be published in Russia in October and I need my notebook so I can show it to the Russian journalists when they come to interview me. This poetry book can help the Russian editor to advertise the book I wrote though I have no royalties rights on it. I regret I wrote it because the actual victims of it were my chil-dren who had no opportunity to learn and develop skills for a pro-fession. Dona Julieta advised me to enroll them at *SENAI* [a government-run training institute] when they got in the 4th grade. I couldn't do it because I had urgent tasks in the favela.

I went to shop at the Casa Santo Amaro store. Japanese people are nice and they sell good food products. After I paid they gave me the receipt which I kept in order to participate in the Talão da Ilusão contest [a lottery]. I intended to go back home but before I stopped to buy some cheese and oil. The bags were heavy. A black woman helped me to carry them to the bus stop and helped me to get on the bus with them. There was no place to sit down and I stood up all the way back.

I looked around and the view was plain of ample fields full of trees. We note that the population is really spread out only along the seacoast. I sat down as soon as a seat got free. A mulatto man sat by me. I was surprised because, usually, mulatto men prefer to stand up the whole way rather than to sit close to a black woman. He told me he is building a *granja* [farmhouse] on the outskirts of Parelheiros. When it is ready he will bring his wife to live there with him because it is too expensive to pay the bus every day. The place is being financed by the Bank of Brazil. We got to the 34th Km and I had to get off the bus.

The man who is building the granja helped me with the bags. I want to thank this mulatto man who is not haughty with blacks. It was an ordeal to carry the bags. My children were not waiting for me. The bags were heavy because I was carrying corn for the animals. A woman tried to help me but she gave up, the bags were too heavy. We all know that [Sampson] belongs in the Bible. I felt relieved when I saw my son José Carlos and Vera. José Carlos told me: You know mom, the black man Negro Aço [Black like steel] went to the police and sued you. Sr. José, Negro Aço's employee brought and gave me the summons. You have to be there at 8 P.M.

I had just got home at 7:30 P.M. and I got nervous because I don't like arguments. My dream was to be able to be nice to everybody. However, this Negro Aço is arrogant and has a psychological complex as if he were rich. I went to bed without eating because I was nervous. But I have to be ready for whatever may happen.

Arlindo Sebastiane Paschoalini asked me to loan him 1,000 cruzeiros. I did. I sold him a female pig through his employee, Jorge. The pig ran away from him and came back to my house because it had nothing to eat there and it was starving. Even animals cannot stand famine. The female pig stayed with us for six days. José Carlos notified him and told him to go pick it up. João, my son, told him that he was going to charge them 1,000 for the food we gave the pig. In the afternoon Arlindo sent Jorge, his employee, to get the pig back.

I told him I wouldn't give it back if he didn't pay me! I am tired of being exploited by these opportunists. There are some types of men who like to exploit others. Jorge left my home and told Arlindo Sebastiane Paschoalini that I did not want to give the pig back to him. Arlindo came to my place and called me. I didn't receive him because I was frying sardines. I told him that if he wanted the pig he should bring the money. He got mad! —You, disgusting black tramp. You are a sculpture made of shit! You are a thief!

—What did I steal from you, dog? When you needed money I gave it to you. Those who resist to pay are those who don't like to give back the money they owe. To think that you wanted me to lend you 20,000 . . .

—Your place is in the favela, filthy woman!

—You are a dog. You left Jundiaí because your father in law prohibited you from playing cards! You are avaricious [because] You complained about inviting Paulo the Japanese's family for a *feijoada* lunch. You charged 1,000 cruzeiros for a package of cigarettes that my children went to buy for me.

Arlindo kept saying that I should find a man to help me in my life. I told him to show me one and that I doubted he could find a real man in this whole country. If he did I would like to be introduced to him because up till now I had only seen free samples of them. I don't see men. I see miniatures of them. And he was one of these miniatures. While I was arguing with him, Vera kept saying

—That is enough, mommy!

—I am going to complain to Sr. José Gomes, because the way things are going . . .

Sr. José Gomes is the owner of the plot [where Arlindo works]. It only takes to pronounce this name to make the argument get to an end. It is an epigraph for any quarrel. Arlindo Sebastiane Paschoalini took the money out of his pocket and told Vera that the pig was already with him and he would never have kept it without paying for it. Arlindo is Bocage's pupil, he puts his shoes on and runs away.

I shouted as he left that black people should not favor white people because they get spoiled and think that can have everything for free. They think they don't have to pay us because we are black.

—I pay for the food I have home.

[Arlindo said:]—Don't you want to be friends with your neighbors?

—C'mon Arlindo! Who in Brazil has a neighbor? Brazilian people are haughty, they don't go to each other's place. In this country, when we get sick neighbors run away from you afraid of being asked to help. You wait for my sons and make the deal with them.

He gave 5,000 to Antonio, the printer's son, to go to Sr. Manoel, the Portuguese, to get it changed. The money Arlindo had must have had been lent. I noticed he was not happy about being poor. These days we are living now make people to want to be rich, instead of getting rich they become neurotics and rude.

7 September 1966 I woke up at 5 A.M. to help Vera to get ready, because she is going to march in the parade, though I told her not to go. However she answered me that when a child is in school she has to obey the teachers. I thanked her for the lesson she gave me for being so sensible. I walked her through the most dangerous part of the road. After it I came back picking up woods on the way because it has been two months since they last delivered gas home. As soon as I got home I made coffee and fried some small cakes because bread, poor people cannot buy it. For poor people, bread is going to be something to remember. They will tell their grandchildren about the old year of 1966 when the president of Brazil was

Marshall Humberto de Alencar Castello Branco—a government that came after the 1964 revolution. He didn't know he was going to be the president of Brazil, he had no political preparation and his government was very confusing. Cost of living became unbearable. People live as they may. [These were] tragic times. Millions of people contracted tuberculosis, 900 people per day. Women and children cried with hunger in the streets.

Newspapers and radio got united to address the cost of living issue. However, selfishness won. Finally, I hope [that] abundance will predominate in the world. All for one and one for all.

My children had their coffee and I was doing my laundry when Sr. José, a poor black man, showed up. He is Negro Aço's employee. Negro Aço pays him 1,000 cruzeiros daily and demands that he calls him boss and that he calls his son little boss. As I said before he has a psychological complex of being rich. This arrogance is outdated. Sr. José delivered to José Carlos another summons against me. I was pissed off and I cursed because I have work to do and it takes time to go to the delegacy in Parelheiros.

This is my situation, I have to show up at [the delegacy at] 8 P.M. because it was alleged that my pigs were ruining my neighbor's plantings. The fact is that Negro Aço bought a plot next to mine. He is the ugliest man I have ever seen in my life. And, he is married! This woman who got married to Negro Aço has a courage that is admirable! My dog, Tiger, is more beautiful than he is. I have never sued anybody. I believe that those who make harm will pay for it. We just have to be patient and wait [for justice].

When Sr. Rubens Ribas arrived, I waited for an opportunity to complain about his employee and to ask him to restrain him. When I saw that he was leaving, I went to talk to him:

—Good morning Sr. Rubens.

He was surprised because I had never talked to him before. He is a mulatto and I have heard that he dislikes black people. I have already said in my book Quarto de Despejo: mulattos are the children of blacks but they dislike black people. In the bus, a mulatto prefers to stand up all the way rather than sit by a black. Even the poet Gonçalves Dias was a racist and wanted to marry a white woman.

9 September 1966 I [finally] made it to the Parelheiros police station. Negro Aço, whom I baptized "werewolf," showed up, too. The subordinate delegate and the civil guard, Sergeant Reinaldo Rocha who was very educated, [were there]. I noticed that negro aço was sad. He was under the influence of alcohol. The guard wished to be a singer. I promised I would help him by buying all his records. I told them that I was going to sell the pigs in order to make them stop bothering my neighbors. I learned that whenever I live there will always be a neighbor to bother me.

The state [government] should build schools and pharmacies in rural areas, there should be dentists, social welfare centers and clinics to teach hygiene to the people. For most Brazilians, Brazil is only Rio de Janeiro and São Paulo. These are urban areas and people forget about the rural areas. . . .

If Christ comes back he won't die crucified. He will die of hunger and because of the cost of living.

Politicians who didn't complain when their terms were suspended did so because they had no strength to prove their suitability. I don't believe in it.

If Christ comes back he will die in a car accident because of the new laws regarding traffic in São Paulo. . . .

16 October 1966 Today is Sunday and I intended to spend the day calmly reading and writing. However, negro-aço's mistress started to curse me. She said that the pigs invaded her backyard. There is nothing planted there but some cauliflower. I asked her how much destruction had the pigs caused. This only question was enough to show how a Northern Brazilian woman can be a macho person.

Negro aço filled another complaint against me at the Parelheiros station. He did so backed by his companion who is a Northerner and illiterate person. She is also an alcoholic. What a pain in the neck and ugly woman! I cursed at her. I hate polemics and I am interested in everything related to women's issues.

She wants to change the fences and she cuts the barbed wires I set causing me a great financial cost waste. I demanded José Carlos look for Sr. José Gomes, the plot owner. He sent a message and José Carlos showed this message to Sr. Rubens Ribas, negro-aço's boss. What an ugly man he is! His body has spots just like a frog does. Sr. Rubens told me that he had found a new tenant. I wondered where was negro-aço going to find himself a new job. He has nothing in his favor to get a good job because employers require people to be good-looking. In the evening, José Carlos went to the delegacy. Negro Aço and his Northern woman went too. I didn't show up. He is Sr. Rubens Ribas's employee however he is never working but always he spends the hours sitting under the trees [and] listening to the radio.

It is sowing time and negro-aço didn't prepare the land yet. That is the way it is. It is stupid to trust small farms to tenants. They don't produce. Negro aço cut my barbed wires. The policeman told him that the only solution to finish his quarrel with me would be a club. I believe that there are men who dislike me because I am a person who never bends or breaks. I don't like parties. I like to be with myself and with God. I don't take alcohol. The men I choose and appreciate are very educated. When I get interested in a man it is because he has distinction. I don't like banal men. . . . These following men I admire: Jacinto Figueira Jr.; Sr. José de Sá Gomes Mendoza Enriquez, the Chilean; Moacir Franco; Ronaldo de Morais; Remo Pongella; Dr. Adhemar de Barros; Oito Velho; the Cuban Aleixo Carpentier; Ignacio de Loyola [the Saint].

In Brazil, we have no problem with the soil. Everything we plant will be harvested. But we don't have a great production. What do we lack? Courage, good will, culture, or government help?

It is touching to see people grieving and not to be able to help them.

A Portuguese man told me—Those who carry Brazil are Portuguese and Japanese people. I wonder if this is really true.

People should verify this saying because I don't conceive of people hurting Brazilians' moral strength.

What I notice is that Portuguese who discovered Brazil had no culture to manage and administer this country. What I notice is that it became too difficult to live among illiterate blacks and [they] promulgated a law that permitted blacks to attend school. In 1920 blacks were allowed to register. My grandfather was happy and said:

—White people are getting better. They created a fund to give free books to blacks.

But the spoiled Portuguese remained in the corners gossiping. I remember these times. After the abolition and the Republic there was in Brazil a majority of illiterate people. Brazil was coveted [because of] the gold it possessed. Gold that should had been used in culture for the people. Those who remained here intended to go back again to their country. However, if Brazil is still such a big country, in territorial extension, we owe this to the Portuguese who have the right to be considered the homeowners.

People talk about reforms. To me, the best reform would involve the returning to rural areas those who have no conditions of living in the cities. What is lacking is action.

As well as we need light to see in the dark, we also need to be good.

The best match in the world are honesty and goodness.

[No month and date, 1966] Brazil. He is a 6'2" young man who considers himself a mature man whose heart is weak. This person feels very ill and discouraged because he used the cruzeiro to heal his disease and this treatment proved to be ineffective. He remained anemic.

Therefore, it was decided to bring a doctor from the United States. This physician gave Brazil some dollar injections. He got better for a while but the treatment didn't heal him. Since Brazil wanted to be wealthy and strong he went to see an English doctor who gave him some pound [£] pill medication. This remedy didn't bring the desired result and Brazil was almost losing his hopes of gaining back his strength. Nevertheless Brazil didn't give up and he consulted a German doctor who gave him some pills made from marks. Brazil's hopes were renewed and he felt like being competitive again. However, after a while, his hopes started to fade again. Then, Brazil was advised to consult a Russian doctor but he refused to do so. He was afraid of taking the ruble medicine which was similar to a bandage which would restrict his movements. As a result, he preferred to remain weak rather than to become impaired by this medication. This medication wouldn't allow Brazil and his peers to play the three-day Carnival festivity and would make them work during the three-day party dedicated to the [carnival] Momo king.

Anyway, Brazil is now considering heart transplant surgery. He wants to change his military heart into a civilian heart. [In a smaller but bolder handwriting:] Brazil went under a transplant surgery even before [Dr. Christian] Barnard, when he changed his civil heart and put a military heart in its place. Brazil is getting better from his inflation disease and the tropical anemia is already cured. However he still has tuberculosis, a disease he acquired from his old times of starvation. . . .

There are ill-bred and insolent daughters whose sorrowful parents regret their birthday. I wrote Quarto de Despejo, the book that made me known. According to others, that book was worth millions. However, it brought me, the author, no financial independence. The reason was that it was contracted to the international publishing houses that [do not] give me a dime. My royalties were irritants and disappointments—Fatal Royalties.

Afterword

The Significance of the Unedited Diaries

Carolina Maria de Jesus's newly found unedited writings provide the only first-person description and analysis of life at the bottom of Latin American society written by a member of that marginalized population. Moreover, they depict a wholly different woman than the one presented in her two published diaries. They show that she was much more critical, much more wide-ranging in her observations, and much more nuanced than her published memoirs reveal. Dantas edited out what was controversial or what he thought would impede commercial sales. This should not detract from the recognition that Dantas deserves for what he did in 1958. Had he not recognized the importance of Carolina's writing and spent months nagging publishers to take her diary, its author would have lived and died in squalor, her writings unknown. Dantas was one of a handful of investigative journalists during the late 1950s and early 1960s who challenged the complacent tradition of the Brazilian press of echoing the elite's outlook. His stories quoted ordinary people; it was his quest for sources that led him to Carolina in the first place.

The published diaries—*Quarto de Despejo* and *Casa de Alvenaria*—provide a clear road map to Dantas's editing. Dantas's text contains ellipsis points enclosed in parentheses, contrasting with unenclosed ellipsis points, Carolina's own device for showing the passage of time. It is telling, moreover, where the enclosed ellipsis points occur. More often than not, Dantas removed material directly following a disparaging statement by Carolina about one subject or another or, in several places, a clash between the two of them. Dantas likely edited sections out of the diary when he thought they would be too controversial: when her son José Carlos, for example, arranges for a white woman to work for them as a servant. Nor did Dantas evidently want Carolina to explain fully her complaints again him in their complicated relationship, which she does at length. The editor's practice of taking out potentially controversial portions of the diary suggests further that although he did not write words for Carolina, he believed that he had the right to censor her and that he did this for her protection.

Carolina Maria de Jesus's unedited notebook entries run three to four times longer than the selections in the two published diaries. The language is vigorous, displaying inexhaustible energy. Frequently Dantas took eight to ten pages of entries and boiled them down to a paragraph. One section of more than a hundred diary pages was shrunk to four pages of published text. Some of what was edited out was detail, some of it repetitive, but most of it consisted of nuanced depictions of local politics and Carolina's opinions about her life. Her unedited diaries contain sections on political chicanery, on abortion, and on the daily lives of her children. We have, then, a much more complete picture of Carolina.

Comparing the pages of Carolina Maria de Jesus's diary published in 1960 and the unedited original diary entries, as well as examining entries written after her second diary was published in 1961, sheds important new light on the life and personality of the black

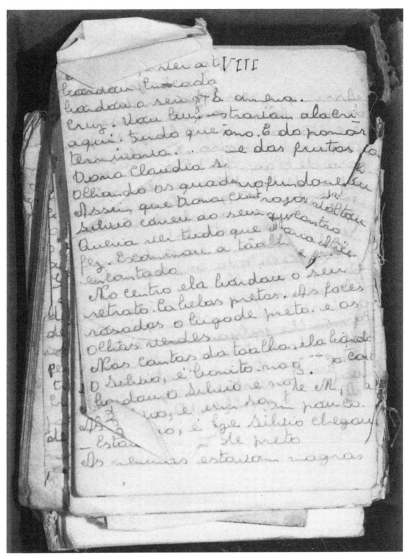

7. Fragments of Carolina's original diary entries. *Vera Eunice de Jesus Lima collection.*

favela dweller who defied all odds in managing to escape with her children from her shanty-town dungeon. Unlike many other Latin American female memoir writers (Rigoberta Menchú, for example, the Guatemalan winner of the Nobel Peace Prize, whose diaries were dictated to a researcher), she wrote everything herself, in her own hand. Carolina reflected on her childhood, work in the fields, her move to the city of São Paulo from the rural interior, and her jobs. She worked as a domestic servant in the homes of the wealthy and, when she was fired from these more steady positions because she had become pregnant, as an oddjobber and eventually a street scavenger, who kept her family alive by foraging for bottles, tin cans, and newspapers to sell for the equivalent of a few cents a day. Sometimes she had to carry more than 220 pounds of paper a day to earn enough to purchase some rice and coffee. And, as she pointed out, her work made her smell like a skunk. It is no wonder that she recoiled when people lauded her after she became famous; by then, she had built a hardened shell of defensiveness around her. She had become bitter: she felt, she said, like a piece of discarded candy in the street being devoured by ants.

Her unedited diary entries offer new insights into the personality of Carolina Maria de Jesus. Dantas knew that Carolina's lack of tact would irritate readers who demanded that lower-class celebrities know their place; as a good journalist he also knew the importance of clear, straightforward writing and of keeping Carolina's message simple. The problem is that the editing muted her personality, which in reality was more feisty and angry than that of the published diaries. Readers of her first diary wonder why Carolina remained so docile. In truth, she was angry and frustrated much of the time. She had a much deeper insight into how Brazilian society functioned, and she was willing to name names. She may not always have been accurate—she was, of course, entirely dependent on her own resources—but her perceptions were tenaciously held. Her experience shows us that indigents were capable of engaging the system that trapped them and that if that system produced individuals whom society considered loose cannons there were many reasons for this. These reasons come through in her unedited writing loud and clear.

Brazilian Society and Politics
Carolina Maria de Jesus's initial success resulted in large part from fortuitous timing. The mid-1950s were a time of anxiety and fear of military intervention after president Getúlio Vargas's suicide in office in 1954. By 1960, however, Brazil had reached a crest of national optimism over economic development and populist reform under Juscelino Kubitschek. Brasília had just been completed. Many Brazilians were coming to believe that it was possible to bring about genuine social change. To Brazilians in 1960, Carolina became a powerful symbol of the belief that with help people could rise out of poverty and transform themselves. Carolina's personal honesty and her unwillingness to fall into despair contributed to the popular view of favela residents as "poor but honest."

Quarto de Despejo probably would not have been published at all if Carolina's diaries had been discovered before 1958 or after 1961. Juscelino Kubitschek's successor in the presidency in 1960 was the mercurial reformer Jânio Quadros. He resigned abruptly in 1961 and fled the country when his government became paralyzed in the midst of rising tensions. His successor was João Goulart, who further polarized politics and heightened ideological rhetoric. In this climate, Carolina's diary would have been dismissed as being too introspective, if not naive. The military dictatorship that seized power by overthrowing Goulart in 1964 was little interested in social reforms. It initiated an era of Chicago-school economic development that greatly increased the disparity between rich and poor and left many Brazilians feeling helpless and angry.[1] When the black performer Josephine Baker revisited Brazil in 1971 after an absence of twenty years, she was staggered by the poverty she saw, especially by black beggar women with infants in their arms. Once, when she was sitting in an elegant Copacabana outdoor cafe, a poor woman with a child approached her table. Josephine Baker took the child in her arms and collected money from her hosts for the woman. "Don't do it," they told her; "these beggars rent children for the day to win sympathy."

What Baker saw was that Brazilian society had become more divided than ever between an affluent world of whites and an almost universally marginalized world of blacks and persons of mixed racial ancestry. Women fared much worse than men in this world. Until 1988, Brazilian civil laws discriminated against women. Before a battered wife could press charges against her husband, he had to give his written permission. Carolina was a poor black woman possessing an iron will and a strong sense of what she wanted. She was aware of the legacies of racism, gender prejudice, and political neglect of the marginalized and the oppressed, but she dealt with these burdens only as they directly affected her.

As a poor black Brazilian woman Carolina faced deplorable prejudice. Given Carolina's unprecedented achievement, it is difficult to understand why so few women rose to her defense when attacks began after her first

flush of fame. Female Brazilian journalists generally treated her as harshly, or more harshly, than did their male counterparts. If Carolina had been a man and therefore had not been considered unemployable in São Paulo after her first pregnancy, she might not have ended up in the favela. The disdain directed at Carolina after her publishing success was a predictable response to an unconstrained, outspoken black female. Romário, the soccer star and luminary of Brazil's 1994 World Cup champions, displayed more petulant and rude behavior than Carolina ever did—in one widely quoted interview, for example, he called Pelé (Brazil's greatest soccer hero) "mentally retarded"—but journalists shrugged off this rudeness as an attribute of Romário's *machismo.* Had Carolina spoken out half as aggressively as Romário, she would have been crucified by the press, not merely deprecated.

Throughout her life Carolina was beaten down by the scorn heaped upon her by society. Even though she shielded herself and her children from the squalid aspects of slum life, these conditions took their toll. By the time she was liberated from the favela by a stroke of fate, it was too late. She was exhausted, too beaten to learn middle-class manners, to censor her thoughts, to remove the layers of suffering from her psyche, or to prescribe solutions for society's ills.

Racial Prejudice

Hostility to her blackness, as well, plagued Carolina ceaselessly. Educated Brazilians accepted the myth of Brazilian racial democracy, despite the clear evidence of racism surrounding them, especially discrimination against people of very dark skin. Carolina's writings describe racist incidents constantly, almost matter-of-factly, long before other Brazilians acknowledged racial prejudice. She casually mentions little things about daily life that most people did not see. She meets a woman named Nair who is so depressed at being black that she does not go to "dances for blacks," a cogent reference to the entirely segregated lives of blacks and whites in her country and especially in São Paulo. She quietly hopes for racial harmony.

When she sees whites and blacks, together she comments on how good this makes her feel, just as she is glad when she visits her black friend Ivete and finds that she lives in a house that is comfortable and well furnished. Her comments about her disappointment in the lack of traditional May Day commemorations in 1961 and her astute observations about the black youth who has lost the use of his hand in an industrial accident but for whom Vargas's labor legislation has done nothing reveal much about the legacy of Getúlio Vargas, who committed suicide before he was to be ousted as president in 1954 and who left nostalgic memories among poor people like Carolina for his populist rhetoric in behalf of ordinary Brazilians.

Foreigners less influenced by the Brazilian racial mythology often recognized race prejudice when they visited Brazil. The Hollywood film director Orson Welles, invited in 1941 to participate in a birthday celebration broadcast for the dictator Getúlio Vargas, was told that he could not bring a black friend with him into the studio. Welles's attempt to film *It's All True,* an anthology film with segments about the Brazilian Carnival and the plight of northeastern raft fishermen, was criticized in a secret letter from Welles's Brazilian production manager to the police in which he complained about Welles's "insistence on emphasizing the unsavory Negro element and mixture of the races."[2]

The attacks on Carolina Maria de Jesus were not seen by Brazilians as examples of antiblack prejudice or discrimination against poor women. At a meeting in São Paulo in December 1992 of students who had read *Quarto de Despejo* for the first time, respondents identified her as a "social victim," "a marginal," and a "favela dweller," not as a black when asked to describe the author. When questioned, not a single participant recalled the passages in her book in which she expressed her pride in being black or her statement that if she were born again she still would want to be black.

In the United States, Carolina's diary was but one of what critics have described, in the 1990s, as a growing "good and valuable stream of . . . books recapturing the life experiences" of blacks. No such stream has yet appeared in Brazil. There, Carolina Maria de Jesus became a heroine for a small group of marginalized black intellectuals and lives vaguely in the memory of scattered groups of poor black women. She did not become "the hope of her community." Brazilian intellectuals on the Left rejected her because she was not, in the words of one of them, a "typical proletarian." She was not a revolutionary; her quest was personal, to fend for and protect her family. Nor did conservatives recognize her, even though she advocated a deeply felt work ethic, did not drink, favored tough police treatment, believed that only rich people should serve in the government, and after 1964 gave statements to the press that seemed to support the military dictatorship. Her political views, in fact, were very much like those of O. J. Simpson in the United States, who declined to support the Olympic boycott in 1968 by blacks for the same reasons that Carolina gave for her lack of political activism: that "you can't change the world until you change yourself."

Why have Brazilians remained

8. Carolina carrying bundles in the street. This photograph probably dates from the mid-1970s and may have been posed. It is not clear whether she is carrying trash or items for her family's use. By now she and her children were living in Parelheiros, on the outskirts of São Paulo, although this photograph seems to have been taken elsewhere, possibly to publicize a collection of her autobiographical essays published in France; the book did not come out in Brazil until 1986 under the title *Diário de Bitita*. *Photographer unknown.*

so silent about Carolina's fate? Why have Brazilian intellectuals like Wilson Martins refused to acknowledge the significance of the fact that a poor, semiliterate black woman published a diary that became a runaway bestseller? Brazilians deal with race on the personal level; in the United States, society is divided into all-encompassing groups (blacks, whites, Hispanics, Asians), and race therefore becomes a matter for governments and laws. Is this explanation sufficient? By choosing to reject Carolina de Jesus's historical importance because her writings are flawed as literature, her detractors have calculatingly shifted the debate away from the causes and consequences of racism and human suffering. Still, it is difficult to understand why Carolina's critics have directed as much personal animosity against her and her writing as they have done. Few Brazilians believe the myth of their nation's supposed racial democracy, fewer still seem willing to acknowledge the need for social injustice to be exposed, except on the level of theoretical abstraction.

Rocketed unexpectedly into fame, Carolina Maria de Jesus went from one kind of pariah status to another: from a woman reviled for her blackness and her illegitimacy and her poverty to a woman mocked for her supposed ingratitude and for her lack of docility. No one attempted to understand her. Brazilian feminists ignored her painful, extraordinarily detailed, and revealing autobiographical writings, about her childhood and her strategies of coping with extreme hardship. They ignored the abuse hurled at her because of the way she expressed her sexuality. Carolina died a broken woman, forgotten in Brazil, her miseries only fractionally relieved, her remarkable life overlooked. She had lived independently with a self-sufficiency that was taken as a rebuke, but she had never lost her way. She stubbornly refused to accept what was considered to be the role of the poor, and especially poor black women, to suffer in silence.[3] Many rejected her because once she became prominent she seemed to them "common" and "ordinary" in the way she behaved. For a society like Brazil's, where being "ordinary" is not admired, few were able to recognize that she was, in fact, an extraordinary human being.

From Favela to Fame

Another contribution is the welter of new information we receive about Carolina's life and, by extension, the lives of the poor in modern society. Her asides provide a rich glimpse into the material culture of shantytown poverty. Carolina goes to bed hungry, but she insists on leading a normal life. As carnival approaches, she obtains four kilos of chicken feathers from an abattoir. Wealthy Brazilians dress in satin and lace; she wears chicken feathers but is equally proud. Her discussions of how her children fare in school reveal the exaggerated dignity with which school officials dealt with her—just as when as a child she was for two years on a scholarship in Sacramento and her teacher insisted on calling her by the formal " senhora" and using her given name, not her nickname.[4] And she is not embarrassed to tell how she disciplines her children, at one point beating one of her sons with a metal rod and chain. She did this because to her the world was so dangerous and inhospitable that beating sense into them was the only parental behavior that she knew. In some ways, Carolina was a Brazilian Tocqueville, exploring the nuances of Brazilian life as if she were a foreign traveler, because her status as an outcast rendered her an alien. Like Tocqueville in 1830s America, Carolina brilliantly described social contradictions and singular secrets.[5] Carolina, moreover, did not only view the social conditions of her country, the way Tocqueville did: she was forced to live them.

The diary entries Carolina wrote after her two diaries were published contain valuable new material. We also have additional detail about the periods those diary entries cover. This information is especially valuable for the insights it offers about Carolina's new role as a celebrity. Brazilian society was not accustomed to indigent black, single mothers talking to reporters, being interviewed on television, or writing about their lives. We should not be surprised at how she reacted. The woeful circumstances of her early life had steeled her against

9. Carolina signing copies of a new edition of *Quarto de Despejo* in São Paulo, 1976. By now, the most repressive phase of the military dictatorship had passed. *Photographer unknown.*

rejection and had given her a tough coat of psychological armor, which she had used in order to survive. As an illegitimate black female brought up in Sacramento in a society of mulattos and whites and a sexually active woman who took whites as lovers, Carolina was always an outsider. Yet, unlike many outsiders, she craved to be accepted, to revel in glory, to be recognized as a writer, to achieve upward mobility. Her comments about why she did not marry offer powerful insights into gender relations among members of her social class.

We learn lessons about the implications of poverty in Brazil. Carolina considered herself rich when Dantas opened her first bank account for her in an amount equivalent to U.S. $858. Her royalties for the sale of her first diary were 12¢ a copy, bringing her, after the first edition of ten thousand copies sold out,

$1,170. Still, the fact that she had to break bills for 1,000 cruzeiros ($4.88) to make change amazed her and her children. She earned the equivalent of $20,000 or $30,000 (in 1999 value) and a few thousand from American and European royalties, an undreamed-of fortune. On her earnings she was able to have a maid, whom she paid $22 a month. When she needed to withdraw $10 from her bank account to pay for supplies to fix her house or for some other purpose, she had to take the bus downtown and wait for hours until Dantas showed up and walked with her to the bank to sign for her. Her wealth disappeared quickly, however. She was besieged by requests to give charity to others, and she did so generously. She had to pay for the unsuccessful manufacture of a samba recording, and she may have subsidized the poorly received publication of her later books. By 1963 she bitterly relates that her family is hungry again and that she had to sell her typewriter to buy food. She died in barren austerity, yet she was the Brazilian author who sold the most copies of books in Brazil or anywhere in the world.

It seems extraordinary that no one in Brazil bothered to speak out against the contempt with which she was treated by most members of the press or to suggest that the conditions Carolina had exposed merited greater national debate. Critics blamed Carolina for failing to adjust to the middle-class life her success had made possible. Reporters who were sent to write about her from time to time consistently showed irritation that this black woman turned social critic was still a complainer. No one acknowledged that for a former slum dweller to have ups and downs or to have difficulty adjusting to a world that reviled people like her was perfectly understandable. By emphasizing her brusqueness and eccentricities the media deflected attention from what she was trying to say. They applied a double standard: after she became famous, reporters mocked her purchases of elegant clothing and her use of cosmetics. Yet, when the novelist Patrícia Galvão (Pagú) dressed the same way two decades earlier, giving an even more garish impression, she became the darling of the cultural elite, especially its leftist members. She was, after all, white, a member of the literary vanguard, the wife of modernist icon Oswald de Andrade, and a communist.

Carolina was human. She revelled in the prominence that came to her in 1960 and was susceptible to notice and flattery, especially from men with higher social status. She was receptive to reporters and other promoters of her talents, and she often confided in them, a trust that they often betrayed. She was quick to report instances of hypocritical behavior or attitudes that she saw as demeaning or derogatory toward the poor, especially blacks. She recorded her horror at hearing a well-dressed Argentine member of the elite claim that the rich were the descendants of Abel and the poor the descendants of Cain. She did unusual things. She tried to learn to drive a car. Perhaps this was the fulfillment of her yearning for middle-class status; perhaps she thought that being seen behind the wheel of an automobile would bring her respect. Instead, it had the opposite effect: when

she drove the driving school car through her neighborhood, her neighbors, who had been hostile to her from the first day she moved in, stared at her as if, in her words, she had "come from another planet."

There is a world of difference in the entries written prior to for 1958 and those written after *Quarto* was published. From a world of violence and hunger she has been transported to a place where people go on diets and take taxis and have their hair done by hairdressers. Before her fame she painstakingly wrote down the addresses of shops and depots where she sold her trash; now she writes down the names of reporters and television personalities and consuls and the addresses of newspapers and national magazines. She has enough to eat, but she often feels tired, even exhausted. The way people treat her confuses her. In the favela she trusted nobody. Now she trusts others, although they often betray her. Her life becomes more complicated, and she loses her self-confidence. A wistfulness takes hold of her personality, and she is much less feisty now, but she continues to

10. Carolina on her property in Parelheiros, c. 1976. *Photographer unknown.*

struggle to raise her children in the midst of her confusion. She writes increasingly of her desire to leave the city and live on a farm, in solitude. She has learned the bitter truth that even as a celebrity she will never be treated like other celebrities; she will always be expected to know her place. Sometimes she is so lonely that she goes back to visit the streets where she used to scavenge for paper.

There are delicious ironies as well. Once a pariah, she now has a maid named Dona Alba— Carolina is careful to put "Dona" before her name, a symbol of respect—who is from Uberaba, near where Carolina was born. Alba is Italian and, as Carolina notes, resentful at having to work for her, even though sometimes she is obsequious. She cooks foods like cornmeal polenta, which Carolina does not like, but Carolina is too intimidated to tell her. Living in a two-story house brings privileges, but some of them are dubious. Now that

Carolina is famous, her white neighbors permit their daughters to play with Vera. But Carolina notices that they do so reluctantly, as if they were afraid to dirty themselves by playing with a black.

Questions remain that we cannot answer. Where did Carolina acquire the books that she mentions she was reading in her shack when the weather was too bad for her to go out and scavenge for junk? What services did the social worker assigned to the Canindé favela provide? Why did she refuse to work full time for Dona Julita, who frequently gave her things she needed and for whom she occasionally cleaned house? Did she value her independence that much? What means did Carolina use to reach the mayor's office, which provided hospitalization for her after a woman in the favela stabbed her? Where did her suitor Luiz come from? Who is Ely da Cruz, the woman she takes into her house to live with her? What was in the notebooks Carolina mailed by registered mail to publishers in New York? Did she keep copies? Were the packages acknowledged? This

was after Dantas discovered her but more than a year before *Quarto* appeared in print. Sending the notebooks by airmail cost her a small fortune: to buy the stamps she had to sell 360 scrap oilcans and 60 wax containers, and still she came up short when she went to the post office. She never recounts the full story, and we can only guess.

Moral Principles

Her diary entries reveal a homespun philosophy that demands honesty in relationships mainly between people, mainly men and women. Carolina, whether she knew it or not, was a practicing feminist in a society that was overwhelmingly dominated by males. She refused offers of marriage because she knew that the men would not respect her and would treat her as their servant. "I have loved," she wrote, "but I have never been in love." She defied the Roman Catholic Church's insistence on marriage as the basis for having children and raising them, and she insisted on choosing her own sexual partners, in all known cases white men. Even living amidst garbage and sometimes covered with sores, she found herself to be sexually attractive to white men from higher social classes, yet she never betrayed her independence to exploit this, even for the benefit of her children.

She decried the suffering of undernourished and illiterate children and preached basic family values, which she held as guiding principles, not only after she became famous but before. She understood that children of alcoholic mothers may be developmentally disabled. She insisted that mothers were duty bound to observe their children, care for them and protect them from danger, and discipline them when they were in error. Other favela parents shrugged when their children stole or cursed or acted irresponsibly; Carolina thrashed her children when they did something she considered improper. In a society in which the poor had for centuries drowned their pain in *cachaça,* she refused alcohol and tried (ultimately in vain) to keep her sons from liquor as well.

She lashed out at sycophants, playboys, perverts, unfaithful husbands, drunks, layabouts, and people who refused to work and who lived on the dole. She scored politicians who cynically promised what they never intended to deliver. She demanded that society show responsibility in providing education and health care and housing for the poor, and she always protested within the system; she was not a revolutionary and showed no sympathy for those who called for radical reform. She criticized Brazil out of her love for her country. She never alienated herself from the law or from political authorities, and she cultivated some of them to obtain favors, as when she got the mayor of the city, Adhemar de Barros, to pay for a hospital stay. She took landlords and uncaring politicians to task. Her newspaper interviews and statements to the press gave her a passport to the offices (but not the hearts) of local officials, publishers, media people, and some members of the elite. Despite her generally favorable disposition toward the have-nots in society, her observations about people constantly staring at her rather than helping her when she had a hard task to perform were a reminder to her of how people perceived her—as a dirty black woman.

Her writings reveal how far Carolina served as an intermediary, a kind of tour guide through the usually hidden world of poverty for the curious and for those who advocated reform. As soon as her diaries were serialized by Dantas's newspaper and before the first diary was published, she guided not only Dantas but other newspapermen and photographers through her favela. Even after her celebrity had passed, she served as a conduit into the slums for film makers, out-of-town journalists, and politicians. When the Finnish writer Eva Vastari stayed at her house, she turned over her children's bedroom to the visitor. Eva paid her nothing, although she paid for food; Carolina acted as her personal escort. These visits must have been difficult for Carolina. Reporters judged her clothing and the way she kept her house. On one occasion, Vastari accused Carolina's children of stealing money from her purse. Carolina defended her children tooth and nail, yet she pulled her son José Carlos aside and told him that if he was guilty she will feed him poison.

She provides rich evidence about the changing composition of favelas in São Paulo as migrants from Brazil's north and northeast poured into the slums of the industrialized cities of the south. Blunt and opinionated, Carolina looked down on these migrants, in part because she was from the interior of Minas Gerais—a place of higher status than the northeast—but mostly because the hapless migrants seemed to her to gave given up. They lacked her burning work ethic and her sense of civic duty. Carolina's frequent calls to the radio patrol—the Brazilian equivalent of calling 911—and to the police document her determination to rid the favela of troublemakers and lawbreakers. She was especially harsh on gypsies, because they were unclean and because their habit of walking naked titillated the other favelados and therefore raised tension in an already volatile environment. Foreigners, namely, Portuguese but also some Japanese, were also changing the character of the favela population. Carolina was astonished by a Japanese woman who claimed that children were "worse than the devil" and in her diaries

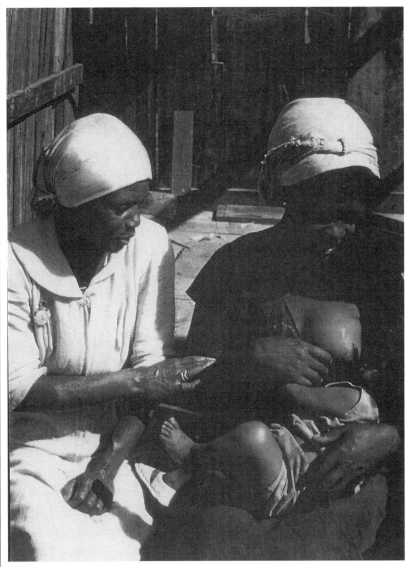

11. Carolina with a nursing mother, c. 1976. *Photographer unknown.*

derided the woman for "engaging her mouth before engaging her brain." On the other hand, she admired Japanese men, whom she considered hardworking, eager to better themselves, and not disdainful, like the northeasterners.

Her writing about her calls to the radio patrol and the police, her conversations in the street, and her appeals for medical assistance all were aimed at dispelling what she considered the elite's contempt for those forced to live in slums and shantytowns. This is significant given that Carolina wrote during a period of peak interest in Brazil in social reform and at a time when public sentiment (and real estate speculation) focused on favela removal as a leading solution for the expanding urban centers. After she became a celebrity, she was always aware of the tenuousness of her fame, and she flailed away at social ills as if she knew that she had little time left before she would fade from public attention.

The role she assumed as spokeswoman for the downtrodden empowered her. She maintained her stoic impatience and did not let insults get her down. She sat quietly outside offices of would-be publishers, waiting to speak with people whom she knew were inside although their secretaries had assured her that they had not returned from lunch. It irked her that her desire to purchase a new house in the countryside and pay the installments from the rent of her present house was repudiated by her sponsors and publishers. Still, she persisted, resisting affronts to her social status, her skin color, and her gender. She refused to be defeated by people who inwardly snubbed her while they outwardly, and often begrudgingly accorded her her due. She shocked and charmed, cajoled and flirted. At the height of her popularity as a public figure she threatened to cancel her publicity trip to Argentina and Chile if her sponsors did not guarantee that in her absence they would provide money to buy food for her children, who stayed behind in São Paulo. She knew that despite the clamor about her diary no one really cared for her and that she was and always would be a loner, the sole responsible person in her life and the lives of her young children.

Not surprisingly, Carolina's

written observations were sometimes confusing. Some readers will find her contradictory; others, elusive and inconsistent. Not only was she a self-taught writer, but her life was tormented by hunger and by the frequent crises that afflicted favela dwellers. When the rainy season came to São Paulo, her shack, along with all the others in her favela on the banks of the Tieté River, was flooded, and her family had to find alternative housing. Often this amounted to living in doorways or under bridges until the waters subsided. Frequently her routine was disrupted by the necessity to protect her children from threatened violence or by her inability to find sufficient amounts of paper and metal to buy food. She had to spend hours each day spanding in line at the single water spigot in the favela to draw water. Given all of this and her personal rejection of what she considered the immoral and lazy character of her neighbors, she underwent mercurial mood shifts from despair to joy to hope to dejection. At the height of her fame her writing style became more reflective. She never shed her depression though,

although she had an astonishing ability to rise to the occasion and recover when—a reviled, unemployed black single mother—she had to fend for her children and keep her family afloat. Consider her use of the word *povo* or 'people.' Sometimes she seems to refer to people in general; other times she clearly means the poor people, her fellow members of the Brazilian underclass. In her publicity tour of Argentina in 1961 after the publication of the Spanish translation of her first diary, she used the same word, *povo,* to refer to the Argentine population at large and to the inhabitants of the Buenos Aires slums, the notorious *villas miserias.*

The Unedited Diary Entries

For the published versions of *Quarto de Despejo* and *Casa de Alvenaria,* Audálio Dantas shortened most of the entries and cut out large sections he considered repetitious or otherwise unnecessary. He deleted details of her morning routine, her repetitive comments about neighbors, and her accounts of repaying loans or paying off bills to local merchants. For some reason, Dantas switched around the dates of some of the entries, adding sections from other entries, and in general taking small liberties with the diaries to enhance their readability.

As a result the first diary, *Quarto de Despejo,* ran only 181 pages with fairly large type and wide margins. More than two-thirds of Carolina's diary entries covering the period of the published diary were deleted and only reappeared twenty-five years later when her daughter, Vera, revealed to us their existence. Yet this is not to say that *Quarto* suffered because of the deletions: its simple brevity contributed to its power as a social document and testimony. But the edited notebooks projected an image of the author that shortchanged her personality, simplifying it and robbing it of the contradictory elements that made Carolina more human than the packaged diaries suggested.

The edited Carolina Maria de Jesus, then, comes to us as a poor, black single mother and shantytown dweller who is observant, conscious of her surroundings, dutiful toward her children, and judgmental toward favela neighbors of whom she disapproved. In contrast, the unedited diaries show her in a far less restrictive way. The questions that fly off the pages of her published diaries—why she was always so docile, so single-minded, so patient—come closer to being answered. Instead of being resigned, her personality flares up unpredictably and then subsides. She suffers mood swings. She spends a fortune to repair an old radio someone gives her, then throws it to the floor and smashes it when her son João taunts her. Sometimes she is feisty and manic; other times she lapses into depression. She not only records her observations but she describes them in great detail, belying the common stereotype that marginalized victims of society do not have complex explanations for their plight. She is astute and politically savvy in her criticisms, so much so that Dantas felt that he had to sanitize them lest her militant tone compromise her promoters and publishers and those who sympathized with her.

Carolina's two published diaries appeared in 1960 and 1961, at the height of national and local political reformism in Brazil. But this was reformism held in check—not the leftism of militants but a measured set of demands that stopped well short of calling for structural social change. By packaging her as a simple woman whose complaints seemed poetic in their innocence, Dantas managed to create diaries that neither threatened readers nor motivated them to demand political reform. What she really said in her diaries would not have ingratiated her with the authorities in São Paulo. Had Dantas's cuts not been made, it is likely that the editors at Francisco Alves would not have taken the chance of publishing them, and, had this occurred, with certainty Carolina's writings, recorded in stained notebooks that she found in the trash, would have vanished into oblivion.

She minces no words: her observations about sexuality among her fellow favelados is more explicit that anything published in the late 1950s. The exactness of her charges shatters our preconceptions about how marginalized people relate to the system that overwhelms them.

Dantas's editing retains some of the shocking revelations but on the whole obscures the extent to which favelados like Carolina struggled to engage the system. Carolina recorded people's reactions to what they perceived as unjust prices and fare increases; she reacted to measures taken by São Paulo's mayor, Adhemar de Barros, to use police to prevent riots. She demanded accountability for public figures, particularly for actions that affected poor people. In so doing, she was advocating active political citizenship for people denied voices by a system that gave them the vote but that paternalistically doled out to them empty rewards, such as the set of playground equipment donated to Carolina's favela on the eve of the 1958 mayoral election—an act that, ironically, made it possible for Dantas to meet Carolina and bring to light her diaries. Her diaries show us that even favelados wanted to be informed, wanted to be consulted, wanted explanations for urban renewal, fare increases, the unavailability of hospital beds in emergency wards. An outspoken nobody, she risked arrest for her militancy.

How sad it is that after she was discovered she was showcased as a sideshow freak—an illegitimate black scavenger who dreamed about heaven—while her courage was ignored and her prescriptions for needed social change brushed aside.

We see Carolina Maria de Jesus as a much more nuanced, complex person than the one we knew before. *Quarto de Despejo* offered details of her daily life as well, but Dantas carefully balanced her criticisms with passages of idealism and hope. Taken as a whole, Carolina's written output swings the balance to the darker side. Her unedited words, phrases, and paragraphs provide invaluable new evidence about the way poor people related to their world and how they coped with it. Her diary entries were consistent in some ways, but not in others. She started most of them in the same way, recounting when she woke up in the morning and what chores she set out to do, and then following the day's activities hour by hour. Some of her entries were brief; others went on for pages. However rambling her

style, she is relentless in her opinions. Politicians stir unrest, she says over and over again, because they do not subsidize the prices for basic foodstuffs and because they forget their promises once elections are over. Her words are stern: a man says that someone will kill the mayor if he does not help the people; criminals and drunks will overrun the shantytowns unless there are more police.

To gauge the extent of Dantas's deletions, compare the English version of *Quarto de Despejo* with Carolina's original, unedited entries, set in italics, for 31 October 1958.

I went to get water. How wonderful! No line! because it is raining. The women of the favela were upset and chattering. I asked what happened. They said that Orlando Lopes, now the owner of the electricity, had beat Zefa. And she reported him and he was arrested. I asked Geraldina if it was true. She said that it was.

Nena said that Orlando hit Zefa for real. I went for some paper.

If he beats up Pitita, he will see Pitita is the biggest whore in the shantytown.

I heard the women say that people with children should behave themselves. At the door of Zefa's house there is a line of men. *I made coffee and sent João to buy 10* [cruzeiros] *worth of bread.*

They went off to school, and I went out with Vera. The policemen are still on the streets. I met Nena and her mother Dona Dindita.

Vera went past the slaughterhouse and asked for a sausage. I earned 106 cruzeiros. Vera got six cruzeiros, because she went into a bar to ask for some water and they thought she was asking for money.

The people are saying that Dr. Adhemar raised the fares to punish the people because he lost at the ballot box. *At the bus stop I heard a man say he was a supporter of Adhemar. The others in the line reacted and an argument began. First there were only 2. Then others. There is a rumor that Dr. Adhemar is in Rio de Janeiro. I think: when a politician's decisions displease the people he should not disappear He should stay around and explain why it was necessary to raise the fares He who does something and flees, is a rogue. That he wants to replace what he spent. The people are saying that Dr. Adhemar raised fares to get back at them for not voting for him. Politicians don't lose anything. When he loses at the polls he grabs the voters and tans their hides, and then, after using them in this way, forgets how they helped him get into office.*

I paid the shoemaker for fixing Vera's shoes. Then I went shopping. I bought rice, black beans and soap and the 100

cruzeiros disappeared. I remembered the words of the black man who gave Vera 5 cruzeiros. That the paulistas are wrong, [that] the strike should be a general one. Fight the food prices that oppress us. That it is not only the CMTC [Municipal Transport Company] that exploits the people, exploitation is general.*

When I got home the boys were already there. I heated the food. There was very little. And they stayed hungry. *I'm not irritable because I know that it doesn't solve anything.*

In all the streetcars they've put a policeman. And the buses too. The people don't know how to fight back. They should go to the Ibirapuera Palace [the mayor's office] and the State Assembly and give a kick to those shamefaced political pygmies who don't know how to run the country.

I am unhappy because I didn't have anything to eat.

I don't know what we are going to do. If you work you go hungry, if you don't work you go hungry.

Many people are saying that we must kill Dr. Adhemar. That he is ruining the country.

Whoever travels 4 times on the bus contributes 600 to the CMTC. Whoever takes the streetcar and the bus spends 1000 on transportation only. At this rate nobody can save for the future. Bus fares are too expensive. It can't go on like this. Nobody can take it anymore.

In the morning when I was leaving, Orlando and Joaquim

Paraíba came back, returning from jail.[6]

Carolina's entry for 7 November 1958 was omitted entirely from *Quarto de Despejo*. The following selection is a literal translation of her diary entry:

I couldn't sleep: Vera began to cough I got up and went to Dona Black Maria to ask for a Melhoral [a brand name for aspirin]. She have me 1 Cibalena [another brand]. I was afraid to give it to Vera because [when] she had the injection at the Central Senhor João Pires told me that for 2 days she could not injure herself because the injection could not be reapplied. I thought about the horrible life of Brazil's poor people. And I am also one of them.

I got up and went to fetch water at 5:30 a.m. I lit the stove and didn't go to buy bread since I had no money. I made a porridge of cornmeal and asked my children to do me the favor of eating it. They agreed to. Vera didn't want to. I went to ask Rosalina to lend me her cart to take scrap metal pieces to the depot. She said that she had lent the cart [to someone else]. That when the guy returned from the market I could use it. I got João ready for school and I went after the cart. I waited for the guy to empty it. I went to sell scrap metal bits. I took Vera and José Carlos.

As I approached the Guine bakery, there was a woman washing the pavement and cussing out dr. Adhemar. —It is the mayor who ought to live on this dusty street. The only thing that he wants is our money. He ought to wet down the road. I am tired of cleaning the dust, and the house is always dusty—i thought of the Vicious Circle [because] if it rains, there is mud, the mayor is no good because he doesn't pave the streets. If it is sunny and there is dust, the mayor is no good because he doesn't wet down the streets. When will the people understand that when it rains it is muddy. And when it shines it is dusty. Political careers are thorny Senhor Manoel weighed the scrap metal pieces I earned 70. I bought bread, and a cup of coffee with milk for the kids. Two bars of soap 9 cruzeiros each. I was horrified! 1 bar of soap 9 cruzeiros—at this rate the poor is a candidate for dirtiness It only took Adhemar to back one price rise, everything went up. If Dr. Adhemar wins over the people and the fare increase holds, things are going to get worse at this end.

Dr. Adhemar isn't affected because he doesn't use public transportation.

—He only uses it to inaugurate it. It is injustice to increase the only transportation of the poor.

The people ennoble dr. Adhemar's philanthropic qualities and said:

—Dr. Adhemar . . . he is a saint. Even my daughter Vera Eunice said: that he is a saint. I heard a lot of people say that body and soul dr. Adhemar was or is going to heaven.

—*Nowadays I hear people say he is going to hell. That he is the devil's assistant.* —*The people say: that dr. Adhemar is no good.*
—*That dona Leonor* [the mayor's wife] *is good.*
So let's adopt the old proverb: for the saint they kiss stones.
I went after José Carlos who was taking his time. I told him to buy meat. When I passed the warehouse I saw the Municipal trucks moving people evicted from Municipal land. They are cussing dr. Adhemar—but, they haven't paid rent for 4 years. They should have said: Thank you, City Hall. But, more thankless are born than thankful.
The weeds multiply easily. The owner of the dona Neusa candy factory watched the women fighting with the supervisor. . . .

Dantas did the same kind of editing with *Casa de Alvenaria*. Consider the diary entries for 18 November 1961, written while Carolina was in Argentina on a publicity tour.[7] Both diary entries begin with Carolina awakening at 3 A.M. and writing until 9 A.M. Both offer an account of her autograph session; the edited entry lists the event to have taken place at a book store, Libraria Atlántida, on Calle Florida; the unedited diary mentions the Libraria Florida: perhaps Carolina was mistaken. The sentences Dantas deleted are shown in italics:

We spoke about the resignation of [Brazilian president] Janio [Quadros]. *I predicted his downfall. It wasn't a surprise for me. he is an actor. He is not a politician. There are two politicians: Dr. Leonel Brizola and Dr. Adhemar de Barros. But the people do not understand Dr. Adhemar.* The table was full of sweets and liquors. . . . The women elegant and polite. I thought: this is a reprise of Victor Hugo's story of the nobles and the paupers. They asked me to recite a poem. I recited "The Landowner and the Peasant," as requested by Audálio. *And I told them that it was the landowners who planted the favelas in the major cities. The condition of a pauper who lives near a rich person is such that the rich person is always thinking that the poor one is going to rob him of something.* I was horrified listening to a woman say that the poor are the sons of Cain. And the rich are the sons of Abel. But Abel didn't leave a son. They requested that I sing. I sang a waltz from Rio Grande do Sul.
I went to see the grandson of Dr. Ignacio Winizky. He was sleeping. The house is sumptuous. I sensed that Dr. Ignacio Winizky is a friend of Culture. So many books. He appreciated books and painters. The Argentine painter Manuel Kantar was present. . . . We spoke of Brazil. The poverty of the North and Northeast. *The misery, and* [about] *literary terms. Brazilians eat little. He doesn't drink wine, doesn't use olive oil which thins the blood. He doesn't drink milk. The lack of schools in*

*the North gives the impression
that the Brazilian is listless. But it
is only an impression. We talked
about our parliamentary government—teledirected. I would not
accept a teledirected government.
I would want to be the proprietor
of my actions. I am horrified. Men
enter power poor and exit rich to
buy palaces in London.* Dr.
Ignacio Winizky requested me to
write my autograph on the buffalo
table—I wrote a verse. Everybody
loved it. . . .

Audálio Dantas was not the
only one to choose selectively
from Carolina's words. In the
early 1960s, filmmakers from the
West German Institut für Film
und Bild produced a documentary reenactment of Carolina and
her life before the publication of
her diary.* The twenty-five-
minute film portrays Carolina as
a bitter woman unrelentingly
angry at the misery faced by
Brazil's poor and the callous
indifference of the government
and the rich. From beginning to
end, the film depicts pain and
misery. "If I try to be friendly
when I am in the street," she says
as she rummages through garbage

cans, "people look at me with hate.
Do they feel guilty because São
Paulo has poor people?"

Unlike her written diaries, the
film offers no relief, little sense of
Carolina's pride, her love of life,
her positive work ethic.
Manipulative and one-
dimensional, the film pounds
away at the sordidness of
Brazilian slum life and warns of
social unrest. It is telling that
foreigners produced the film,
electing to see Carolina as a
heroine and a voice of protest.
Leftists in Brazil, by contrast,
dismissed her as not sufficiently
committed to overturning the
system, perceiving her as selfish
and as a nuisance and refusing to
take her seriously.

Last Years

Carolina's diary entries are filled
with detail recorded by a woman
determined to hold others to the
high standards she set for herself. No revolutionary—she ultimately respected people in
authority and did not seek radical social change—she nonetheless was never reluctant to name
names and to criticize with sting-
ing words. Her 1966 diary entries,
written after the overthrow of the

---

* In 1974, only a few years before
Carolina's death, an English version of
the film was distributed by Films
Incorporated in the United States as
Favela: Diary of a Slum.

constitutional government and the imposition on 31 March 1964 of the first of a series of generals as head of state, reveal the most about the toll taken on Carolina's personality by her roller-coaster life. They represent her last known writing; she was by then living in her isolated house in Paralheiros, almost as a hermit, and within another decade she would be dead. Her writing has lost some of its edge; it seems tired. It demonstrates, however, the underlying conservative tone of her outlook that drove leftish intellectuals to consider her a pariah. She does not want the military government to continue, though: its intervention cured the country's anemia, but now it "has tuberculosis." Within her story remains her sense of national pride, of compassion for her country's ills.

By 1966 she had withdrawn to the point that she was nearly dysfunctional. *Quarto de Despejo*, she wrote angrily, brought her no financial independence; her international publishers, she claimed, were "told not to give me a dime." This is inaccurate, but it is how she came to feel about the matter. Yet she does not seem to mind that the Russians have paid her nothing; she will show her poetry notebook to a visiting Russian journalist who has arranged to interview her.[8]

Things were better in the 1920s, she argues. People had less education but they lived better. She reports her quarrels with her neighbors, one of whom, Arlindo Sebastiane Paschoalini, calls her a "disgusting black tramp" and a woman who belongs in the favela. She responds by cursing him in the same manner, just as she had to do in the Canindé favela to defend herself. She is ordered to report to the police station because neighbors have filed a complaint against her that her pigs are ruining their gardens. Her neighbor drinks too much, she writes; to make herself feel better she calls him a "werewolf." There is a second complaint by a neighbor from the northeast who is also an alcoholic. "What a pain in the neck," she writes, "and ugly woman."

Still, she maintains her pride. When Paschoalini tells her that she should find a man to help her—he means, of course, to control and silence her—she reminds herself that she had always refused to marry because she knew that this would happen to her. When people continue to ask her for moneẏ, she tells them to visit her house to see "the real living conditions of a miserable writer."

Her sense of racial injustice has not diminished. She writes down thoughts that were never spoken out loud—that blacks were unwelcome in the new capital of Brasília, for example. Whites, she says, see blacks as fit only to live in favelas or to be thrown into the street. Her sense of social criticism has become sharper over time: blacks are still not free; there are no black entrepreneurs; beacks remain socially marginalized. Carolina wrote some of these things in her 1950s diaries, but her tone is more bitter now; she talks about whites selling blacks "as if they were animals." She talks warily about racial conditions in the United States, which she feels are harsher than in Brazil, and she worries that Brazilian whites will copy the behavior of American whites and things will be worse. She criticizes mixed-race Brazilian mulattos, who, she argues, hate blacks more than anyone in Brazilian society. They would rather stand up in a bus than sit next to a black person. This was no intellectual theory: her treatment as a pariah by her own mulatto relatives was one of the most traumatic episodes of her unhappy childhood.[9]

She looks with envy at black women, who by the mid-1960s have managed to go much further than she could have dreamed of. Nowadays black women are able to study through high school, she notes, although she adds that nowadays "it is much more expensive to be a lawyer, engineer, dentist, or physician." She notes the subtle changes that have occurred in Brazilian life. In the old days, she says, the word *bola* was used to describe a piece of poisoned meat used to trick and kill a dog. Nowadays, she adds, *bola* is used to describe bribes that officials collect in exchange for favored treatment.

Her unedited writing is filled with biting social commentary. She dreamed of painting her house red, she says, but if she did this the church would label her a communist. It has already excommunicated Fidel Castro, she adds, and she knows that she is a candidate for excommunication too. She also knows that she is strong. "I am a person who never bends or breaks," she writes. "I like to be with myself and with God. I don't take alcohol." She remains to the end an optimist. "We need light to see in the dark," she concludes. "The best matches in the world are honesty and goodness."

Concluding Thoughts

Carolina never understood the symbolism of her ascent from misery. Fame for her was a path to having food to eat every day and a house in which to live. She never saw herself as a role model or as a crusader. This is one of the main reasons that Brazilian intellectuals rejected her: they considered her selfish, looking out only for herself and her children. Yet how could it have been otherwise? Few really listened to her or took her observations seriously. Her resolve never to marry because of how men treated her and because she feared the loss of her independence was a courageous feminist act, but female Brazilian intellectuals never rec-

ognized this; women reporters who interviewed her criticized her incessantly for wearing ill-matched clothing and for not knowing how to walk on high-heeled shoes.

Even after her success, most Brazilians saw her as a sideshow freak. Foreign journalists wrote that her diaries represented the voice of poverty, a cry out of the undeveloped world, a justification for the Alliance for Progress and other programs to eradicate lower-class suffering. Most Brazilians, in contrast, never saw her as more than a curiosity. It is also likely that some of her contemporaries resented the fact that the fathers of her children had all been white men, a prejudice expressed more openly in the Brazil of the 1950s and 1960s than after. Even the marriage during the early 1960s of the great soccer star Pelé to a blond white woman was severely criticized, and Pelé's wedding was held in Germany, not in the country that revered him for his athleticism.

Only a small number of Brazilians saw in her published diary entries ammunition for advocating social reform, and

12. Carolina during the last year of her life, 1977. *Photographer unknown.*

these voices were silenced after the military coup of 31 March 1964. The media frenzy that briefly enveloped her in Brazil came from her curiosity value, because social norms could not accept a black favelada to be an author. A tiny group of black São Paulo intellectuals, the manager of the Pinheiro Sport Club, who held a dance in her honor, and a few others, embraced her unconditionally. Although city officials, in the harsh light of her first diary, soon tore down the Canindé favela, the number of favela dwellers in São Paulo rose precipitously over the years. Today they live under conditions much worse than those suffered by Carolina, with much higher rates of drug abuse, overcrowding, crime, and disease.

How is Carolina Maria de Jesus remembered today in North America? People still read her diary; public libraries still have (by now well-worn) copies of the hardcover version of her diary, and people still check them out when they want to read about Brazil although newer and more updated books are also available. These include Alma Guillermoprieto's excellent

Samba[10] and Joseph A. Page's 1995 interpretation of current Brazilian life, *The Brazilians,*[11] as well as translations of novels by the Brazilian Academy of Letters author Nélida Piñon and other novelists. Most books for nonspecialists on Brazil, however, offer little insight into the relationship between the poverty and wealth that coexist in Brazil, much as in Carolina Maria de Jesus's Brazil three decades ago.

Much of the interest in Carolina in the United States remains within academic confines. Survey courses on Latin American and on Brazilian history at the undergraduate level typically have 40 or 50 students enrolled, with some classes at large universities sometimes reaching 150. The late E. Bradford Burns of UCLA (University of California at Los Angeles) always had a large number of students in his courses, and he frequently assigned *Child of the Dark* as required reading. The book also has remained important at the two-year, or community college, level. Craig Hendricks, for example, has regularly assigned it to his students in courses on the comparative history of the

Americas. Wilson Martins may feel that in the United States academics are "typically naive," as he describes them, but the fact remains that they have kept the diary alive, using it not to show what Brazil is like today but to raise questions in students' minds about the reasons for the docility of poor people, whether in Brazil, the inner cities of the United States, or anywhere else.

The fact that *Child of the Dark* is assigned reading in an estimated fifty to three hundred college courses each semester—the figure is based on the fact that the Conference on Latin American History lists more than 850 members, most of whom teach courses in which the diary would be appropriate, and the Latin American Studies Association has several thousand members—means that Carolina's written memoirs are read more by students than by the general public. But, unlike Brazilians, millions of North Americans obtain their reading material not from bookstores (which increasingly are becoming supermarkets for popular, nonliterary books) but from their local public libraries. In Madison, Wisconsin, for example, libraries lend an average of twenty-nine books per resident each year. This means that hardcover books like Carolina's diary may continue to be read dozens of times a year by different patrons. My videotape is still available for showing—I list it along with some others I have made on the Latin American Studies home page at the University of Miami—although the master copy has deteriorated and the sound quality is poor. Nevertheless, I am frequently told by colleagues at other universities that their students were captivated by it and by its message, and some were moved to tears.[12]

What are the main lessons to be learned from Carolina's life? Her feisty personality, so often criticized by her contemporaries, served her well as a defense mechanism and permitted her not only to cope but to fend for herself against long odds. From their birth, she protected her children fiercely, shielding them from danger to the point of taking knife thrusts from an angry prostitute running after her son. Carolina received personal assistance from politicians even before she became famous, a testimony to her assertiveness and refusal to play the docile role assigned to the destitute.

Her fame neither diminished her curiosity about the world nor her self-confidence. Her mentors grew tired of her, but in part because they forced her to be dependent on them. Her publisher did not permit her to open a bank account for her royalties, because no one believed that she could handle money. Carolina never shied from telling what she considered to be the truth, even if her bluntness embarrassed those trained in the social skills of flattery and telling white lies. One of the reasons that she abandoned her dream house and moved to live a hermit's existence on the city's edge was her resolute desire to live without pretense. Reporters hounded her even when she sought solace, mocking her clothing, her sparse furnishings, and her too honest answers to their silly questions.

For a brief period of time in the early 1960s, Carolina Maria de Jesus earned the respect of university students, reform-minded citizens, and Brazil's minuscule Afro-Brazilian intellectual community. Most intellec-

tuals mocked her or dismissed her as an odd curiosity. Conservatives deprecated her lack of manners; leftists considered her selfish and lacking in class consciousness. Once her fame faded, she dropped from sight. From 1964 to 1978 Brazilians lived under a military dictatorship that branded all social criticism as communist; academics left for exile, were chased from their jobs, or retreated behind walls of theory and esoteric scholarship. Reform journalism died in the 1964 coup, replaced by tabloids and porno films.

In the early and middle 1990s, when the efforts to find Carolina's children produced a flurry of publications about her, a revival of interest in her occurred, but on a very limited scale. Benedita da Silva, the black woman born in a Rio de Janeiro favela who narrowly lost the election as mayor of Rio de Janeiro and who later was sent to the federal senate, admitted to researchers that she had known nothing about the woman whose past in some ways so closely resembled hers. Leaders of the black-consciousness movement

13. Vera, her husband, and her children at Vera's house at Santo André, São Paulo, 1993. The girl on the left is José Carlos's daughter, who is being raised by Vera. *Photograph by Robert M. Levine.*

centered in Salvador, in the state of Bahia, pointedly ignored Carolina in their speeches and publications. University students who read about her showed little interest in reading her books. Those who did tended to see her as a historical anachronism rather than as a women of color. Brazilians who read *Quarto de Despejo* invariably overlooked her ideas about race, which run through all of her writing; rather, they accepted her as a victim, without searching for the causes of urban poverty and lower-class hopelessness.

Brazilian intellectuals seemed more willing to accept exposés about life in the slums when they were not written by women. In August 1997 Paulo Lins, a favelado from Rio de Janeiro's grim Cidade de Deus (God's city), published a three-part, six-hundred-page novel with that title.[13] A Cidade de Deus resident since the age of eight, Lins had attended public school, was drafted into the army, but left to become a university student; he dropped out, but in 1986 he went back. In the mid-1980s he joined the "independent poetry" movement and published a book of poems in 1986. A decade later, working as a middle-school teacher, he turned to fiction. Each of the three parts of *Cidade de Deus* takes place in a different decade, starting in the 1960s. The novel is frenzied, "a vomit-filled narrative of rapes, murders, gang battles, robberies, spectacular assaults, rapes again—six or seven violent acts per page," in the words of Wilson Bueno.[14] It is telling that of all the reviewers of *Cidade de Deus,* the only one that compared the author directly to Carolina Maria de Jesus was Bueno, a Paraguayan writer living and working in Brazil. Lins's language, like Carolina's, is the language of the favela, "replicating, faithfully and spontaneously, the everyday life of beggars," although Lins's book is far more aggressive and filled with chaos.[15]

Readers outside of Brazil, quick to cast Carolina in the role of Third World heroine, might have reacted less warmly to her writing had it been published in its original form. Dantas edited it by taking out the most grating parts, statements he considered opinionated, and attacks on himself as a manipulating Svengali.

Carolina, after all, did not know that her diaries would be read by millions; nor did she cultivate any consistency in what she wrote. Her original manuscripts are difficult to read—how many drafts written under similar conditions would be less difficult? They reveal anger and frustration, they pontificate, sometimes they infuriate, but for this very reason they open a window into the lower depths of Brazilian society. The refusal of Brazilians to look into this window by marginalizing her as unworthy or irrelevant speaks volumes about their own way of looking at the world.

It is difficult to guess how reading Carolina's writings in 1998 differs for a North American or European from reading them in 1962 when the translations began to appear. The early 1960s were times when many believed that poverty could be combated by the application of massive amounts of foreign aid. Some saw the question in the progressive context of the First World's responsibility to help the Third World; others saw it as a means of preventing favelados and peasants and the hapless from becoming communists. In the cynical and selfish 1990s, neither view holds much weight. Carolina herself offered no clear advice. In some ways she was deeply conservative: she abhorred drinking, she hated people who cursed, and she wrote that people evicted from city land ought not to complain but thank the city for permitting them to be squatters up until then. In other ways she was progressive, seeking assistance from authorities to combat inflation, to subsidize food prices, and to provide good schools.

The world of the Brazilian poor has evolved since the days when Carolina wrote her diaries. Things are different. Many favelas have been torn down to make way for highways and high-rise buildings; others, mostly in Rio de Janeiro, have had some sections improved, mostly because of the actions of residents, who exchanged votes for political favors. Pollution is even worse than during the 1970s when Carolina died of what the doctors said was a breathing ailment. Most of Brazil's urban poor live under conditions more precarious and squalid than Carolina and her three children did. Drug lords control most shantytowns now, and violence is rife. The rich are getting richer and the poor poorer. Following the fall of the Berlin Wall, free-market economics has become the ideology of choice in much of Latin America. In turn, budgets for social welfare have declined. Opportunities for people like Carolina Maria de Jesus to escape from their hopelessness are far fewer. Poverty is no longer the only obstacle faced by favelados; in addition, they now have to deal with the scourge of illicit drugs, persistent—and rising—violence, and the indifference of the affluent, who cloister themselves behind guarded residences and elegant shopping malls.

Notes

Introduction

1. Carolina Maria de Jesus, *Quarto de Despejo,* ed. Audálio Dantas (São Paulo: Editora Franciso Alves, 1960).
2. Carolina Maria de Jesus, *Casa de Alvenaria,* ed. Audálio Dantas (São Paulo: Editora Francisco Alves, 1961).
3. Marilene Felinto, "Clichês nascidos na favela," *Folha de São Paulo,* 29 September 1996, sec. 5, p. 11.
4. Carolina Maria de Jesus, *Child of the Dark,* trans. David St. Clair (New York: E. P. Dutton, 1962).
5. See Marisa Lajolo, "The North American Accent of the North American Version of Carolina Maria de Jesus's Diary" (paper presented at BRASA IV, Washington, DC, 13 November 1997).
6. Carolina Maria de Jesus, *I'm Going to Have a Little House,* trans. Melvin S. Arrington Jr. and Robert M. Levine (Lincoln: University of Nebraska Press, 1997).
7. David St. Clair, based on his interview with Carolina Maria de Jesus, Rio de Janeiro, 1960, in Carolina Maria de Jesus, *Child of the Dark* (New York: Signet Mentor Books, 1962), 9. For Carolina's early life, see Robert M. Levine, ed. and trans., *Bitita's Diary,* by Maria Carolina de Jesus (New York: M. E. Sharpe Publishers, 1997).
8. See Daphne Patai, introduction to *Brazilian Women Speak* (New Brunswick, NJ: Rutgers University Press, 1988), 1–35.
9. *Child of the Dark,* p. 44.
10. St. Clair, *Child of the Dark,* 15.
11. St. Clair, *Child of the Dark,* 15.

12. Comments typical of those made to the authors in Brazil after the publication of *Cinderela Negra* in 1994.
13. Maura Lopes Cançado, *Hospício é Deus* (Rio de Janeiro: José Alvaro Editora, 1965).
14. Reynaldo Jardim, Preface to Lopes Cançado, *Hospício é Deus,* 9.
15. Francisca Souza da Silva, *Ai de Vós!* (Rio de Janeiro: Civilização Brasileira, 1986).
16. Wilson Martins, *Jornal do Brasil,* 23 October 1993, p. 4. In a second newspaper essay, Martins wrote: "With the characteristic naivete of foreign intellectuals, Robert M. Levine assigned the book as required reading in his Latin American history survey course" ("Lendo Carolina," *Gazeta do Povo,* 29 April 1995, p. 28).
17. *Jornal do Brasil,* 11 December 1993, p. 4.
18. Robert M. Levine and José Carlos Sebe Bom Meihy, *The Life and Death of Carolina Maria de Jesus* (Albuquerque: University of New Mexico Press, 1995).
19. José Carlos Sebe Bom Meihy and Robert M. Levine, *Ciderela Negra* (Rio de Janeiro: Ed. UFRJ, 1994).
20. *Jornal da Tarde,* 11 October 1996, p. 4.
21. Some of these comments were added to the home page. See http://www.as.miami.edu/las.
22. Robert M. Levine, Letter to Julie Charlip, 20 April 1997.

Afterword

1. For a statement of this frustration, see Marcelo Rubens Paiva, *Happy Old Year,* trans. David George (Pittsburgh, PA: Latin American Literary Review Press, 1991), published in Brazil as *Feliz Ano Velho* (São Paulo: Editora Brasiliense, 1981).
2. C. 1942. Courtesy of Peter Reznikoff, New York. See Robert M. Levine, *The Brazilian Photographs of Genevieve Naylor* (Durham, NC: Duke University Press, 1998).
3. This sentiment still held fast a generation after Carolina's diary was published. See the statement "Sofrer e calar" by "Flávia" in Frances O'Gorman, *Morro, Mulher* (São Paulo: Ed. Paulinas, 1984), 21.
4. See Levine, *Bitita's Diary.*
5. See George Wilson Pierson, *Tocqueville in America* (Baltimore: Johns Hopkins University Press, 1996).
6. David St. Clair, translation of Carolina Maria de Jesus, *Child of the Dark* (New York: Mentor Books, 1963), 111–112.
7. The comparison was made from the Spanish edition of the book (1962), translated by Robert M. Levine from the Portuguese original.
8. She received so little in foreign royalties because the rights to her book in many countries—including the Spanish, German, and Italian editions—were sold to middle-level literary agents before the scope of her success was known. Further, the Communist-bloc countries, in which her book sold extremely well, paid nothing. She did receive royalties over the years from France and from the United States. See Levine and Sebe, *Life and Death.*
9. See Carolina Maria de Jesus, *Diário de Bitita* (Rio de Janeiro: Ed. Nova Fronteira, 1986). English translation published in 1997 by M. E. Sharpe Publishers.
10. Alma Guillermoprieto, *Samba* (London: Bloomsbury, 1991).
11. Joseph A. Page, *The Brazilians* (Reading, MA: Addison Wesley, 1995).

12. See http://www.as.miami.edu/las.
13. Paulo Lins, *Cidade de Deus: romance* (São Paulo: Companhia das Letras, 1997).
14. See Wilson Bueno's untitled review in *O Estado do São Paulo,* 23 August 1997, see 2, p. D4.
15. Bueno, review.

Glossary

bola	Poisoned meat thrown to dogs by robbers.
cachaça	Powerful sugar-cane liquor.
Catete Palace	Residence of the president of the Republic.
cruzeiro	Brazilian monetary unit (1 cruzeiro = 100 centavos).
D., Da.	Abbreviated forms of *Dona*.
Dona	Mrs., used together with first name (for example, Dona Ana).
Dr.	Doctor. Used in Brazil for a person with a university degree, but also used by persons of low status to address persons of higher status, regardless of their formal education. Carolina usually capitalizes "Dr." although she usually writes "Senhor" (Mr.) in lower case.
favela	Shantytown; urban slum.
favelado, -a	Inhabitant of a *favela*.
fazenda	Ranch; rural agricultural property.
fazendeiro	Owner or proprietor of a *fazenda*.
feijoada	Traditional meal of rice, beans, and meats.

gaúcho	Generally, a cowboy of the South American pampas; here: inhabitant of the state of Rio Grande do Sul.
granja	Farm house.
João	Carolina's oldest son.
José Carlos	Carolina's younger son.
kilogram	1000 grams (2.2046 pounds avoirdupois).
linguiça	Hard sausage.
macumba	Spiritist fetishist ceremony of African origin with some Roman Catholic elements, accompanied by chants and percussion instruments; related to voodoo.
mineiro	Inhabitant of the city of Minas Gerais.
pátria	Country; homeland.
paulista	Inhabitant of the State of São Paulo.
portenho	Portuguese spelling of porteño, a native of Buenos Aires, Argentina.
SENAI	Government-run training institute.
Senhor	Mr.
seu	Informal way of saying Mr.
Vera; Vera Eunice	Carolina's daughter.
villas miserias	Argentine phrase for urban slums.

Index

About the Editors

Robert M. Levine is the author of more than twenty books on Latin American history and is the director of Latin American studies at the University of Miami, Coral Gables. He is the past chair of the Columbia University seminars on Latin America and on Brazil and since 1989 has been coeditor of the *Luso-Brazilian Review*.

José Carlos Sebe Bom Meihy is a professor of history at the University of São Paulo and the academic director of the CIEE (Council of International Educational Exchange) Interuniversity Study Program in Brazil. He has written numerous books on the history of Brazil and Spain and is one of the founders of the field of oral history in his country.